Ageing and the Labor Market in Japan

ESRI STUDIES SERIES ON AGEING

In April 2000 the Japanese government launched a series of comprehensive, interdisciplinary and international research projects called 'the Millennium Projects' and as part of this initiative the Economic and Social Research Institute (ESRI) of the Cabinet Office of Japan initiated a two year project entitled 'A Study on Sustainable Economic and Social Structures in the 21st Century', which focuses on ageing and environmental problems in the Japanese and international context.

The *ESRI Studies Series on Ageing* provides a forum for the publication of a limited number of books, which are the result of this international collaboration, on the three main issues of macroeconomics, pension and social security reform, and the labor market. The series is invaluable to students and scholars of public economics and public finance as well as policymakers and consultants.

Titles in the series include:

Ageing and the Labor Market in Japan

Problems and Policies

Edited by

Koichi Hamada

Tuntex Professor of Economics, Yale University, USA

and

Hiromi Kato

Professor, Faculty of Economics, Tokyo Keizai University, Japan

ESRI STUDIES SERIES ON AGEING

Edward Elgar
Cheltenham, UK • Northampton, MA, USA

Published by
Edward Elgar Publishing Limited
The Lypiatts
15 Lansdown Road
Cheltenham
Glos GL50 2JA
UK

Edward Elgar Publishing, Inc.
William Pratt House
9 Dewey Court
Northampton
Massachusetts 01060
USA

Reprinted 2016

A catalogue record for this book
is available from the British Library

Library of Congress Cataloguing in Publication Data
Koichi Hamada and Hiromi Kato.
    p. cm. — (ESRI studies series on ageing)
    Includes bibliographical references and index.
    1. Japan — Population — Economic aspects. 2. Age distribution
    (Demography) — Economic aspects — Japan. 3. Ageing — Economic aspects
    — Japan. 4. Labor market — Japan. I. Hamada, Koichi, 1936–.
    II. Kato, Hiromi, 1947–. III. Series.

    HB3651.A62 2006
    331.11'430952—dc22   2006012074

ISBN 978 1 84542 849 5

Printed and bound in Great Britain by T.J. International Ltd, Padstow

Contents

Contributors

Asaoka, Hitoshi: Senior Economist, Mitsubishi Research Institute, Inc., and Lecturer, Department of Economics, Sophia University, Japan.

Genda, Yuji: Assistant Professor, Institute of Social Science, Tokyo University, Japan.

Goto, Junichi: Director and Professor, Research Institute for Economics and Business Administration, Kobe University, Japan.

Hamada, Koichi: Tuntex Professor of Economics, Yale University, USA.

Hernæs, Erik: Managing Director, the Frisch Centre, Oslo, Norway.

Ishihara, Mamiko: Lecturer, Faculty of Economics, Josai University.

Kambayashi, Ryo: Assistant Professor, Institute of Economic Research, Hitotsubashi University, Japan.

Kato, Hiromi: Professor, Faculty of Economics, Tokyo Keizai University, Japan.

Makino, Tatsuji: Graduate School of Economics, Chuo University, Japan.

Ohta, Souichi: Professor in Economics, Keio University, Japan.

Raut, Lakshmi K.: Economist, Social Security Administration, Washington DC, USA, and California State University at Fullerton, California, USA.

Sakai, Hirotsugu: Research Director, Mitsubishi Research Institute, Inc., and Visiting Professor, Graduate School of Environment and Information Sciences, Yokohama National University, Japan.

Sakuragawa, Masaya: Professor, Department of Economics, Keio University, Japan.

Strøm, Steinar: Professor in Economics, University of Oslo, Norway and Turin, Italy.

Teruyama, Hiroshi: Professor, Institute of Economic Research, Kyoto University, Japan.

Zhiyang, Jia: Research Fellow, Statistics, Norway.

Preface

At the beginning of the twenty-first century the world must place the highest priority on constructing a sustainable socioeconomic system that can cope with the rapid ageing of populations in developed countries and with the limited environmental resources available in both developed and developing countries. At first glance, the problems of ageing and the environment may seem to be quite separate issues. However, they share a common feature: they both deal with intergenerational problems. The essence of the ageing problem is how to find effective ways for a smaller, working generation to support a larger, ageing generation. The crux of the environmental problem is to find a feasible way to leave environmental resources to future generations. Moreover, in terms of consumption, slower population growth may slow consumption and help to alleviate environmental problems. On the other hand, a rapidly ageing society may use more energy-intensive technology to compensate for the inevitable labor shortage, and thus cause deterioration on the natural environment.

Today, these concerns are highly applicable in Japan. The pressure created by the rapid ageing of the Japanese population is becoming acute; Japan must construct a sustainable society that does not create intergenerational inequity or erode the public welfare. At the same time, Japan cannot deplete its environmental resources and energy, as this would leave future generations with an unbearably heavy burden.

The Japanese government has recognized the vital importance of both problems. To explore and implement solutions for this difficult task, in April 2000 former Prime Minister Keizo Obuchi launched several comprehensive and interdisciplinary research projects known collectively as the 'Millennium Project'. As a consequence in the same month, the Economic and Social Research Institute (ESRI), Cabinet Office, Government of Japan, initiated a two-year project entitled 'A Study on Sustainable Economic and Social Structure in the Twenty-first Century'. While the Millennium Project covers a wide range of topics and disciplines such as natural science and technological innovation, the project conducted by ESRI places major emphasis on social science. While taking into account technological innovation and feasibility, it focuses on ageing and environmental problems. It aims to design a desirable socioeconomic structure under the pressure of an ageing population and environmental constraints by identifying the necessary policy tools to attain stable and sustainable growth.

AGEING SOCIETY

The Japanese population is graying rapidly, and the elderly are expected to account for a quarter of the nation's total population in 2020. Japan needs to reform its social security system, pension management schemes, financial/capital markets and labor markets if it hopes to create a better and sustainable future society. When looking at Japan's problems head on, we see giant fiscal deficits, bad-loan problems, and long-term structural problems that must be fixed aggressively or suffered indefinitely. The clock is ticking, and the time to act is short, but our problems are not insurmountable. Pessimism is not our rallying call. Rather, we are optimistic, and encouraged by the European example. In Europe, countries have worked hard to improve fiscal conditions and social security, and they have attained positive results and succeeded in uniting their separate markets.

Studies on ageing populations can be divided roughly into three categories: (i) macroeconomic problems related to the decline in the workforce due to ageing; (ii) social security systems, with many of the studies looking at pension systems; and (iii) the labor market, for example, employment of the elderly, competition with younger workers, the female workforce, and immigrant workers. We have made a specialized study of our theme from these perspectives.

Many people are pessimistic about the effect of ageing on the macroeconomy due to the reduction in the labor force. However, in this study, there were others who expressed a challenging view that various impacts, including those on economic growth, can be coped with fully and overcome by technological progress and other measures. Some strongly suggested that the current economic and social system would need to be reformed to achieve the flexibility required. Accelerated return to prosperity and the realization of economic growth at a comparatively high level would reduce costs and alleviate the distress that a change in the system in the transition period would involve, helping to carry forward the reform smoothly. In other words, measures to be taken to improve the present situation of the Japanese economy do not differ significantly from what is required to build the future sustainable economy and society.

In order to continue the current recovery from a recession for a decade, it is necessary to reconstruct the financial system in such a way as would bring about efficiency of fund allocation and recover efficiency of the labor market. Some also pointed out that it will be difficult to achieve economic growth amid an increasingly ageing population unless a sound labor market and an efficient financial and capital market are established. Finding solutions for the bad loans and forming an efficient financial and capital market will not only make it possible to diversify portfolio selection and pension asset management of individuals but will allow enterprises to raise their funds efficiently. At the same time, there were many who expressed the opinion that the soundness of the Japanese economy would be recovered and a sustainable economy and society will be realized by defining public participation in the social security system (defining the roles which the public and the private sectors should play in social security) and building a safety net against various risks. As a timeworn story, it is pointed out that the formation of an efficient market through the improvement of various regulations and systems in the labor market will not only stimulate participation of the aged and women in the market and make up for the labor shortage but will also make a variety of employment forms feasible and contribute to the formation of a society in which people will feel that their life is worth living. There are also some who see the necessity of establishing the concept of equity in the social security system and employment of the aged since these factors bear a significant relationship to the age at which payment of pensions is started, sustainability of the system and fair sharing of the pension cost between the young and the aged.

RESOURCE AND ENVIRONMENTAL PROBLEMS

Studies on resource/environmental problems reflect a closed-loop model of the economy and society. These studies are divided into four themes: (i) studies on waste management, which cover a wide variety of empirical studies; (ii) studies on sustainability and technological innovation related to resources/energy; (iii) studies on potential policies for addressing changes in climate; and (iv) studies on the relationship between environmental policies and economic policies, including employment policies.

From the standpoint of long-term sustainability of global resources, official involvement including policy measures and the development of new technology to remove environmental restriction will be called for. There is a high possibility that new technology creates new products, stimulating demand, developing new industries with high productivity, and bringing about a renewed sustainable economic growth. New technology in the 21st century should contribute to the construction of the closed-loop economy and society and enhance resources and energy efficiency, properly dispose of waste and increase efficiency of reusing resources. Furthermore, it must generate renewable energy efficiently and on a large scale. It may sound para-doxical, but past experience suggests that various restrictions imposed on economic activities, and the existence of regulation actually stimulates new technological development which helps to break through the restrictions.

Today, environmental issues encompass a very wide range of problems from territorial disposal of waste to the global environmental issues. It has been pointed out that policy mix ingeniously combining such methods as regulatory and economic instruments, voluntary agreements and inter-national emissions trading is essential for coping with these issues. What is important then is a policy which skillfully uses incentives, making use of market mechanisms. Japan is one of the most advanced countries in environment-related technology in the world. However, further technolog-ical breakthroughs will be called for in the future and it has been pointed out that use of market incentive and official support is essential in the fields where long-term risks are uncertain.

It is suggested that concrete behavior by a community based on shared information (bottom-up approach) and a change in behavior of individual as consumers provide one of the keys in the closed-loop economy and society. Such change in the behavior of individuals is caused by the diffusion and permeation of concepts such as precautionary principle, one of the environmental principles in the EU.

Addressing the construction of the closed-loop materials-cycle economy and society is an effort that is particularly called for in the Japanese economy which is faced with restrictions on resources and energy and it may be said to be a way by which we must seek sustainable progress and growth of a Japanese type. Furthermore, some pointed out that, for its cli-matic and topographical conditions and for its population density, the waste management system in larger cities of Japan can be a model for Asia, and Japan will play an important role in the Asian area in coping with global environment issues.

SYNTHETIC CONSIDERATION

None of the various issues dealt with in this project are independent issues. They are issues closely related to each other and they will require simulta-neous decision-making, all of them when a desirable scenario is to be visu-alized. And both issues of ageing and environment will have a strong impact not only on the welfare of our generation but also on that of future generations. An awareness of issues that are common to the ageing popu-lation and the issue of environment is the context in which we should make use of market mechanisms.

There is a case for saying that we should make good use of market mechanisms by utilizing economic means in order to efficiently attain goals in health care and annuity, employment of the aged, women in the labor force, climatic change and waste disposal. However, many of these issues are examples of market mechanisms not functioning efficiently, or what one calls a failure of the market. Utilizing market mechanisms in this domain involves various difficulties such as internalizing externalities and we cannot avoid classical problems such as efficiency and equity and what roles should be played by the public and private sector.

Research into the ageing population and the environment has thrown into relief the importance of technological innovation. Looking back on human history, we find that restrictive conditions gave birth to technological innovation which presented a way out of the difficulties faced. When we think the 21st century has severe restrictions imposed upon it, such as resources, energy, labor force and population, we may take a positive view of things and say that, conversely, the century carries full conditions that will give birth to technological innovation. If we could succeed in achieving technological innovation in this global situation, formation of more enriched economy and society would be materialized.

In the short term, countries with ageing populations will likely elect to consume more energy – without any thought to the long-term impact of their consumption patterns and economic activity. This tendency must be offset with a new sense of sustainability, one that looks to the future, one that thrives on improved resource/energy efficiencies, one based on eco-friendly waste disposal and new eco-friendly technologies. Without lowering living standards, we must solve global environmental problems, and overcome the constraints of limited energy resources. To do so will require the creation of a closed-looped economy/society. Failure to do so may spell the end to our way of life in the not-so-distant future.

In this project, we explore optimal solutions to social optimization problems. After taking into account the political and social constraints we face, and after alignment and coordination with the results of the studies, we will sketch out an ideal design and examine the possible direction of future research.

This project came to an end in March 2002. It solved many theoretical and empirical issues, but has created new debates. Twice a year, all the members of the project, along with selected participants, met to discuss the results of the research. Regrettably, it has not been possible to reproduce the fruitful discussion in this volume.

Overall, the papers presented in the project were extremely challenging, and covered a wide range of topics. In the near future we very much hope we will have a chance to discuss the research once more from a common standpoint.

The result of this research appears in print from Edward Elgar Publishing Ltd as part of the ESRI studies series, available to policy makers, academics and business people with a keen interest in these subjects. The series on ageing problems covers macroeconomics, social security and the labor market. Unfortunately, because of space limitations we regret that we are able to publish only selected papers from the total research effort. The research papers to be published were selected by the Editorial Board members. We would like to acknowledge the ceaseless efforts of the members of ESRI throughout the project period, especially those of the Department of Administration Affairs. Last but not least, we would like to thank Matthew Pitman, Nep Elverd and Karen McCarthy from Edward Elgar Publishing.

Masahiro Kuroda, President, ESRI

Acknowledgments

This book is the outgrowth of the research that was carried out during a two-year project organized by the Economic and Social Research Institute (ESRI), Cabinet Office, the Japanese Government, entitled 'A Study on Sustainable Economic and Social Structure in the Twenty-first Century'. We would like to express our sincere gratitude to all the staff members of the Institute for their support throughout the project and during several conferences held in Osaka and Tokyo. We are particularly grateful to Megumi Sagara for her extensive assistance with all the editorial work. We also thank Junko Kiyuna for her expertise in administrative assistance, and Carolyn M. Beaudin for her help with style and overall improvements.

Introduction

Koichi Hamada and Hiromi Kato

With the advent of the Millennium, substantial qualitative changes have been taking place in environmental, technological, economic and social conditions on earth. One of the most conspicuous changes in Japan is the ageing and decline of its population. It was expected that the population in Japan would decline before long, but it was still shocking to hear the confirmation of Japan's government statistics to that effect for last year's population.

The Millennium Project at the Economic and Social Research Institute (ESRI), Cabinet Office of Japan, gathered distinguished scholars from all over the world who studied the impact of ageing on the Japanese economy and its society from various angles. This book is a collection of several studies from this project and the chapters deal more specifically with the impact of ageing on the labor market in Japan. The content of the chapters observes the surprising phenomena of drastic ageing and the declining population, and explores new directions of research. Since we face a new set of problems that were not anticipated, some chapters may carry a flavor of being a simulcast of current situations as well as a scientific observation of the ageing trend.

At the turn of the new century, Japan has been encountering the advent of a rapidly ageing population. In 2000, about 17.2 per cent of its population was over 65 years old, and about 7 per cent was over 75 years old. In 2025, 27.5 per cent of Japan's population is expected to be over 65 years old, and about 11.9 per cent is expected to be over 75 years old. This means that there will be about 2.5 people in the active population for every adult aged 65 years or more.

This tendency is not a feature peculiar only to Japan; many other developed countries are following the same trend. The proportion of those over 65 years of age in the population of the United States, Great Britain, Germany, France and Sweden are expected to reach 18.8 per cent, 21.2 per cent, 23.4 per cent, 21.7 per cent and 24.3 per cent, respectively by the year 2025. Thus, similar trends are everywhere in developed countries, but the situation in Japan is probably the most extreme.

The rapid ageing process of the population presents serious questions in terms of its economic and social impact. Japan can be viewed as an experimental ground to test various hypotheses related to these questions. This fact presents a strong contrast to the past state of Japanese economic studies. Formerly, the Japanese economy was used as a field where the already established was to be reconfirmed. Now, Japan faces new problems such as deflation, massive government debt and, in particular, ageing, which other economies have seldom experienced. These novel problems challenge economists to make accurate diagnoses and prescriptions, and they challenge, at the same time, the robustness of conventional theories. It is hoped that new directions of research and fresh insights in economic logic will be found and developed following the experience in Japan in advance of similar occurrences in other countries.

Ageing has diverse effects on the economy, polity and society of a universe. Before facing the ageing problem directly as we are currently forced to do, ageing was often an abstract concept such as the decrease in population growth rate in macroeconomics, unemployment problems in the labor market, and the balance of the social security account. By observing and experiencing the ageing problems first-hand in Japan, however, one finds that the many facets of this phenomenon seriously affect other parts of a nation's life. Not only through the macroeconomic route but also through various structural, sociological, behavioral and cultural routes, does ageing exert a strong influence on a country.

Literature illustrates various types of serious old age problems. Elderly people in ancient Japanese villages used to be sent, or sometimes even voluntarily went into the wilderness of the mountains in order to 'reduce the number of mouths in a family'. A female novelist, Sawako Ariyoshi, describes with black irony a Japanese housewife's ordeal of taking care of her father-in-law – a quite common pattern of care of the elderly in Japan where nursing homes and other public facilities are yet to be fully developed.

Since social changes have been rapidly taking place along with these demographic trends, new phrases and jargon that reflect these changes have become a part of the lexicon. Normally, a graying labor population would mean a higher demand for young workers and college (or high school) graduates. In reality, however, the conventional pattern of lifetime employment still persists and prevents young people from obtaining the status of full employees. This is reflected by a new phrase, 'parasite single' (*parasaito shinguru* as paraphrased in Japanese). 'Parasite single' is an unmarried young person who lives with his (or her) parents, and whose basic expenses are taken care of by the parents. They are not constrained by the regimen of regular employees, and conduct elegant lifestyles. Masahiro Yamada, a sociologist who coined this phrase in his book of the same title, points out that a child, now a scarcity in a family, is often capable of commanding a greater cash flow from parents than before.

The above depicts the nature of the supply side of the 'parasite single'. At the same time, as Genda et al. analyze below, this lifestyle also stems from the nature of the demand side of employment. Employers are now reluctant to hire many employees on a permanent basis because of increasing uncertainty as well as the difficulty in firing employees, a tradition based on legal practices. For those reasons, we observe the somewhat ironical phenomenon of 'parasite singles', a lack of demand for younger workers in spite of the drastic ageing of the population.

Along with this trend, a Japanese–English term, 'freeter', was coined. A 'freeter' describes a young person who does not have a constant job but earns a living by irregular and part-time work. This category of young people is also created by the interaction of supply and demand. More simply put, workers are not willing to settle or commit to a lifetime job. Firms are also reluctant to hire many new workers because the firms have to provide fringe benefits and employment protection if young people are taken on as regular employees. Currently the number of 'freeters' is said to exceed 2.1 million in Japan.

Incidentally, 'NEET' (not in education, employment or training) is a word created in England, and describes young people who neither intend to obtain jobs nor have vocational training. These NEETs in England are usually considered to belong to the lower income classes. By contrast, NEETs in Japan were considered to come more often than not from relatively well-to-do families. However, recent statistics suggest that NEETs in Japan also drastically changed around 2002 so that they began to come from lower and middle income classes.[1] They rely on the parents' income and do not study or work. The often expressed reasons for not working are that they do not find attractive work or that they do not want to be involved in an interpersonal network or to be subordinate to bosses. The number of NEETs in Japan is estimated to exceed 0.64 million in 2004.

Thus the increase in the numbers of young people who make no lifelong plan independently exacerbates the severity of the ageing problem. 'Parasite singles' depend on their parents for basic expenses and housework, although they work. 'Freeters' only work on a day-to-day basis. 'NEETs' cannot even take care of their everyday needs, let alone plan for their own bright future. Because 'parasite singles' feel little dissatisfaction about their life, the status quo continues and leads to the tendency towards late marriage or no marriage, which aggravates the ageing of the population. Quality of labor improves when a worker commits to a single job for a considerable duration. If 'NEETs' and 'freeters' stay uncommitted to a job, they may give up opportunities for improving their skills.

In short, these new phenomena are caused by the interaction of the supply side and the demand side. On the supply side, there is a behavioral basis for the choices of young workers. On the demand side, the pattern of Japan's typical, firm-based lifetime employment and seniority wage system is changing to the extent that firms are no longer demanding a large source of regular employees.

The increase in the type of young people described here has its own repercussions. This trend makes the process of on-the-job training in a firm more difficult, a process that was considered to be a key factor in the success of Japanese firms. This absence of OJT candidates makes it more difficult to accumulate workers with firm-specific skills. The social security system suffers from a lack of new membership. Moreover, these phenomena themselves tend to delay the age of marriage and also to reduce the number of children in a household. They work to aggravate the problem of an ageing population in a kind of vicious circle.

If we turn to the field of academic economics, an ageing and declining population also creates new puzzles in economics. First, take the case of growth theory. What happens to the long-run growth path in the economy with a declining population? Even the definition of a balanced growth path in growth theory should be replaced by the definition of a balanced contraction path, but it is not easy to define such a path. On such a path, both labor and capital must be declining at the same rate. Yet, though capital can often be obsolete, it cannot be depleted easily. Therefore, it is difficult to define a balanced contraction path in a national economy with a decreasing population. Under the old view of growth theory, the welfare effect of an economy with a declining population may appear to be a blessing because the same capital stock serves fewer people. It presents a harder problem in practice, however, because the working generation is shrinking relative to the retired generation. Producers are gradually outnumbered by mere consumers.

Second, can the international economy help the problem of a shrinking working population? Definitely. Immigration of younger labor from abroad would help in the abstract sense. It is the first best policy to cope with an ageing population. On the positive side of immigration, one can learn from the US immigration policy which allows only a limited number of immigrants with selective categories of workers. In practice, migration involves various social and cultural problems as the past Gastarbeiter problem in Germany illustrated. Goto argues below, taking those problems into account, that the increasing job participation of women, more active trade, and foreign investment would fill in the gap posed by this apparently natural policy response towards increasing immigration.

In any case, a reasonable response of an economy to a declining population, aside from migration, is that a younger generation, anticipating the ageing of the economy, will save and invest abroad to prepare for the hardship of the future silvering of the population. In other words, younger generations facing the ageing population structure in the future will work and save abroad with the hope of cashing in the results of their savings in their old age. This process is not without problems, however. If it is not feasible to import eldercare services, and these same services are not completely supplied by robots or through other technology, then the use of savings accumulated at a younger age will have its limitations. An aged society needs young workers, and cannot exist solely on the accumulation of past savings unless these same savings can be transformed into labor. Is this process still possible even if we exclude migration? These realistic questions motivate the theoretical analysis by Hamada and Raut.

In the United States, for example, the government selects those groups of workers wishing to be immigrants, and makes them compete with each other as well as with domestic workers. Thus immigration is a natural instrument to keep the vitality of the national economy sound and flexible. In Japan, which has a long history of homogeneity on a somewhat secluded island, resistance to immigration is strong, as is suggested by Goto. It is now a serious question as to whether or not Japan can continue to be a viable economy if it insists on rigorously limiting foreign workers as it has done for a long time.

Declining numbers of young workers also create serious incentive problems. Suppose a hypothetical country succeeded in enforcing 'a single child per family' rule as tried for some time in China. It would be amazing to observe that the population in such a country would reduce by half in one cycle of reproduction and to one quarter of the initial population in two cycles. Every child would have two parents and four grandparents who could extend care. It would not be surprising that a child might lose the incentive to compete for a good education or to struggle to improve his or her skills. This is the point emphasized in Makino and Sakuragawa.

Intergenerational transfers are, and should be, primarily based on love and trust. Often, however, they are also subject to explicit and implicit calculations and negotiations. The citation from *King Lear* at the beginning of Chapter 4 is a sincere but frank admission of this strategic maneuvering by Cordelia, and it anticipates the tragic saga of the Lear dynasty. Nowadays, game theory not only predicts the outcome of rational behavior but also allows us to test what kind of strategic assumptions are implied from the data. Chapter 6 is a pioneering attempt in this direction, and because of its novelty, we decided to include the chapter even though it is not directly related to Japan.

Let us now give a short synopsis of each chapter and its relationship to our main motifs.

Chapter 1, 'Ageing and employment in Japan' is the result of a collaboration of many economists in the ESRI Labor Market Study Group under the leadership of Yuji Genda. This chapter starts off with a concise but thoughtful examination of ageing from the macroeconomic and the micro-economic standpoints. In its macroeconomic section, the chapter breaks down the incidence of unemployment into the unemployment of each age cohort and the age distribution of the population. Comparing these results with results in the United States (Katz and Krueger, 1999), this chapter concludes that the contribution of the age structure is much more import-ant than the effect of cohort-specific unemployment in Japan. Genda et al. also find that the effect of age, education and gender on unemployment is of little importance.

The microeconomic part of this chapter highlights, by way of cross-section analysis, the negative effect of increases in middle-aged and older employees on the total downsizing of firms. The age composition effect dominates the effect of decreases in labor demand in general. The legal decisions made in Japan's courts do not allow outright dismissals though statutory laws do not have any prohibitions against this. The difficulty in dismissing old employees is in fact reducing the demand for young workers. The above-mentioned and well publicized 'parasite singles' – young persons relying on their parents after graduation and without steady jobs – are not necessarily the result of behavioral problems of youngsters but the demand problem on the part of firms. The traditional schemes of transferring employees between firms – often used among *keiretsu* firms – are no longer sufficient to absorb redundant old-age workers. This brief chapter will convey a current and vivid picture of the Japanese market as it is under the wave of rapid ageing.

Chapter 2, 'Factors affecting labor force participation in Japan', by Hirotsugu Sakai and Hitoshi Asaoka presents a suitable companion piece to the first chapter by conducting quantitative analyses of labor participa-tion. The authors' main methodology is the estimation of participation probability. The propensity to participate in labor markets is decreasing as a function of age, bad health and flexibility of the working system. The authors also evaluate the impact of Japanese tax law which acts as a disin-centive on the spouse of the main wage earner in the household. More often than not the spouse under this tax treatment is a woman. Typically, a part-timer – say a wife– who earns more than 1300 thousand yen has to pay income tax even though she (or he) does not need to pay the tax if she earns less than 1300 thousand yen. Again a probit estimation is carried out of the spouse's income-adjusting behavior by withholding labor participation. Income-adjusting behavior can be clearly seen if the female is well edu-cated, but can be mitigated by a family-friendly child care system.

Given the premise that labor participation should be encouraged in order to cope with the ageing problem, this chapter argues that: more flexible as well as more child-care-friendly working conditions should be offered; discouraging tax and social security treatment of labor participation should be legislated; and that the government should respect and train the elderly because they have a wealth of accumulated professional experience. The reader may find a subtle difference in tone between this chapter and the previous chapter regarding the treatment of elderly workers. This chapter recommends that we keep elderly workers participating as much as possible, while the first chapter points out the side effects of keeping too many elderly workers in the market. We marvel at and are intellectually attracted by the analysis in Chapter 1, but at the same time we learn much from the objective and quantitative analysis in Chapter 2. Certainly, more careful analysis is needed to make comparisons between Chapters 1 and 2.

Chapter 3, 'Labor force ageing and economic growth in Japan' by Masaya Sakuragawa and Tatsuji Makino, takes a long-run view of the economy that is more or less on a full employment path. It offers a contrast to the previous two chapters which traced the fluctuations in unemployment and labor supply decisions along the business cycle. Because of the ageing of the population, Sakuragawa and Makino argue that younger people become relatively scarce. They tend to be employed in favorable conditions with relatively high real wages. The lifetime wage profile that faces younger workers becomes flatter. Then, younger people will lose incentives to accumulate human capital in order to enjoy the higher returns to human capital in their later ages. In short, younger workers become more relaxed in terms of self education and self training. Thus ageing reduces growth rate not only because of the reduction of labor input in the process (direct effect), but also because of the loss of incentives for investments in human capital (adverse growth effect) resulting from the flattening of the lifetime wage profile. By calibration in an overlapping generation model where skilled labor and unskilled labor are imperfect substitutes, the authors indicate that the loss due to the drastic transition of population decline can be quite substantial. According to their calculation, direct effects may account for 19.1 per cent of per capita consumption decline and the growth effect may account for 11.5 per cent of per capita consumption decline. (In contrast to the context of Chapter 1 where the pressure of large numbers of elderly workers discourages younger ones, in this full employment scenario, scarce younger workers are spoiled by improving working conditions and tend to neglect investing in their human capital for the future.)

In Chapter 4, Hamada and Raut draw direct attention to the need for caring people in a country where the population is rapidly ageing. Naturally, costs of medical care for the elderly grow rapidly and at greater proportions than the pace of an ageing population. The process requires not only material costs but input of direct human care as indicated by classic literature described above. More capital-intensive medical care may substitute for a part of nursing care for the elderly, but *robots* can never replace a substantial part of the care needed for the elderly. Indeed, they are never able to be a substitute for the essential human ingredients, attention and loving care.

To capture the basic nature of nursing needs in terms of human labor, the authors develop a simple overlapping generation model in which a person works when young and consumes as well as demands nursing care during old age. In order to prepare for the need for care during old age, a person will need to save more from the present consumption than in the absence of elderly care. When nursing services cannot be substituted for by physical equipment, a nation is forced to import foreign young labor or to export capital abroad in order to buy more goods and shift workers from the production sector to the nursing sector.

In Chapter 5, Raut elaborates on this international aspect of an elderly population. He asks the question regarding to what extent capital movements can substitute for labor immigration as a means of mitigating the seriousness of old age problems that are magnified in present day Japan. To deal with an extended model of the previous chapter, he appeals to both a theoretical and a calibrating approach, allowing technological differences between developing and developed countries.

He indicates that under plausible values of production and consumption parameters for Japan and its surroundings, immigration of labor is likely to be more effective than exporting capital. In an extreme case, if all the young labor were absorbed for elderly care, immigration would be the only choice. This example is certainly a hypothetical case, but it is a strong one.

It seems natural to consider the use of immigrants if Japan is experiencing a crisis of a precipitous population decline. If the deficiency is in the supply of labor, why do we not replenish it by importing from abroad? In Chapter 6, 'Ageing society and the choice of Japan: migration, FDI and trade liberalization', Junichi Goto develops a completely different view. He argues that the social cost of importing substantial immigrant labor to Japan is enormous and that labor import can be detrimental to a national economy that is under import protection of consumption goods. (The second effect is generally known as the Dias–Alejandros–Brecher effect. In Japan it is known as the Uzawa effect based on his contribution in Japanese.) On the positive side, Goto emphasizes that female labor can be utilized more effectively in Japan and that capital outflows as well as freer trade will be good substitutes for labor inflow. In a neoclassical environment, his economic logic may hold theoretically. Then he proceeds to calibrate these effects for seven countries/areas in Asia, China (including the Province of Taiwan), Indonesia, Korea, Malaysia, the Philippines and

Thailand. He concludes that Japan can cope with the ageing problem even without relying substantially on immigration.

We find insightful observations in this chapter. For example, low fertility is not necessarily an outright labor shortage problem because the ratio of a supporting population may increase for a while when fertility declines. The author's theory and calibrations may seem to dissent strongly from conventional views concerning migration in Japan, but we consider that the examination of somewhat extreme views helps us to clarify the nature of this important issue. It is politically impossible to realize the free flow of labor around Japan's archipelago, but the proper policy mix seems to lie in the middle ground between free migration and its complete ban, that is, a skillful combination of selective immigration policies and other policies discussed in this chapter.

In the final chapter, 'Retirement in non-cooperative and cooperative families', Erik Hernæs, Zhiyang Jia and Steinar Strøm challenge the difficult but valuable task of testing strategic behavior using microeconomic household data. Because of its importance, we include their work though it is concerned with data other than those of Japan. In the conventional theory, a household is usually considered to be a standard economic decision unit. In practice, however, individual members in the household engage in mutual interactions and then form the household behavior. Similarly, a husband and a wife can be regarded as playing a dynamic game regarding their individual employment, retirement and saving decisions. These decisions and their strategic interplays are naturally affected by pension systems.

Hernæs et al. use the data from an 'early retirement program' (abbreviated as AFM in Norwegian) and ask the following questions: how do households decide on their retirement? The husband and the wife decide non-cooperatively, given the other spouse's decision, in the manner of Nash equilibrium. Or does a husband or a wife initiate the decision as a Stackelberg leader? Or do they cooperate completely to achieve the joint maximization of the household utility? What kind of strategic structure can be explained most reasonably by the data? Their answer for the Norwegian data can be most reasonably explained by assuming that the husband is the Stackelberg leader.

In other words, the husband takes into account how his wife may respond to his decision whether or not to retire, and then he takes the decision whether or not to retire early. In this sense the husband is the leader when retirement decisions are made and the wife is the follower. Preferences of both husband and wife matter for the husband's decision to retire early, but it matters in this asymmetric Stackelberg leadership way. Note that the wife's decision to work or not depends on her own preferences as well as on the preferences of her husband. This result may be due to the data that have been used – the Norwegian men in the sample are born between 1930 and 1935. For other (and younger) cohorts and from other countries with a different social structure, it may well be that the female is the leader or more likely that the decisions are made jointly in a symmetric way.

The preferred model yields estimates of the effects of such variables as age and health history of partners. Calibration results suggest that economic incentives matter to a great extent, and that less generous taxation of pension benefits would postpone the age of retirement.

Game theory was once considered a normative science that cannot be tested by empirical data. Now, particularly combined with the probit analysis, this chapter shows that testing strategic analysis is within our reach.

In short, ageing problems manifest their most conspicuous patterns in the current Japanese economy. Naturally, the demographic trends present serious social and economic problems to Japan, and affect the way Japan interacts with the world. It is hard to summarize lessons for Japan's policies obtained from the chapters, but the following would indicate the common denominators of the collected chapters.

Ageing creates the problem of supporting the growing cohorts of elderly by financial transfers and actual elderly-care services. Also, it affects the labor market of young cohorts and generates various social phenomena exemplified by the existence of 'parasite singles'. In order to cope with the labor shortage, tax treatment of incomes of married couples should be corrected to encourage increased participation of women in the labor force. Part of Japan's current account surpluses in the past can be explained by the need to prepare for the aged population, and the current account surpluses will most likely end in the near future. Immigration of labor is not only an easy way out to solve the shortage of young workers, but also an effective way of stimulating competition to build up human capital. At the same time, a country must be braced for the social and cultural issues associated with immigration, if it is willing to utilize foreign sources of labor.

The problems of an ageing population present challenging puzzles and questions for economists. This volume is a serious attempt to investigate and answer these puzzles. The rapid ageing problems enrich the menu of macroeconomic and microeconomic problems, and studying Japan's experience is crucial, we may say almost indispensable, for learning about the ageing problem, because here in Japan all the symptoms are so acute. This book records our attempts to face and tackle these problems. The methodologies used here are diverse, and the reader may detect subtle differences in policy prescriptions. The diversity and differences, however, reflect the richness of the subject. Also they reflect incipient stages of the ageing problem in Japan, and they suggest the need for multiple paths of investigation into the future. We hope the present volume will be a useful reference for the many different phases of adjustments that nations will face in an immediate or intermediate future.

NOTE

1. The percentage of NEETs, not searching for jobs, who came from households with (their parents') income levels of more than 10 million yen reduced from 25.7 per cent in 1997 to 17.0 per cent in 2002, and the percentage of NEETs from households with income levels of less than 3 million yen increased from 15.2 per cent to 20.8 per cent during the same period (Cabinet Office, 2002, 'Seisho-nen no shuro ni kansuru chosa-kenkyu' (survey on the working style of the younger generation), Japan).

REFERENCE

Katz, Lawrence F. and Alan B. Krueger (1999), 'The high-pressure US labor market of the 1990s', *Brookings Papers on Economic Activity*, **1**, pp. 1–65.

1. Ageing and employment in Japan

Yuji Genda, Hiroshi Teruyama, Souichi Ohta, Ryo Kambayashi and Mamiko Ishihara*

1. INTRODUCTION

This chapter uses two basic approaches to examine the effects of ageing on employment to determine the relationship between economic shifts and the labor market.

The first approach evaluates the impact of labor supply shifts towards the older population at the macro economy level. The unemployment rate in Japan has continued to increase over a long period, and it increased sharply in the 1990s. We examine how the demographic shifts to higher levels of older workers affect the unemployment rate. In a previous study that examined the effect of ageing on unemployment in the United States, it was found that shifts in the labor supply contributed considerably to decreases in the unemployment rate (Katz and Kruger, 1999). We compare the effects in the United States with those in Japan.

The second approach, on the other hand, looks at the effects of ageing at the establishment level instead of the macro level. The proportion of older and senior workers steadily increased within firms in the 1990s; labor costs were also raised because of the seniority wage system which, although slightly transformed, is still largely maintained. During the recession following the burst of the bubble economy, most Japanese firms continued to avoid hiring young workers and, after the serious financial recession of 1997 and 1998, firms were also forced to undertake significant levels of downsizing, which led to the retrenchment of existing senior employees.

The composition of this short report is as follows. In the next section, we use several different methods to study the effect of ageing on the unemployment rate. In the third section, we examine the influence of ageing on the decline in labor demand at the establishment level. The fourth section summarizes the empirical results.

2. AGEING AND UNEMPLOYMENT

Contribution of Age Composition to Male Unemployment

For nearly 30 years, the unemployment rate in Japan has been on an upward trend. This section first gives an overview of the extent to which each age group affects secular movements in the unemployment rate; it also discerns a few trends. We then analyze changes in the trends of some age groups since 1998, when the unemployment rate started rising drastically.

We first assessed the influence of each age group by using published data from the *Annual Report on the Labor Force Survey* between 1974 and 2000, conducted by the Statistics Bureau. We divided the male labor force into 11 age groups (15–19, 20–24, 25–29, . . . , 55–59, 60–64, and 65 or more) and calculated the contribution rate for each age-sex group to the annual unemployment rate. The contribution rate for the group is defined by the number of unemployed people in the group relative to the overall number of unemployed.

Figure 1.1 shows the results for some age categories among the male labor force. The contribution rate for male workers aged 60–64 grew most during the period 1974–2000. Since the middle of the 1980s, the contribution rate for that group has been as high as that for young workers aged 20–24, which is dominant not only for males but also for females during the period. It indicates that the group of males aged 60–64, as well as young workers, has continued to have a considerable influence on unemployment in Japan.

Figure 1.1 also clarifies the fact that the contribution rate for male workers aged 55–59 was high from 1980 to 1987, after which it fell. Their unemployment rate also began to fall from 1988. Because the age of mandatory retirement changed from 55 to 60 years in most Japanese firms during the late 1980s, the figure suggests that the behaviors of age groups after mandatory retirement play important roles in raising overall unemployment rates.

Although the contribution of males aged 60–64 to the overall unemployment rate is large and increasing over the long run, it has been falling since 1999. This indicates that a different mechanism is operating behind the recent sudden rise in unemployment. Because the group's unemployment rate and workforce share have not decreased, the declining influence of the unemployed aged 60–64 must be due to an increase in other group's contributions to the overall unemployment rate.

Figure 1.1 shows that male workers aged 50–54 have had a considerable rise in their contribution to the overall unemployment rate since 1998. Their unemployment rates and their labor force shares increased simultaneously. However, this trend is not likely to last for long, because it is due to the so-called 'baby boomers', those born in Japan between 1947 and

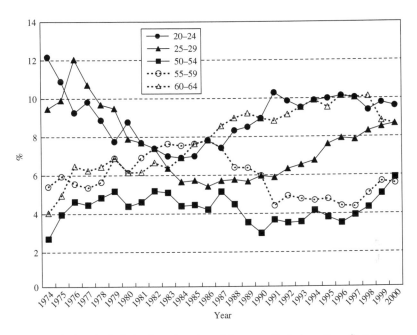

Source: Authors' calculation based on *Annual Report on the Labour Force Survey*, 1974–2000.

Figure 1.1 Contribution rates to annual unemployment rates among males

1949, and so the influence must be somewhat generation-specific. However, for the group of workers after mandatory retirement, we expect a large increase in the unemployment rate when the baby boom generation reaches the age of 60, around 2007–2009. At that time, the trend towards a high contribution by workers aged slightly over 60 to the overall unemployment rate will strengthen.

Another important feature represented in Figure 1.1 is the steady increase in the contribution of the 25–29 year-olds during the 1990s. With the continuation of the ageing society, young workers have been less likely to find suitable jobs and, at the same time, more likely to change jobs in Japan (Genda, 2003). Details of this serious situation among young Japanese are given in the third section.

A Comparison with the USA

We next quantitatively examine the extent to which the ageing labor force affects the unemployment rate in the long run. Changes in the age structure of the workforce affect the unemployment rate considerably, because unemployment rates differ sharply between age groups, as we saw before. To capture more precisely the impact of age-structure changes on trends in unemployment, we can calculate hypothetical age-constant unemployment rates and age-driven unemployment rates by using micro-data from the *Annual Report on the Labor Force Survey* between 1974 and 2000. This follows the procedure provided by Katz and Krueger (1999) which examined the effect of ageing on unemployment in the United States.

The actual overall unemployment rate at time t (U_t) equals the weighted average of the group-specific unemployment rates (u_{jt}) using the actual labor force shares (w_{jt}) as weights; that is,

$$U_t = \Sigma_j w_{jt} u_{jt}. \tag{1.1}$$

The age-constant unemployment rate at time t (UW_t) is then defined as

$$UW_t = \Sigma_j w_{jo} u_{jt}. \tag{1.2}$$

Here, we use a fixed set of age-group weights for some baseline time period (w_{jo}) instead of the actual labor force shares. The age adjustment to the unemployment rate at time t (the age-composition effect) is simply given by the difference between the actual and the age-constant unemployment rates, that is, ($U_t - UW_t$).

As an alternative approach for examining the impact of changes in the age structure on the unemployment rate, we can also define the age-driven unemployment rate at time t (UA_t) as

$$UA_t = \Sigma_j w_{jt} u_{jo}, \tag{1.3}$$

where u_{jo} is the group-specific unemployment rate for group j in a baseline period. Changes in UA_t are all driven by the ageing composition of labor forces (for details, see Genda and the ESRI Labor Market Study Group (2003, chapter 6)).

The center column of Table 1.1 represents the difference between the actual and the age-constant unemployment rates ($U_t - UW_t$) in Japan and the United States. Then, a fixed set of age-group weights in 1979 is used for some baseline time period in both countries. It is quite clear that the negative age adjustment effect is larger and is observed more clearly in the United States than in Japan. As the unemployment rate basically ceases with age in the United States, ageing shifts clearly contribute to the lowering of the unemployment rate by up to almost 0.7 per cent.

Table 1.1 Effects of changes in age structure on unemployment rates in Japan and USA

Year	Age adjustment					
	Unemployment rate		Using 1979 labour force shares		Age-driven unemployment rate	
	Japan	USA	Japan	USA	Japan	USA
1960		5.5		−0.63		5.69
1963		5.7		−0.60		5.74
1966		3.8		−0.35		5.96
1969		3.5		−0.33		6.04
1973		4.9		−0.29		6.32
1974	1.40		0.06		2.16	
1975	1.91		0.05		2.14	
1976	2.01	7.7	0.05	−0.02	2.12	6.38
1977	2.05		0.03		2.11	
1978	2.24		0.01		2.09	
1979	2.07	5.8	0.00	0.00	2.07	6.40
1980	2.02		−0.01		2.07	
1981	2.28		−0.01		2.06	
1982	2.34	9.7	−0.01	−0.19	2.06	6.22
1983	2.67		0.00		2.06	
1984	2.68	7.5	0.00	−0.29	2.06	6.12
1985	2.63	7.2	−0.02	−0.33	2.06	6.08
1986	2.76		0.00		2.07	
1987	2.88		0.01		2.07	
1988	2.53		0.00		2.08	
1989	2.25	5.3	0.00	−0.44	2.08	5.90
1990	2.10		0.00		2.09	
1991	2.09		0.00		2.10	
1992	2.16	7.5	0.00	−0.69	2.11	5.76
1993	2.54		0.00		2.11	
1994	2.89		0.00		2.11	
1995	3.15	5.6	−0.01	−0.67	2.11	5.72
1996	3.38		−0.01		2.11	
1997	3.37		−0.02		2.12	
1998	4.08	4.5	−0.03	−0.63	2.12	5.67
1999	4.68		−0.06		2.12	
2000	4.77		−0.05		2.11	

Source: Results for US are from Katz and Krueger (1999, Table 10) while those for Japan come from authors' calculation based on *Annual Report on the Labour Force Survey*, 1974–2000.

In contrast, the effects of age-structure changes on the unemployment rate in Japan are comparably minimal, and have a slight downward trend over the given period. The recent change in age structure also lowers the overall unemployment rate in Japan, but it has a smaller effect in Japan than in the United States.

The right-hand column in Table 1.1 represents the age-driven unemployment rate in each country. As the group-specific unemployment rate for group *j* in a baseline period, the average unemployment rate for each age group between 1960 and 1998 is given for the United States, whereas the actual rate in 1979 is used to calculate UA_t for Japan. The age-driven unemployment rate is more than 5 per cent for the United States in most years, but it is at most 2 per cent for Japan. The age-driven unemployment rate is 2.07 per cent in the base year (1979) and it goes up to 2.11 per cent in 2000. The changes in age structure have a quite modest impact on the unemployment rate in Japan, compared with the United States.

These results suggest that the effect within age groups dominates the age-composition effect and the overall unemployment rises in Japan. The reason for this is that some factors would cancel each other out in Japan. We break down the change in the Japanese overall unemployment rate between 1974 and 2000 into the age-composition effect, the effect within each age group, and their interaction term as follows:

$$U_{00} - U_{74} = \Sigma_j(w_{j00} - w_{j74})u_{j00} + \Sigma_j(u_{j00} - u_{j74})w_{j00}$$

$$- \Sigma_j(w_{j00} - W_{j74})(u_{j00} - u_{j74}). \tag{1.4}$$

The subscripts $_{00}$ and $_{74}$ express the periods 2000 and 1974 respectively. The first term denotes the age-composition effect, the second term the within-age-group effect, and the third term their interaction term.

Table 1.2 summarizes the breakdown by age group given by equation (1.4). The age-composition effect by age group indicates that the increase in the older workforce (those aged more than 45 years) raises the overall unemployment rate, whereas the decline in the younger workforce moves to reduce it. An increase in ageing decreases the proportion of young workers whose unemployment rate is high and, as a result, it has a negative impact on overall unemployment. However, at the same time, the ageing shift will increase the proportion of 60–64-year-old workers with high unemployment rates, resulting in an increase in the overall unemployment rate. Therefore, these two effects of ageing cancel each other out, and the overall age-composition effect slightly lowers the unemployment rate because the former effect is slightly larger than the latter.

Table 1.2 Effects between and within age group from 1974 to 2000

Age category	15–19	20–24	25–29	30–34	35–39	40–44	45–49	50–54	55–59	60–64	65+	Total
(1) Age composition effect	−0.20	−0.34	−0.06	−0.12	−0.09	−0.07	0.02	0.17	0.16	0.15	0.07	−0.32
(2) Effect within age group	0.18	0.58	0.56	0.37	0.22	0.20	0.25	0.32	0.22	0.41	0.12	3.44
(3) Cross term	−0.15	−0.25	−0.04	−0.09	−0.06	−0.05	0.01	0.12	0.09	0.12	0.04	−0.25
(4) (1)+(2)−(3)	0.12	0.49	0.55	0.34	0.19	0.18	0.26	0.37	0.29	0.44	0.14	3.37

Source: Authors' calculation based on *Annual Report on the Labour Force Survey, 1974–2000*.

Additionally we can observe in Table 1.2 that the effects within age groups are positive for all age groups, which implies that changes in age-group-specific unemployment rates raise the overall unemployment rate in all age groups. In particular, the unemployment rate within specific age groups increased sharply, especially among young workers aged 20–34. The overall increase in the unemployment rate is largely due to an increase in the likelihood of unemployment among these young workers as well as those aged 60–64 in Japan.

Age, Education and Sex

Our analysis so far has clarified that the ageing of the labor force accounts little for the deteriorating Japanese employment situation. There seem to be, however, at least two limitations concerning the methodology used above. First, the age-composition effects captured in Tables 1.1 and 1.2 need not be the 'pure effects' of ageing on unemployment because age distribution is probably correlated with the distribution of other worker attributes such as education level. Thus, controlling for other attributes of workers is required to obtain the 'pure effect' of ageing in the Japanese labor market. Second, the age distribution of the labor force is an endogenous variable determined by labor market participation decisions by workers in each age category. That is, the age distribution of the labor force is affected by the age distribution of the population; what we ultimately want to know is the effect of the change in age distribution of the population on the overall unemployment rate. Thus, a more formal analysis is required to treat these problems.

The method used here to adjust these remarks is quite simple. We first estimate the probabilities of becoming employed, unemployed, and not in the labor force, by using a multinomial logit specification. The explanatory variables are a sex dummy, three education dummies, and 10 age class dummies. The data period is from 1988 to 2000, and regressions are run for each year. Treating the status 'employed' as a base category, the probabilities can be expressed as below.

$$\Pr(E)_t = \frac{1}{1 + \exp(\beta'_{ut} x_t) + \exp(\beta'_{nt} x_t)}$$

(Probability of employment)   (1.5)

$$\Pr(U)_t = \frac{\exp(\beta'_{ut} x_t)}{1 + \exp(\beta'_{ut} x_t) + \exp(\beta'_{nt} x_t)}$$

(Probability of unemployment)   (1.6)

$$\Pr(N)_t = \frac{\exp(\beta'_{nt}x_t)}{1 + \exp(\beta'_{ut}x_t) + \exp(\beta'_{nt}x_t)}$$

(Probability of not being in labor force) (1.7)

where x_t is the vector of explanatory variables at time t, and β_{ut} and β_{nt} are the vectors of coefficients for unemployment and not being in the labor force, respectively. Now, we define the 'estimated' overall unemployment rate at time t by

$$\hat{u}_t = \frac{1}{1 + \exp[-\hat{\beta}'_{ut}\bar{x}_t + bias]} \qquad (1.8)$$

Here, $\bar{x}_t$ is the average of the explanatory variables at time t, and *bias* is the term for correcting the bias. The value of this *bias* term is chosen such that $\hat{u}_t$ is equal to the actual unemployment rate at time t. This procedure is somewhat arbitrary, but considerably simplifies the analysis.

Let $\bar{x}_0$ be the average of the explanatory variables in 1988. If we replace $\bar{x}_t$ with $\bar{x}_0$ in equation (1.8), we can obtain the estimated unemployment rate at time t that would have been realized if the distribution of the population had remained the same as in 1988. The pure age/education-composition effect can be obtained by replacing only the age/education-related terms in $\bar{x}_t$ with the average values at 1988.

Table 1.3 shows the share-adjusted series of unemployment. It can be seen that both the fixed age share and the fixed education share unemployment rates are higher than the actual unemployment rates, except for the base year. This shows that the shifts in the distribution of ageing and higher educational attainment among the population had a *negative* effect on the unemployment rate because young and less-educated workers are more likely to be unemployed. Without ageing and higher average education, the unemployment rate in 2000 would have been 5.44 per cent, which exceeds the actual overall unemployment rate by 0.58 percentage points, about half of which can be accounted for by each effect.

Next, we study the case in which the estimated coefficients had remained constant through 1988 to 2000. This can be examined by replacing β_{ut} with β_{u0} in equation (1.8) and following a similar procedure as before. The results are presented in Table 1.4. Let us first look at column (F), which shows the adjusted unemployment series when all the estimated coefficients are fixed at the 1988 level. The estimated unemployment rate in 2000 is 2.62 per cent, which is 2.25 percentage points below the actual unemployment rate at column (A) and 0.28 percentage points below the unemployment rate in 1988. This leads to the conclusion that most of the change in the

Table 1.3   Effects of change in population composition on unemployment rate, 1988–2000 (%)

Year	Actual unemployment rate (A)	Age share fixed at 1988 (B)	Education share fixed at 1988 (C)	All shares fixed at 1988 (D)	Contribution (age) [(A)−(B)]	Contribution (education) [(A)−(C)]	contribution (total) [(A)−(D)]
1988	2.90	2.90	2.90	2.90	0.00	0.00	0.00
1989	2.49	2.49	2.52	2.52	0.00	−0.02	−0.02
1990	2.29	2.30	2.33	2.33	0.00	−0.03	−0.04
1991	2.16	2.17	2.20	2.21	−0.01	−0.04	−0.05
1992	2.13	2.15	2.17	2.19	−0.02	−0.04	−0.06
1993	2.44	2.51	2.51	2.58	−0.07	−0.07	−0.14
1994	3.00	3.07	3.08	3.15	−0.07	−0.08	−0.15
1995	3.06	3.12	3.14	3.21	−0.06	−0.08	−0.14
1996	3.45	3.55	3.53	3.63	−0.10	−0.08	−0.19
1997	3.47	3.61	3.61	3.76	−0.15	−0.15	−0.30
1998	3.70	3.86	3.83	3.99	−0.16	−0.13	−0.29
1999	4.73	4.99	4.92	5.19	−0.26	−0.20	−0.47
2000	4.87	5.15	5.14	5.44	−0.28	−0.28	−0.58

Note: See text for the derivation of these figures.

Source: Authors' calculation based on Special Survey of the Labor Force.

Table 1.4   *Effects of change in unemployment propensity on unemployment rate, 1988–2000 (%)*

Year	Actual unemploy-ment rate (A)	Age coefficients fixed at 1988 (B)	Education coefficients fixed at 1988 (C)	Sex coefficient fixed at 1988 (D)	Constant term fixed at 1988 (E)	All coefficients fixed at 1988 (F)
1988	2.90	2.90	2.90	2.90	2.90	2.90
1989	2.49	2.25	2.36	2.70	3.10	2.86
1990	2.29	2.10	2.15	2.46	3.02	2.77
1991	2.16	2.18	2.06	2.19	2.93	2.86
1992	2.13	2.26	1.94	2.28	2.70	2.80
1993	2.44	3.12	2.21	2.69	2.27	2.88
1994	3.00	3.43	2.66	3.33	2.35	2.65
1995	3.06	2.89	2.95	3.18	2.97	2.81
1996	3.45	3.61	3.00	3.56	2.92	2.75
1997	3.47	4.04	3.46	3.61	2.27	2.75
1998	3.70	3.94	3.46	3.65	2.86	2.80
1999	4.73	4.66	4.45	4.73	2.87	2.66
2000	4.87	5.16	4.47	4.75	2.76	2.62
	(A)–(B)	(A)–(C)	(A)–(D)	(A)–(E)	(A)–(F)	
1988	0.00	0.00	0.00	0.00	0.00	
1989	0.24	0.14	−0.20	−0.60	−0.37	
1990	0.20	0.15	−0.16	−0.73	−0.47	
1991	−0.02	0.10	−0.03	−0.77	−0.69	
1992	−0.14	0.19	−0.15	−0.57	−0.67	
1993	−0.68	0.23	−0.25	0.18	−0.44	
1994	−0.43	0.34	−0.33	0.65	0.35	
1995	0.17	0.11	−0.12	0.09	0.25	
1996	−0.16	0.44	−0.11	0.53	0.70	
1997	−0.57	0.01	−0.14	1.20	0.72	
1998	−0.24	0.24	0.05	0.84	0.90	
1999	0.07	0.28	0.00	1.85	2.06	
2000	−0.29	0.40	0.11	2.11	2.25	

Note: See text for the derivation of these figures.

Source: Authors' calculation based on *Special Survey of the Labor Force.*

Japanese unemployment rate is attributable to the change in unemployment propensity, rather than to the change in overall demographic compositions of age, education and sex.

Column (B) shows the age-adjusted unemployment rates that are obtained when only age-related coefficients are fixed at 1988 values. Although the degree is modest, the age-adjusted unemployment rates mostly exceed the actual unemployment rates, which suggests that the age-coefficient effect contributed to the alleviation of rising unemployment during the 1990s as well as the age-composition effect. On the other hand, education-adjusted unemployment rates in column (C) have always been a little below the actual unemployment rates. The sex-adjusted unemployment rate (D) in 2000 is also below the actual unemployment rate, but this is only a recent phenomenon. Furthermore, the degree is not very substantial.

In contrast, what is most impressive in this table is the effect of constant terms on the estimated unemployment rates, which are shown in column (E). If only the constant term had remained the same as in 1988, the unemployment rate would have become just 2.76 per cent in 2000, which is more than 2 per cent lower than the actual unemployment rate. This clearly indicates that, irrespective of worker attributes, the employment situation has worsened, the impact of which dominates the demographic effects.

3. AGEING AT THE ESTABLISHMENT LEVEL

A Decline in Hiring Young Workers

The previous section examined the effect of ageing on employment opportunities with demographic shifts of labor forces at the aggregate level; that is, it focused on how the change in labor supply composition toward older workforces played a role in the overall unemployment rate. It was found that such supply shifts had minor effects on unemployment in Japan.

However, the ageing effect may not be attributed only to the labor supply side but also to the labor demand. After the so-called bubble economy burst, business performance declined in most Japanese firms. Further, the graying of the workforce, that is, the increasing numbers of middle-aged and older employees, has raised labor costs, particularly within Japanese firms that are most likely to be maintaining seniority-based compensation practices. Figure 1.2 shows that the ratio of workers aged over 45 among full-time workers soared from 32 per cent in 1990 to 37 per cent in 1997. In large firms with 1000 or more employees, the ratio rose from 27 to 34 per cent in the same period.

The creation of such a demographic structure clustered around older workers within firms is the result of both demographic and economic factors. Broad demographic shifts have resulted in an ageing of the population and a shrinking of the birth rate. Further, members of the baby boom generation – those born between 1947 and 1949 in Japan, and employed en masse during the economic boom years in the 1960s and early 1970s – were aged over 50 by the late 1990s. Finally, the oil crisis curbed employment of the succeeding generations.

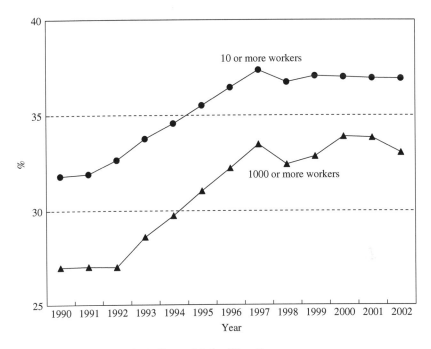

Source: Ministry of Health, Welfare and Labor Wage Census.

Figure 1.2 Proportion of workers aged over 45 among full-time workers (%)

An increase in labor costs through ageing within firms would result in a fall in optimal labor demand. Generally, separation costs of existing employees are quite high for firms in Japan because of legal constraints generated by case laws to prohibit dismissals. Consequently, firms tend to concentrate on employment adjustment by reducing the number of young recruits. The remaining employment adjustment option available to achieve an optimal level of employment during poor business performance is to enhance labor mobility between firms, including transfers and reallocation. Until the mid-1990s, sufficient demand for labor from small and medium-sized firms enabled large firms with excess labor to adjust employment levels by promoting the transfer of workers to smaller firms. However, the recession of the late 1990s, unlike those preceding it, has substantially reduced labor demand even from small and medium-sized firms. Consequently, to reduce their employment level, large firms have no choice but to cut the employment of young people.

The situation of declining employment opportunities for youth may be conceptualized in terms of a job displacement effect; that is, middle-aged and older workers displacing young workers (Ohta, 2002). To examine the job displacement effect precisely, it is useful to focus directly on employment adjustment from the labor demand side. However, the unemployment rate may be influenced by adjustments in both labor demand and supply. By focusing on job openings for recent graduates, which is a direct measure of labor demand, Genda (2003) confirms that establishments with more middle-aged and older workers tended to depress the labor demand of new graduates in the 1990s. As a result, ageing at the establishment further accelerated the increase in the proportion of older workers by reducing the hiring of young workers. In this sense, ageing has a negative impact on job opportunities through a decline in labor demand, especially demand for young workers, at the establishment level.

Downsizing of Ageing Firms 1998–2003

Until the mid-1990s, ageing establishments tended to reduce their hiring of young workers but, on the other hand, they attempted to maintain existing employees and avoid massive dismissals as much as possible. One distinct feature of Japanese labor practice is the large proportion of workers who acquire a wide range of problem-solving skills through on-the-job training (Koike, 1988). While this kind of skill-formation is common among white-collar employees in Japan and other developed countries, Japan is unique in that blue-collar workers in large firms also accumulate a variety of skills similar to white-collar workers. As a result, most middle-aged and older employees have acquired skills along with experience in large firms. Facing business downturns, this skill accumulation encourages employers to maintain experienced employees, in whom human capital investment specific to the firm has already been made.

From 1998 to 2003, however, under the pressure of the serious recession and acceleration of a deflated economy, ageing firms could not avoid reducing the massive numbers of existing older employees, such as the 45–54 year-old workers, through the promotion of early retirement payments. In what seemed like a daily occurrence in 2001, newspapers ran many stories describing well-known Japanese companies, famous for their lifetime employment practices, being forced to let go not only large numbers of employees but also entire divisions. Some large companies reduced their employee count by more than a thousand, as shown, for example, in Table 1.5. Many workers who had been hired in the 1970s were obliged to give up their jobs because their salaries were too high to be maintained.

Table 1.5   Companies reducing workforce by 1000 or more in 2001

Company	Number of workers' reduction	Time of enforcement	Personnel reduction method etc.
Toshiba	17 000 (whole enterprise group)	By the end of 2003 fiscal year	Emphasis on domestic, 10 000–11 000 workers reduced by means of the retirement aged and reduction in recruitment
Fujitsu	16 400 (whole enterprise group)	By the end of 2001 fiscal year	Emphasis on the overseas branch, cutting back 2500 employees by the business reorganization in Japan
Hitachi	14 700 (whole enterprise group)	By the end of 2001 fiscal year	12 000 employees are reduced by means of the retirement aged and reduction in recruitment and by the business reorganization in Japan
Kyosera	10 000 (whole enterprise group)	By the end of 2001	Cutting back the employees in the overseas branch
AIWA	5000 (whole enterprise group)	By the end of 2001 fiscal year	Reducing the number of total employees by half
NEC	4000 (whole enterprise group)	By the end of 2001 fiscal year	2500 employees are cut back by the business reorganization in Japan
Showa Denko	2800(whole enterprise group)	By the end of 2002	Employees reduced by 20% by means of the early retirement system and the retirement aged
Mazda	2210	2001.3	Adopting the early retirement system
OKI Electric Industry	2200 (whole enterprise group)	2001–02 fiscal year	Adopting the early retirement system and selling off some enterprise sections
The Central Mitsui Trust & Banking	2000	From 2001 fiscal year to 2004 fiscal year	Cutting down by the transfer of domicile to the subsidiaries and adopting the early retirement system
MYCAL	1700 (whole enterprise group)	2001.4	Adopting the early retirement system for people over 40

Table 1.5 (continued)

Company	Number of workers' reduction	Time of enforcement	Personnel reduction method etc.
Kenwood	1700 (whole enterprise group)	2004.3	Cutting down 1000 employees in the first stage
Mitsubishi Motors	1382	2001.9	Adopting the early retirement system for people over 52
Nisshin Steel	1000	From 2001 fiscal year to 2003 fiscal year	Emphasis on cutting down by the retirement aged and reducing recruitment, transference and early retirement systems
Daiei	1000	2001.5	Cutting down total 2000, by the retirement aged, decreasing new employment and adopting early retirement system

Source: The Weekly Diamond 29 September 2001.

One notable characteristic of such downsizing today is that many companies make their plans and implement them within a very short time. Interviews with these companies indicated that many completed their downsizing plans within half a year of their announcements. Whereas it had taken substantially more time for Japanese firms to sound and reach agreement with labor unions and at the same time to realize personnel reduction in the past, from the historical view of Japanese industrial relations, the downsizing at the end of the 1990s and at the beginning of the new century appears unique.

Regression Results

A simple regression analysis can confirm the above interpretation. Using the microdata on the establishment survey, that is, the *Employment Trend Survey* conducted in 2000 by the Ministry of Health, Labor and Welfare, the determinant of the employment growth rate is examined at the establishment level.

As an explanatory variable to represent the degree of ageing at the establishment level, the following regression includes the ratio of middle-aged and older employees aged 45 or over among regular employees in addition to firm size, industry and region dummy variables. The ratio of those aged

45 or more is that measured at the end of June 2000. As a dependent variable, on the other hand, the growth rate of regular employees at the establishment level is a measure that is focused on several studies of job creation and destruction such as Davis, Haltiwanger and Schuh (1996) for US manufacturing, and Teruyama (2002) and Genda (1998) for Japanese cases. Although these studies usually measure the annual employment growth rate, we examine the growth rate as the change during the second half of that year because the age composition is documented at the end of the first half year, and so the use of annual growth as a dependent variable would involve a serious endogeneity problem for the regression result.

Table 1.6 shows that the coefficient of the ratio of workers aged 45 or more is significantly negative after controlling for differences in industries, firm sizes and regions between firms. That is, a 1 per cent increase in the proportion of these older workers tends to reduce employment growth rate by 1.85 per cent within the following half year, if other factors are held constant. This suggests that the increase in ageing worker composition significantly reduces the net employment and promotes downsizing at the establishment level. This is clearly a substantial effect of ageing on reducing employment opportunities through a decline in labor demand, which is clearly different from the demographic ageing effect of the labor supply side, which has only a small effect on employment opportunities.

The main cause of the large decline in employment in the second half of the year is not the suspension of new hiring, because the decline tends to be highly concentrated at the beginning of the fiscal year (April in Japan). Such a downsizing would be due to the dismissal of existing workers after the serious recession from 1997, especially senior workers such as those aged 45–54.

Encouraging Senior Employees to Retire

Interviews with representatives of several companies indicated that massive downsizing of senior employees at Japanese firms, especially large firms, reduced the number of employees not by direct dismissal but by expanding their early volunteer retirement systems. In Japan, companies have been forbidden from performing outright dismissals by a historical accumulation of case laws since the 1970s. As a result, many big companies tend to decrease their workforce by persuading their senior workers to give up their jobs voluntarily. Most of these companies, therefore, attempted to establish voluntary and early retirement systems for workers over the age of 45.

Such early retirement schemes can be classified into two types. One is used as a way to rationalize the downsizing of employees. Companies decide on the required reduction in the number of employees and encourage workers

Table 1.6   Determinants for employment growth rates from July to December in 2000

Explanatory variables (in the end of June, 2000)	Employment growth rates
Ratio of employees aged 45 or more	−0.0185
	(−3.23)***
More than 1000 employees	−0.0079
	(−2.17)**
300–999 employees	−0.078
	(−1.92)*
100–299 employees	−0.0063
	(0.32)
30–99 employees	−0.0037
	(−0.96)
Large prefecture	0.0001
	(0.06)
Manufacturing	0.0122
	(2.36)**
Electricity, gas, heat and water supply	0.0192
	(1.82)*
Transportation and communication	0.0241
	(3.48)***
Wholesale, retail trade and restaurants	0.0077
	(1.28)
Finance and insurance	0.0130
	(1.69)*
Services	0.0143
	(2.58)***
Constant term	−0.0136
	(−2.23)**
Number of observations	9889
F-value	2.24
adj. R^2	0.0015

Notes:
t-values are in parentheses. ***, **, and * represent the significance levels at 1, 5, and 10% respectively.

The variable 'large prefecture' represents a dummy for an establishment located in a city with a more than 3 million labor force. A reference group for firm size dummy variables is establishments with 5–29 employees while that for industry dummies is 'constructive'.

to retire early – before mandatory retirement – by paying more generous retirement allowances. The other type is one that makes the system a kind of career development program for individual workers. Some companies allow their middle-aged employees to take leave with about 80 per cent of their pay to find new jobs. If they want to use outplacement companies, the enterprises can ask them to offer their services to such workers. These costs are significant for the companies, but the process can effectively decrease their workforce by forcing them to adjust to the market. On the other hand, this process has a serious drawback: companies can lose some excellent workers, for example, those who have prospects of high salaries because of their high productivity.

Transfer of Employees between Firms

Many major companies have systems that incorporate the temporary or permanent transfer of employees to associated companies. Those systems have played an important role in effectively adjusting the workforce (Aoki, 1988). The system has become less effective, however, since the end of the 1990s because such systems were not sufficient to absorb the separated senior workers within corporate groups. Even today, many companies tend to force transfers on their young employees to affiliated corporate groups for the purpose of shaping the careers of those workers. They typically return to the former company within two or three years. Their salaries during the transfer tend to be as high as their former levels.

For middle-aged employees over 45, on the other hand, the transfer has mostly meant moving to smaller enterprises with no possibility of returning; it is a one-way ticket. They are obliged to take lower salaries than before. Many major companies have adopted such systems to maintain the balance of their employment and to give others a chance to obtain executive positions. Those systems, however, are becoming a burden on the affiliated companies because of the persistent recession. Moreover, many small companies are reluctant to accept these senior workers, as their long-term relationship with their parent companies is weakened. To prevent the situation from worsening, many companies have adopted consolidated accounting systems that place priority on total profits within their corporate grouping.

In the twenty-first century, therefore, most senior workers are forced into finding new jobs on their own. Although durations do vary, today many of these workers spend at least four months looking for new employment, even if they ask for the services of the outplacement companies. Job-hunting durations for middle-aged people vary as well, but generally they take about the same time as those using the public organization, the Public Employment Service Agency, to find new jobs. Some workers with special schemes find new jobs through introductions by their former employers. Middle-aged people seem to be able to find new jobs through this kind of introduction or by their own personal network more easily than the younger generation (for a detailed discussion, see Genda, 2001). However, even those lucky enough to find new jobs may earn only about 70 per cent or less of their previous salary.

Development of Outplacement Businesses

There are companies and public organizations that help find jobs for people who want them, including the Public Employment Service Agency (also known as 'Hello Work'), the Organization for Stability of Industry and Employment (the Sangyo Koyo Antei Center), a bank of human resources (the Jinzai Bank), a career employment center (the 'Career Koryu Plaza'), and private outplacement companies (for rich case studies about outplacement businesses in Japan, see Caplan Research Committees, 2003 and Chuma, 2002).

Most of the outplacement companies were founded after 1997, that is, after deregulation allowed fee-based job introduction services. It is said that about 20 000 jobless workers used them in 2001. Outplacement companies support senior workers who are losing jobs and who are looking for new ones by intensive counseling and by attempting to find appropriate job openings. In some cases, they also make plans to restructure companies or to give workers job training. The companies pay for their services; the employees are not required to pay the fees for this support, as Japanese labor law prohibits in principle charging money to workers directly.

The professional career counseling provided by the experts at outplacement companies is quite effective because they can assuage the negative and ambiguous mental and emotional struggles that often accompany job loss. It also motivates the unemployed to persevere with their job search. Some outplacement companies provide a more complete counseling service than does the Public Employment Service Agency. They have middle-aged and skilled counselors who usually take charge of a maximum of 20 unemployed workers, so that the people losing jobs can be provided with proper counseling at any time. Many outplacement companies in Japan are not merely waiting for information about job offers; they also actively search for employment opportunities for their clients.

With the exception of companies undergoing bankruptcy, compulsory dismissals or nominated discharges are not actually carried out in most large sized companies. Many such companies in turn encourage the workers to retire early and to find alternative jobs. However, significant numbers of smaller companies are obliged to enforce compulsory dismissals or nominated discharges to survive. In the case of bankruptcy, no help can be forthcoming. Because the outplacement businesses are not authorized by the enterprise or are licensed by the government, the government does not know much about the activities of these companies. Many of their business hubs are in urban areas because white-collar workers of big companies are located there and hence it is easier to carry on their businesses in these areas.

Therefore, compared with white-collar workers living in metropolitan areas, workers in regional areas and blue-collar workers are less likely to be supported by outplacement businesses. Today, these outplacement companies receive compensation only from companies that are reducing their workforce. As a result, people who worked at companies without asking for outplacement have not been able to use their services. In conclusion, the Japanese government, together with private enterprises, should discuss enacting a new law concerning dismissal. There is also an urgent need for them to work out a new and fair system to support all jobless workers, which should cover the entire country.

4. CONCLUSION

This chapter briefly studied the effect of ageing on employment in the Japanese labor market, examining in particular the unemployment rate at the macro economic level and employment adjustment at the establishment level.

The former specifically focused on the demographic shifts toward ageing labor forces in the overall economy and attempted to capture the extent to which the labor supply shifts affected the unemployment rate. It is common in the United States that ageing itself contributes to a lowering of the unemployment rate, as it reduces the proportion of young workers whose propensity to be unemployed is relatively high. Without ageing and higher average education, the unemployment rate in 2000 would exceed the actual overall unemployment rate by 0.6 percentage points, about half of which can be equally accounted for by ageing and higher educational attainments.

However, the ageing effect on unemployment is slightly negative in Japan, in contrast to the United States, because the unemployment propensity of older workers (aged 60–64) is exceptionally high in Japan, and the ageing shifts increase their contribution. The bulk of the rapid increase in the unemployment rate after the 1990s was attributable to the change in unemployment propensity within each age group rather than to the change in demographic composition. In this sense, ageing, as the demographic shifts, or the labor supply shock, has little impact on the overall unemployment rate in Japan.

The other aspect of ageing, however, had a strong influence on the decline in job opportunities in the 1990s; there was a decrease in labor demand at establishments with a large component of middle-aged or older employees. Our analysis using microdata suggests that establishments with a higher proportion of senior workers experienced, on average, negative employment growth in the 1990s. With the high adjustment cost of employment and inflexible wage payments, the large decline in labor demand because of recession and high labor costs mainly suppressed the hiring of young workers instead of dismissing existing workers. Consequently, the large contractions in labor demand for younger workers through the 1990s have been due to the job displacement effect by the graying workforce, especially within large firms.

In addition, it was not until the end of the 1990s, after the financial recession, that a large amount of downsizing occurred in those firms with a high proportion of senior workers and, as a result, many older workers aged 40–59 chose to retire and attempted to find alternative jobs by themselves or with the support of outplacement businesses that rapidly developed in the Japanese labor market.

In summary, although ageing has little effect on employment as labor supply shifts, the increase in the proportion of older employees, which reduced labor demand at the establishment level, had a significant impact on the Japanese labor market by reducing the number of job opportunities for young workers during the 1990s and for senior workers after the end of the 1990s.

NOTE

*   The ESRI Labor Market Study Group was organized from 2000 to 2003, and comprised these authors. We are ably supported by the researchers of the Economic and Social Research Institute (ESRI), especially Yuji Senuma, Kazuhiro Sasaki, Kentaro Abe, Takayuki Kusajima and Taku Morito. Takehisa Shinozaki and Yoko Takahashi largely contributed to this work as research assistants. We have benefited from comments provided by Hiroyuki Chuma, Noel Gaston and Koichi Hamada. All remaing errors are our own.

REFERENCES

Aoki, Masahiko (1988), *Information, Incentives, and Bargaining in the Japanese Economy*, Cambridge: Cambridge University Press.
Caplan Research Committees (2003), *The 100 Case Studies of Reemployment Challenge for Middle-aged Executives* (in Japanese), Tokyo: Toyo Keizai Shimposha.

Chuma, Hiroyuki (2002), 'Successful careers for job switching among middle and senior workers', in Yuji Genda and Yoshifumi Nakata (eds), *Mechanisms of Turnovers and Restructuring* (in Japanese), Tokyo: Toyo Keizai Shimposha, pp. 51–79.

Davis, Steven J., John C. Haltiwanger and Scott Schuh (1996), *Job Creation and Destruction*, Cambridge: MIT Press.

Genda, Yuji (1998), 'Job creation and destruction in Japan, 1991–1995', *Journal of the Japanese and International Economies*, **12**(1), 1–23.

Genda, Yuji (2001), 'Involuntary separations of middle-aged and older workers under restructuring of Japanese firms', the Third International Forum, ESRI.

Genda, Yuji (2003), 'Who really lost jobs in Japan? Youth employment in an aging Japanese society', in Seiritsu Ogawa, Toshiaki Tachibanaki and David A. Wise (eds), *Labor Markets and Fringe Benefit Policies in Japan and the United States*, Chicago: The University of Chicago Press, pp. 103–133.

Genda, Yuji and the ESRI Labor Market Study Group (2003), 'Empirical studies for job creation and unemployment in Japan', *Keizai Bunseki (Economic Analysis)* No. 168, Economic and Social Research Institute, Cabinet Office, Government of Japan.

Katz, Lawrence F. and Alan B. Krueger (1999), 'The high-pressure US labor market of the 1990s', *Brookings Papers on Economic Activity*, **1**, 1–65.

Koike, Kazuo (1988), *Understanding Industrial Relations in Modern Japan*, New York: St. Martin's Press.

Ohta, Soichi (2002), 'Reexamination of youth unemployment – its economic backgrounds', in Yuji Genda and Yoshifumi Nakata (eds), *Mechanisms of Turnovers and Restructuring* (in Japanese), Tokyo: Toyo Keizai Shimposha, pp. 249–275.

Teruyama, Hiroshi (2002), 'Employment opportunities and worker flows', in Yuji Genda and Yoshifumi Nakata (eds), *Mechanisms of Turnovers and Restructuring* (in Japanese), Tokyo: Toyo Keizai Shimposha, pp. 211–247.

2. Factors affecting labor force participation in Japan[1]: empirical study of labor supply of the elderly and females

Hirotsugu Sakai and Hitoshi Asaoka

1. INTRODUCTION

According to the 'Projection of Japanese Population' by the National Institute of Population and Social Security Research, the productive-age population of Japan, aged 15 to 64, will keep on decreasing due to the drastically decreasing fertility rate which reached its peak in 1995. The labor force population will decrease accordingly, and thus push down the potential growth of GDP. It is necessary to find a way to soften the negative impact of the shrinking working population on economic growth, especially by utilizing the elderly and female population who are willing to participate in the labor force.

Japan's female labor force participation rate by age exhibits a typical M-shaped curve with the troughs existing in the 25–34 years age groups. Its trough is deeper than those of most other developed countries. Thus, one possible and immediate way to increase the current labor force is to promote the labor force participation of the females aged 25–34. Not only from an economic aspect, but also from social and cultural aspects, policy measures to increase the female labor force in Japan today are desirable, considering the fact that more and more females are entering higher education.

Also, since there will be a sharp increase in the proportion of the elderly in Japan's population in the near future, promoting the labor force participation of the elderly would possibly have more quantitative impact on the total labor force. In contrast to the female labor force participation, the elderly's labor force participation rate in Japan has been one of the highest among developed countries. This is mainly due to the high rate of self-employed individuals and family-operated businesses in the primary industry (farming). However, because of the drastic changes in Japan's industry structure, this rate is decreasing. Especially considering the fact that the baby boomers born immediately after WWII mainly consisted of employees who will soon become 'the elderly', raising the labor force participation rate in the elderly is more urgent.

In the first half of this chapter, we study the current working behavior of the elderly in Japan. We consider the conditions that help to promote the employment of various kinds of elderly worker. Our study is distinctive in that it compares the elderly's intention to work and their actual working conditions using ordered probit models and Heckit procedures. The main results are the following: one of the ideal ways of working for the elderly is to work full-time for as long as possible by continuously acquiring skills. But the existing work-related education/training programs are for entry-level or low-skilled workers. Enhancing the programs, along with support measures that enable the elderly to benefit from the programs, is quite important. In addition, flexible work opportunities are not widely available in Japan. Considering that the elderly who are either unhealthy or who are skilled workers may wish to work more flexibly, establishing the working conditions that meet their needs is essential. It is also necessary to improve the image of flexible working by fair evaluation and an appropriate ability rating.

In the latter half of this chapter, we investigate the relationship between the working behavior of females and current institutional backgrounds. First, we try to find out what kind of characteristics married women exhibit under the current tax and social security systems (which are mainly based on the male breadwinner model). As has been widely discussed, the advantageous treatment of housewives under the current tax and social security systems in Japan is preventing females from working to their full potential. It is well-known that an obvious incentive mechanism exists that prevents female part-time workers from working full-time in Japan ('income-adjusting behavior'). We have found here that women's income-adjusting behavior (and thus their reduced labor participation) is more common when their husband's income is higher, implying that current tax and social security systems not only yield an unintended effect on income distribution, but also prevent women from working. When changing tax and social security systems, the government should take these complementary/secondary effects into account so that such changes do not unduly suppress female labor participation.

In Sakai and Asaoka (2001), we showed that reproductive behavior (fertility) and female labor participation is a simultaneous decision. Thus, if the woman chooses to have a child, she is likely to discontinue work. Our concern in this study is then what kind of policies/systems prevent women who face such a decision from discontinuing work. One way to prevent women from discontinuing work is the introduction of family-friendly systems, which have been becoming popular in current Japan. 'Family-friendly systems' are the systems that allow workers (both male and female) to work more flexibly in order to successfully combine child rearing with a career. We have confirmed here that family-friendly systems promote married female (with children) labor participation if systems are better prepared and publicized. Even under the recently introduced Child-Care Leave Law, its effect is limited unless complementary family-friendly systems exist at workplaces. In this respect, the government should promote the introduction of family-friendly systems at the workplace.

2.   EMPIRICAL IMPLEMENTATION OF WORKING BEHAVIOR OF THE ELDERLY

2.1   Issues on the Elderly Labor Supply in Japan

We may overcome the bleak prospects of an increasing social security burden and low economic growth in the ageing society by using the elderly effectively[2]. It is an urgent necessity to overcome the challenges presented by the ageing society by arranging by the working conditions so that the elderly who are willing to work can work as long as possible.

The majority of the elderly want to work until they are 65 and over. Then, what kinds of working conditions are necessary to fulfill their needs? We try to find out the gaps between the intention to work of the elderly and their actual working conditions. First, we give an account of their intention to work and their ideal working conditions by ordered probit models using our original survey data. Then, we try to compare them with the actual working conditions by using Heckit procedures, and explore the way that the elderly, who vary in their willingness to work, can participate in the labor market.

2.2   Data

The dataset used for our analyses is the survey on labor participation of the elderly conducted in August 2001. We randomly chose around 3900 samples, ranging from 50 to 64 years old, both male and female, from available addresses in Japan. More specifically, we chose 1300 samples from the following age group: 50–54, 55–59, and 60–64[3]. To reduce the bias of the dataset, it was collected using a stratified two-stage sampling method, that is, age and area. The questionnaires consisted of 44 questions, mainly focused on detailed individual characteristics on current labor status and the intention to work. We sent and collected them via the postal service, and obtained 1017 valid responses. Because respondents were free to choose whether or not to answer the questionnaire, the dataset might have some bias problems.

2.3 Ordered Probit Estimations of the Intention to Work of the Elderly

Until what age will the elderly want to work without taking into consideration the constraints that they might face? The result of our survey research is shown in Figure 2.1.

The results indicate that only about one-fifth want to retire by the age of 60, which is the most popular mandatory retirement age in Japan. The majority want to work until 65, and about one-fifth prefer to work until 70 or older. It seems that this is closely related to the starting age of pension payments.

In this subsection, we estimate two ordered probit models on the preferred retirement age to determine what factors are important for the elderly when deciding the length of their working years, and how many hours they want to work if they are to work over the age of 60.

Some questions in our survey research are multinomial choice variables that are inherently ordered. If the responses were coded 1, 2, 3, . . ., a linear regression would treat the difference between 3 and 2 the same as that between 2 and 1, when, in fact, they are only rankings. The ordered probit models have been widely used as a framework for analyzing these kinds of data.

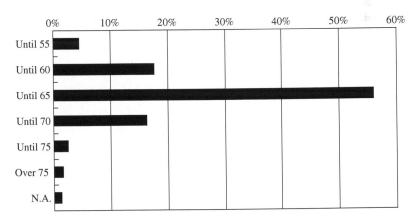

Source: Our survey in August 2001.

Figure 2.1   Preferred working age

The dependent variable of the first model, *preferred working age*, denoting the age one wants to work to is: =1 if the individual wants to work until 55; =2 if until 60; =3 if until 65; =4 if until 70; =5 if until 75; and =6 if over 75. We used the following as explanatory variables in this ordered probit model.

Health problems   Equal to 1 if the person has a health problem;[4] otherwise, 0.

Education attainment   Equal to 1 if the person has a bachelor's degree or more; otherwise, 0.

Work-related education/training[5]   Equal to 1 if the person has participated in work-related education/training programs; otherwise, 0.

Specialist[6]   Equal to 1 if the person is specialized in their work; otherwise, 0.

Changing jobs[7]   Equal to 1 if the person has experience of changing jobs; otherwise, 0.

Flexible work   Equal to 1 if the person wants to work as a temporary, part-time, contract employee, or teleworker if he/she is to work over the age of 60; otherwise, full-time, the variable is 0.

Amount of money one needs other than pension   A reasonable amount of money for living/leisure expenses per month other than pension payments.

Male   Equal to 1 if the person is male, and 0 if female.

Large company   Equal to 1 if the person works at a company with more than 1000 employees; otherwise, 0.

Among the variables, *health problems* and *large company* are negatively significant, and *educational attainment, work-related education/ training, changing jobs, the amount of money one needs other than pension,* and *male* are positively significant for deciding the working years (Table 2.1).

Then, how many hours do the elderly really want to work in a week?[8] According to our survey, about 40 per cent of the elderly want to work 30 hours a week, that is, 4 days a week. About 30 per cent of the elderly want to work 20 hours a week, that is, 3 days a week. About one-fifth of the elderly want to work full-time.

The second ordered probit model is on how many hours one wants to work over the age of 60. The dependent variable of the equation for preferred number of hours worked, *work hours,* is: =1 if he/she wants to work 10 hours; =2 if 20 hours; =3 if 30 hours; =4 if over 30 hours a week. We used the following as explanatory variables in this model. Variables not listed below are the same as before.

Table 2.1   Ordered probit estimation of the preferred working age

Variable	Parameter estimate	Standard error	Asymptotic t-statistic
Constant	0.888	0.152	5.830***
Health problems	−0.351	0.075	−4.690***
Educational attainment	0.225	0.108	2.083**
Work-related education/training	0.200	0.080	2.501**
Specialist	−0.050	0.070	−0.713
Changing jobs	0.148	0.078	1.906*
Flexible work	−0.126	0.083	−1.508
Amount of money one needs other than pension	0.269	0.048	5.605***
Male	0.365	0.108	3.387***
Large company	−0.287	0.080	−3.583***
μ_3	1.002	0.070	14.420***
μ_4	2.709	0.085	31.786***
μ_5	3.712	0.106	34.881***
μ_6	4.129	0.128	32.154***
Scaled $\bar{R}^2$	0.130		
N	991		

Notes:
* Statistically significant at the 10% level, ** statistically significant at the 5% level, *** statistically significant at the 1% level.
   The boundary values between the different categories are estimated parameters, μ_i. The μ_is are given names based on the category value for which they are the lower bound. For example, μ_3 is the lower bound for category with value 3. Negative values are not allowed.
   The scaled R-squared is a measure of goodness-of-fit relative to a model with just a constant term; it is a non-linear transformation of the likelihood ratio test for zero slopes.

Source: Authors' calculation.

Age   The person's age.
Full-time employee   Equal to 1 if the person is a full-time employee; otherwise, 0.
Retirement experience   Equal to 1 if the person has experience of retirement; otherwise, 0.
Pension payments[9]   An amount of public and private pension one receives on average every month.
Double income   Equal to 1 if the spouse of the person is working; otherwise, 0.
Work old   Equal to 1 if the person wants to work over 60 years of age; otherwise, 0.

Table 2.2   Ordered probit estimation on preferred number of hours worked

Variable	Parameter estimate	Standard error	Asymptotic t-statistic
Constant	0.547	0.451	1.214
Age	0.004	0.008	0.459
Health problems	−0.049	0.094	−0.521
Education attainment	0.256	0.113	2.276**
Work-related education/training	−0.001	0.100	−0.004
Specialist	−0.192	0.087	−2.216**
Full-time employee	0.482	0.113	4.258***
Retirement experience	0.472	0.136	3.464***
Pension payments	−0.014	0.005	−2.635***
Double income	0.076	0.089	0.860
Work old	0.927	0.116	7.997***
Large company	−0.082	0.107	−0.768
μ_3	1.456	0.100	14.540***
μ_4	2.857	0.114	25.094***
Scaled $\bar{R}^2$	0.183		
Sample size	672		

Note: See the notes to Table 2.1.

Source: Authors' calculation.

We restrict our sample to those who are working in view of comparing the result with the following Heckit procedures. Coefficients of *education attainment, full-time employee, retirement experience*, and *work old* are positively significant, and *specialist* and *pension payments* are negatively significant (Table 2.2).

The elderly with health problems do not want to enjoy flexible working opportunities by working short hours, while those who want to postpone retirement want to work full time if they are to work beyond the age of 60. *Education attainments* and *work-related education/training* have positive impacts on extending the number of working years. The better-educated also want to work full time even after the age of 60. Preferred retirement age is not affected by whether elderly workers are specialists or generalists, while the aged specialist wants to reduce the number of work hours. This is because the working pattern of specialists is better suited for flexible working arrangements. The elderly who want to work over the age of 60 are willing to work full time as long as possible and expect to develop their capacities by work-related education or training. It seems that they do not like to have the option to extend their working years by working flexibly.

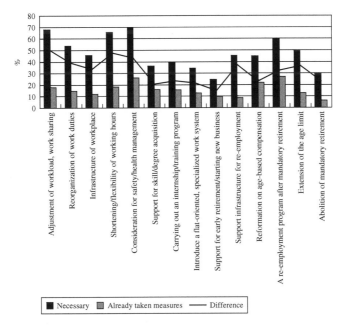

Source: Our survey in August 2001.

Figure 2.2 Working conditions desired by the elderly compared with actual working conditions (total 1017 firms)

On the other hand, Figure 2.2 shows what the elderly consider to be the necessary working conditions if they are to work over the age of 60, and assesses which conditions are already satisfied. Judging from the figure, factors such as adjustment of workload, work sharing, shortening or flexibility of working hours, and consideration for health management are thought to be necessary for elderly workers, but are not given much attention by Japanese firms. It means that flexible work opportunities are not well provided for in Japan. It is possible that the elderly who have professional qualifications and those who have health problems want to retire early because the working environment does not meet their needs.

2.4 Actual Working Conditions of the Elderly using Heckit Procedures

In this subsection, we try demonstrate the actual working conditions of the elderly using Heckit procedures. By comparing the result of ordered probit models and Heckit procedures, we can show clearly the difference between their intention to work and their actual working conditions.

We basically use estimation procedures known as generalized Tobit estimators, also often called Heckit procedures.[10] The data sample consists of 1017 people aged between 50 and 64, with 710 working as of August 2001. We used the following as explanatory variables in the Heckit procedures. Variables not listed below are the same as before.

Housing loans   Equal to 1 if the person was paying off housing loans; otherwise, 0.
Manager   Equal to 1 if the person was holding an administrative position; otherwise, 0.
City/town   Equal to 1, if the person lived in one of the 13 metropolitan cities with a population of over 300 000; otherwise, 0.
Lambda (λ)   Inverse Mill's ratio estimated from the labor participation function.
Wagefit   Predicted wage level calculated from the wage function.

The empirical framework of this section is as follows. A person will participate in the labor market if and only if the market wage exceeds the reservation wage,[11] that is, the minimum wage for which a person will work. This also means that if the reservation wage is higher than the market wage, a person will choose zero hours of work. Thus, the hours-worked function could be written as follows.

$$H_i = \alpha X + a W_m + u_{H_i} \quad \text{if } W_m > W_r,$$

$$H_i = 0, \quad \text{if } W_r > W_m. \tag{2.1}$$

W_r and W_m are the reservation wage and market wage. X is the vector of variables affecting an individual worker's reservation wage which include such factors as age, health conditions, and non-wage income,[12] α is the vector of parameters and a is a parameter, and u_H is an independently normally distributed random variable. Next, consider a model of labor force participation. The respondent either works ($Y=1$) or does not work ($Y=0$) in the period in which our survey is taken. A set of factors such as age, health condition, education level, specialist, public pension payments and others, denoted by vector X, explains the worker's decision, such that

$$\Pr(Y=1) = F(\beta' X)$$

$$\Pr(Y=0) = 1 - F(\beta' X) \tag{2.2}$$

The likelihood function for the labor participation observations from a sample consisting of workers Ω and non-workers Ω' can be written as

$$l = \prod_{i \in \Omega} F \cdot \prod_{i \in \Omega'} [1 - F], \qquad (2.3)$$

where i denotes individuals.

Estimation involves standard probit procedures. The set of parameters β reflect the impact of changes in X on the probability. The results of estimating the participation function by probit estimation are shown in Table 2.3. We show the probit coefficients and marginal effect, which indicates the probability magnitude of the effect of each variable. All the variables except *education attainment* and *work-related education/training* are statistically significant, and all parameter signs are consistent with those predicted.

The function shows that as a person gets older, his/her labor participation probability is reduced. The probability magnitude shows that if a person has health problems, it will reduce the labor participation probability by 6 per cent. The probability will increase by about 11 per cent if a person specializes in his/her work. The sign is consistent because specialists seem to have more opportunities to find appropriate jobs than generalists.

Table 2.3   Empirical results of the participation function by probit estimation

Variable	Parameter estimate	Standard error	Asymptotic t-statistic	Marginal effect
Constant	1.340	0.428	3.131***	0.330
Age	−0.025	0.008	−3.314***	−0.006
Health problems	−0.224	0.101	−2.199**	−0.055
Education attainment	0.193	0.142	1.354	0.047
Work-related education/training	−0.113	0.109	−1.037	−0.028
Specialist	0.462	0.097	4.745***	0.114
Retirement experience	−0.377	0.131	−2.885***	−0.093
Changing jobs	0.231	0.109	2.121**	0.057
Pension payments	−0.042	0.004	−9.593***	−0.010
Housing loans	0.412	0.114	3.624***	0.101
Male	1.086	0.149	7.311***	0.267
City/town	−0.203	0.107	−1.909*	−0.050
Log likelihood	−445.066			
N	1017			

Note: See the notes to Table 2.1.

Source: Authors' calculation.

Once the aged person has experienced mandatory retirement, the probability is reduced by 9 per cent; age discrimination of elderly job applicants by Japanese firms might be one of the reasons for this, as Higuchi (2001) has suggested. Consequently, experience of mandatory retirement becomes a disincentive for the elderly to apply for new jobs. On the other hand, changing jobs increases the probability by 6 per cent. The public pension eligibility was statistically insignificant in the labor participation function in Sakai and Asaoka (2001). However, using the amount of pension payments, instead of pension eligibility, yields significant results. The greater pension one receives, the less one participates in the labor force. Living in metropolitan areas reduces the labor participation probability by 5 per cent. Although it seems easier to find job opportunities in these areas, it might be hard for the elderly to endure the horrendous commutes.

Table 2.4 shows the empirical results for the market wage function by Heckit procedures, that is estimating the following market wage function.

$$\ln(W_m) = \gamma Y + b\lambda + V_m, ^{[13]} \tag{2.4}$$

Table 2.4 Empirical results for the market wage function using Heckit procedures

Variable	Parameter estimate	Standard error	Asymptotic t-statistic
Constant	−1.831	0.206	−8.867***
Age	0.005	0.003	1.316
Education attainment	0.140	0.060	2.351**
Work-related education/training	−0.061	0.047	−1.289
Specialist	0.027	0.044	0.614
Manager	0.322	0.045	7.172***
Full-time employee	0.138	0.056	2.456**
Retirement experience	−0.116	0.064	−1.807*
Changing jobs	−0.093	0.045	−2.057**
Large company	0.281	0.050	5.574***
City/town	0.043	0.046	0.936
λ	−0.172	0.091	−1.885*
Adjusted $\bar{R}^2$	0.212		
N	700		

Note: See the notes to Table 2.1.

Source: Authors' calculation.

where Y is the vector of variables such as the factor of labor demand, λ is inverse Mill's ratio[14] estimated from the labor participation function, γ and b are vectors of parameters, V_m is a random term. The estimate was corrected for sample-selectivity bias using inverse Mill's ratio that was derived from the labor participation function.

Among the variables, the coefficients of *education attainments, manager, full-time employee,* and *large company* are positively significant, and *retirement experience* and *changing jobs* are negatively significant. The statistical significance of λ suggests the importance of correcting for selectivity in estimating a market wage equation. Judging from the coefficients, market wage rate varies greatly according to whether or not an employee works full-time.[15] We also should note that being a specialist is not a significant factor for market wages. Retirement and job-change experiences have tendencies to reduce the wage rate.

Table 2.5 shows the results of estimates of hours-worked function. The function is given by the following:

$$H = \delta X + c \ln (W_m) + d\lambda + V_h, \tag{2.5}$$

Table 2.5 Empirical results for the hours-worked function using Heckit procedures

Variable	Parameter estimate	Standard error	Asymptotic t-statistic
Constant	232.203	27.601	8.413***
Age	−0.487	0.371	−1.312
Health problems	6.003	4.272	1.405
Work-related education/training	4.221	4.803	0.879
Specialist	−4.934	4.164	−1.185
Full-time employee	15.629	6.190	2.525**
Retirement experience	3.940	4.664	0.845
Double income	−4.763	3.885	−1.226
Large company	−9.496	4.215	−2.253**
Wagefit	20.844	10.067	2.071**
λ	−43.459	8.687	−5.003***
Adjusted $\bar{R}^2$	0.143		
N	700		

Note: See the notes to Table 2.1.

Source: Authors' calculation.

where H is the person's monthly hours worked, X is a vector of factors that may affect both labor participation and the optimal hours of work, λ is the inverse Mill's ratio estimated from the labor participation function, δ, c and d are parameters, and V_h is a random term.

Estimated coefficients of *full-time, large company, wagefit* and λ are significant. It is quite interesting, although the significance level is low, that the elderly with health problems tend to work more hours than healthy workers. And the coefficient of *specialist* in the hours-worked function of the Heckit model is insignificant.

2.5 Comparison of the Intention to Work and Actual Working Conditions of the Elderly

The results of ordered probit models show that one of the ideal ways of working for the elderly is to work full time as long as possible by developing their capacities through work-related education or training. Is it really possible? Work-related education/training is not significant in the labor participation function. In addition, while having a low significance level, it has a negative impact on wages using Heckit procedures. This is because the main targets for work-related education/training programs are entry-level or low skilled workers. Current work-related education/training programs are not effective tools for the elderly to develop their competence in the labor market. Under the present system, it might be hard for them to develop their capacities and extend their working years as a full-time employee by participating in the program. They need programs for advanced and sophisticated technologies.

Our ordered probit models show that the elderly do not seem to have any interest in extending their working years by flexible working. Aged specialists want to reduce their working hours, but in reality, the Heckit model tells us that they do not do so. In addition the elderly workers with health problems tend to work more hours. This all suggests that there is little demand for Japanese firms to provide flexible working opportunities for aged workers. At present, Japanese firms do not offer a variety of work opportunities that correspond to the diversified needs of the elderly.

Fair evaluation and an appropriate ability rating system for various types of elderly workers are also lacking in Japanese firms. Our ordered probit models show that the preferred retirement age is not affected by whether the elderly worker is a specialist or a generalist. According to the Heckit models, labor participation probability will increase if a person specializes in his/her work. Specialists are in great demand in the market. However, being a specialist is not a significant factor for market wages. Considering that our labor participation function, shows that they are likely to get a job, specialists are poorly regarded. An ability rating system, along with flexible working arrangements, is of no use to aged specialists. We should also note that there is a great difference in market wage rate between full-time workers and those of other status, such as temporary, part-time, or contract employees. There is some kind of discrimination against them, and this must be addressed in case work sharing is introduced. Fair evaluation and an appropriate ability rating system needs to wipe out the negative images of employees who do not work full time.

3. THE EFFECT OF THE CURRENT TAX AND SOCIAL SECURITY SYSTEMS ON MARRIED WORKING FEMALES

3.1 Issues on Female Labor in Japan

As mentioned in the introduction, Japan's female labor force participation rate displays a distinctive M-shaped curve by age and its trough is deeper than that of most developed countries. This implies that Japanese women tend to leave their jobs after getting married. Promoting the female labor force participation rate is also a desirable measure from the social and cultural point of view. In this section, we examine whether the current tax and social security systems affect their working behaviors.

3.2 Data and Institutional Background

In this study on females, we conducted a survey of female labor participation in August 2001. We randomly chose around 7500 female samples (aged between 20 and 49 years old) from available addresses in Japan. More specifically, we chose 1250 samples from the following age groups: 20–24, 25–29, 30–34, 35–39, 40–44, and 45–49. The questionnaires were sent and collected via the postal service. Eventually, we obtained 1308 valid responses. Since this survey was not collected using personal interviews, and respondents were free to choose whether or not to answer our questionnaire, the dataset generated by this survey will, to a certain extent, have bias problems. The questionnaire consisted of 46 questions. These mainly focused on detailed individual characteristics, such as marital status, financial situation, working status, and others. In particular, we drew up the questionnaire so that we could examine the following issue.

In this section, using only working married female samples from the dataset, we try to find out what kind of characteristics married females exhibit under the current tax and social security systems, and in particular,

Table 2.6   Current tax treatment and part-time worker's income

Part-time worker's annual income (in yen)	Part-time worker's tax treatment		Spouse's (husband's) tax treatment	
	Income tax on part-time worker's income	Residence tax on part-time worker's income	Tax exemption for spouses (wives)	Special tax exemption for spouses (wives)
Under 1 000 000	Exempt	Exempt	Applicable	Applicable
1 000 001 to 1 030 000	Exempt	Not exempt	Applicable	Applicable
1 030 000	Exempt	Not exempt	Applicable	Applicable
1 030 001 to 1 410 000	Not exempt	Not exempt	Not applicable	Applicable
Over 1 410 000	Not exempt	Not exempt	Not applicable	Not applicable

Note: As of February, 2001.

Source: Government data.

if these systems are actually preventing female part-time workers from working full-time in Japan. More precisely, we check if part-time workers adjust their hours worked so that their annual incomes do not exceed a certain amount. The institutional backgrounds are summarized in Table 2.6 and Box 2.1.

Among earlier research, Abe and Ohtake (1995), using the survey of part-time workers conducted by the Ministry of Labour in 1990, examined whether Japan's current tax and social security systems prevent women from working. Using descriptive statistics and estimating the hours-worked function, they find that a special tax exemption for spouses, allowances for spouses provided by their husband's company, and the social security system cause part-time workers to adjust their working hours so that annual income does not exceed 1.0 million yen.

More recently, Kohara (2001) examined the effect of the current tax and social security systems by using households' panel data collected by the Household Economic Research Institute in 1993. Kohara reported that 5.8 per cent of non-working housewives choose not to work in order to stay eligible for tax exemption for spouses, and that 27.5 per cent of working housewives adjust their income for the same reason. Kohara pointed out that for the group of income-adjusting housewives, their husbands' annual income is slightly higher than the non-adjusting group, and that income-adjusting housewives have higher educational backgrounds.

BOX 2.1   CURRENT SOCIAL SECURITY SYSTEM
           AND PART-TIME WORKER'S INCOME

● If the hours worked by the part-time worker (who is married
  and whose spouse is working full-time) exceed three-
  quarters of a full-time worker's hours worked (i.e., around 30
  hours per week), then he/she must self-enroll with the social
  security system and must pay the social security contribution, regardless of his/her annual income.

● If the annual income of the part-time worker (who is married
  and whose spouse is working full-time) does not exceed
  1 300 000 yen and if his/her hours worked do not exceed three-
  quarters of a full-time worker's hours worked, then he/she
  does not have to pay his/her own social security contribution.
  He/she can still receive the full amount of basic pension.

● If the annual income of the part-time worker (who is married
  and whose spouse is working full-time) exceeds 1 300 000
  yen then he/she must self-enroll with the social security
  system and must pay the social security contribution, even
  if his/her hours worked are under three-quarters of a full-
  time worker's hours worked.

Note: As of February, 2001.

Source: Government data.

3.3   Data

In order to determine the type of females who adjust their annual income
level within a certain amount, we have chosen a sample covering both
married and currently working women from our dataset. The size of this
sample becomes 564 out of 1308. However, since some of the respondents
did not provide answers necessary for the explanatory variables we were planning to use, the size of the sample falls to 467 out of 564. Among 467 sample
points, 132 women answered that they adjust their annual income level for a
reason other than to remain under the minimum taxable income level.

3.4   Some Observations on the Dataset

Before implementing an econometric analysis of females' income-adjusting
behavior, Figure 2.3 summarizes the answers to the question in our

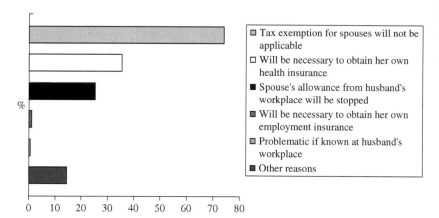

Source: Our survey in August 2001.

Figure 2.3   Reasons for income adjusting

questionnaire that asks for the specific reason for respondents' income-adjusting behavior. The respondents were allowed to choose up to two reasons.

It is shown that 74.0 per cent of the respondents have chosen 'tax exemption for spouses will not be applicable [if they earn more]'. As shown before, this means that they are adjusting their annual income level within 1.03 million yen (to make their husbands eligible for 'tax exemption for spouses') or within 1.41 million yen (to make their husbands eligible for 'special tax exemption for spouses'). Here it is worth mentioning that there are two samples who cannot be eligible for any tax exemption, considering their own and their husbands' annual income level. As Higuchi (1995) pointed out, they might not be well informed about current tax system.

The figure shows that 35.3 per cent of the respondents have chosen '[if they work or earn more, then] it will be necessary to obtain her own health insurance' as a reason, implying that they are adjusting their income level within 1.30 million yen and that their hours worked do not exceed three-quarters of full-time hours worked. 'Spouse's allowance from husband's workplace will be stopped' was selected by 25.4 per cent. Threshold income levels would differ among companies, but they are usually in line with the tax exemption level, namely, around 1.0 million yen.

Next, we would like to see frequency distributions of samples in order to grasp differences between income-adjusting females and non-adjusting females. Figure 2.4(i) exhibits a frequency distribution of annual income. The solid black line corresponds to those who are 'adjusting', and the thin line corresponds to those who are 'not adjusting'. As expected, the

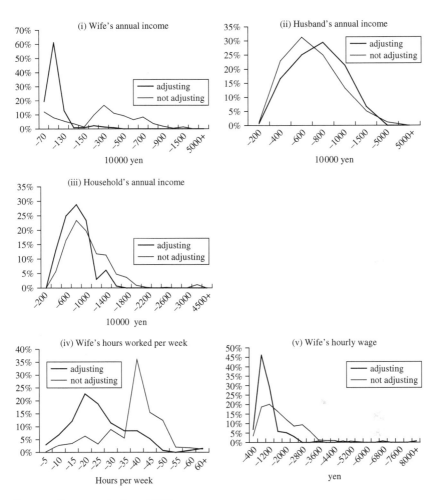

Source: Our survey in August 2001.

Figure 2.4 Frequency distributions

adjusting samples' distribution is significantly spiked at 0.7–1.03 million yen and truncated at 1.41 million yen. Also, even though they identified themselves as 'non-adjusting', a certain number of 'non-adjusting' females are actually eligible for tax exemption. Figure 2.4(ii) shows a frequency distribution of husbands' annual income level. The curves are almost the same as each other, but their peaks are significantly different. Namely, husbands of adjusting samples have higher annual income levels on average than the other group. Although there might be a slight difference, the husbands' income distribution of non-adjusting samples seems to be skewed to the right compared to the other group. Figure 2.4(iii) shows a distribution of households' annual income for both groups. In the questionnaire, we did not ask respondents to write down their exact annual income amount, so we took the average of each annual income level (for example, 2.0–4.0 million yen level = 3.0 million yen) to obtain the households' income. Thus, this graph is possibly misleading, but it can still be inferred that non-adjusting households' distribution is rather skewed to the right.

Figures 2.4(iv) and 2.4(v) exhibit distributions of samples' hours worked and hourly wage respectively. As for Figure 2.4(iv), as expected, the peaks are significantly different, meaning that adjusting samples are working significantly less than the other group. As for Figure 2.4(v), showing distribution of hourly wage (again, we took averages of annual income level to calculate hourly wages; here we asked the exact number of hours worked in the questionnaire), adjusting samples' distribution is heavily spiked at a relatively low wage level. This implies either that adjusting samples might intentionally choose low wage jobs or that they can only find low wage jobs for some reason.

3.5   Probit Estimation of the Factors of Females' Income-adjusting Behavior

Now our concern is to consider what kind of factors lead to females' income-adjusting behavior. In the following, we present an estimate result of a univariate probit model where we took the binary indicator for income-adjusting behavior as a dependent variable (equal to 1 if the female is adjusting her income; otherwise, the variable is 0). As stated before, the sample used here covers both married and currently working women. We used the following as explanatory variables in this probit estimation.

Housing loan   Equal to 1 if the female (household) owns a house with housing loan; otherwise, 0.

Self-employed   Equal to 1 if the female is self-employed; otherwise, 0.

Self-employed (husband)   Equal to 1 if the husband is self-employed; otherwise, 0.

Education I   Equal to 1 if the female has a university degree or higher; otherwise, 0.

Education II   Equal to 1 if the female has a technical school/two-year college degree; otherwise, 0.

Spouse's allowance   Equal to 1 if the husband's workplace offers spouse's allowance and with the limit dependent on the female's income; otherwise, 0.

System to telecommute Equal to 1 if the female's workplace offers telecommuting opportunities; otherwise, 0.

Flex-time system Equal to 1 if the female's workplace offers a flex-time system; otherwise, 0.

City Equal to 1 if the female lives in one of the 13 metropolitan areas or a city with a population of over 0.3 million; otherwise, 0.

Husband's income Natural logarithm for the husband's annual income. (We took an average of each income range to obtain the husband's income. For example, 'Under 2.0 million' = 2.0 million, '2.0 to 4.0 million' = 3.0 million, . . ., '15.0 to 50.0 million' = 32.5 million, 'Over 50.0 million' = 50.0 million.)

We did not use the types of working arrangements (part-time, full-time, and so on) as an explanatory variable, because it perfectly predicts income-adjusting behavior, that is, all of the part-time samples are adjusting their income.

Summary statistics are shown in Appendix Table 2.A2. In this sample, 28.3 per cent of females are adjusting their annual income. Also, it is worth noting that almost half of the husbands' workplaces offer spouse's allowance with the limit dependent on the female's income.

Table 2.7 presents parameter estimates, standard errors, (asymptotic) t-statistics, and marginal effects using a univariate probit model to estimate the binary decision of income-adjusting behavior by the currently working married females.

According to this result, it can be inferred that the female is more likely to adjust her income if she does not have a university degree or higher, her workplace offers a telecommuting facility, and, as expected, her husband's income is higher. *Spouse's allowance* and *City* are significant only at the 25 per cent level. The finding that husbands of income-adjusting females tend to exhibit higher annual income is in line with previous literature (Higuchi, 1995; Kohara, 2001). Although current tax and social security systems were primarily intended to benefit low-income households, in practice they do not.

It is also noteworthy that *system to telecommute* causes income-adjusting behavior. This system indeed allows females to work flexibly, and can primarily be considered to promote female (especially with a child/children) labor participation, but the current tax and social security systems seem to prevent its effect.

The problem here is that most earlier research reports that females with a background of higher education are likely to adjust their income. However, our study is still in line with earlier research but actually adds new findings, considering the following facts.

Table 2.7　Estimate for income-adjusting behavior by probit

	Parameter estimate	Standard error	t-statistic	Marginal effect
Constant	−2.584	0.929	−2.782**	−0.838
Housing loan	−0.047	0.129	−0.362	−0.015
Self-employed	0.026	0.224	0.116	0.008
Self-employed (husband)	−0.019	0.264	−0.074	−0.006
Education I	−0.499	0.184	−2.718***	−0.162
Education II	−0.111	0.147	−0.758	−0.036
Spouse's allowance	0.206	0.134	1.540−	0.067
System to telecommute	0.959	0.433	2.215**	0.311
Flex-time system	−0.219	0.342	−0.641	−0.071
City	0.188	0.133	1.413−	0.061
Husband's Income	0.315	0.149	2.114**	0.102
Log likelihood	−267.429			
N	467			
# of income adjusting	132			

Notes:
* Significant at the 10% level.
** Significant at the 5% level.
*** Significant at the 1% level.
− Significant at the 25% level.

Source:　Authors' calculation.

For example, Higuchi (1995) shows that, using part-time workers' data collected by the Ministry of Health, Labour and Welfare, a female earning a low wage and with a higher education background tends to adjust her income. The important difference between this study and ours is that its dataset does not contain full-time workers at all, while ours contains both. Kohara (2001) shows, as we stated before, that 5.8 per cent of non-working spouses choose not to work in order to remain eligible for tax exemption for spouses and that these females' husbands' average income and their own educational backgrounds are higher than other females, using the samples consisting of currently married females aged from 24 to 34. The difference between this study and ours here is that our dataset does not contain any non-working females.

Therefore, considering the fact that there are no female part-time workers who do not adjust their income in our dataset, and that we are looking at a sample consisting only of women who are currently working, it can be roughly inferred that females with higher educational backgrounds choose not to work at all rather than to work as a part-time worker with a low wage, if they wish to adjust their income under the current tax and social security systems. In other words, if the woman has a background of higher education, then the choice is binary for her. If our conjecture is correct, we may say that currently full-time-working females with higher education backgrounds are not likely to give up their full-time job in order only to adjust their income even if there are just slight changes in the income threshold in the system. For the females with well-accumulated human capital, the opportunity cost might be too expensive.

As Higuchi (1995) showed, it may still be true that the female part-time worker who is adjusting her income tends to have a higher education background, but it does not imply that the female with higher education always chooses to work as a part-time worker with a low wage in order to adjust her income.

4. ARE 'FAMILY-FRIENDLY' SYSTEMS ACTUALLY PROMOTING MARRIED FEMALE LABOR PARTICIPATION?

4.1 How to Successfully Combine Child Rearing with a Career

Promoting the female labor force participation rate will certainly increase the total labor force in Japan, but such measures should not prevent women from having children, as the main reason for the decrease in population in Japan is the rapidly declining fertility rate. Therefore, we also need measures to develop an environment for working women with a child/children. In this section, we examine the effect of the family-friendly systems which are now being introduced more and more at workplaces.

4.2 Earlier Research

Earlier research, especially about the maternity leave system, mostly confirmed that such systems are effective (Higuchi, 1994; Shigeno and Ohkusa, 1998; and others). More recently, Maeda (2000), using female samples in their 30s living in the metropolitan areas, has examined the kind of policies that are actually desired by married females who wish to continue to work. Maeda reported that non-working females (who actually would like to work) preferred flexible work in terms of hours worked rather than compensation for taking leave, or longer maternity leave.

In the following, using married female samples with a child/children from our dataset, we would like to find out whether or not family-friendly systems at workplace are actually promoting female labor participation.

4.3 Data

We use a sample consisting of those who are married and who have a child/children and with current/previous working experience. The size of this sample is 691 from a total sample size of 1308. Eliminating observations with missing values of relevant variables, the number of samples then becomes 644. Among 644 samples, 458 females are currently working.

4.4 Probit Estimation of Female Labor Participation under Family-friendly Systems

Our specific question here is whether or not family-friendly systems at the females' workplaces (particularly those that are intended to promote work flexibility and labor participation) are actually promoting female labor participation. In the questionnaire, we asked both currently working females and currently non-working females with previous work experience if there are/were any family-friendly systems at their workplaces. More specifically, we asked if there were any of the following systems at the workplace (respondents were allowed to choose as many as they liked):

- Holiday system for child rearing, giving birth to a child
- Holiday system for nursing sick parents
- System for telecommuting
- Re-employment system
- Child-care facility
- Flex-time system
- Compensation (cash) for child care.

In what follows, we present three estimate results of univariate probit models where we took the binary indicator of working currently as a dependent variable (equal to 1 if the female is currently working; otherwise, 0). We used the following as explanatory variables in estimation.

Children under 6 Equal to 1 if the female has a child/children under 6 years old; otherwise, 0.
Family member who needs nursing Equal to 1 if the female is living with a family member who needs nursing care; otherwise, 0.

Living with mother(s)   Equal to 1 if the female is living with her own mother or mother-in-law; otherwise, 0.

Three or more systems   Equal to 1 if the number of systems at the female's current workplace/the last workplace exceeds three; otherwise, 0.

One or two systems   Equal to 1 if the number of systems at the female's current workplace/the last workplace are either one or two; otherwise, 0.

Housing loan, Education I, Education II, City, Husband's income   As above in section 3.5.

We considered using seven systems as dummy variables at the same time (that is, if a holiday system for nursing sick parents is present, then 1, 0 otherwise, and so on). However, this model gave us an ambiguous result, possibly due to collinearity. So we omit that result here.

Summary statistics are presented in Appendix Table 2.A3. In this sample, 71.1 per cent of females are currently working. The mean of the number of family-friendly systems at the workplace is only 0.741. Only 285 samples answered that there was at least one system at their current/previous workplace. Here, it must be noted that those systems were counted only when the respondents actually knew that there were such systems at their workplace. Therefore, it is highly possible that the true number of systems available could be higher. But, in the following estimation, we do not think that fact causes problems. Unless the women know that those systems exist at their workplace, they are actually not effective at all.

Table 2.8 presents parameter estimates, standard errors, (asymptotic) t-statistics, and marginal effects by three different univariate probit model to estimate the binary decision faced by currently working married females with a child/children, who have experience of working.

Table 2.8 presents the result where we use two binary indicators (*Three or more family-friendly systems* and *One or two systems*) as explanatory variables. It shows that even if family-friendly systems exist at the workplace, if the number of systems available is small, then the female is not likely to continue to work, since the *One or two systems* dummy variable is not found to be statistically significant.

4.5 Characteristics of Companies with Family-friendly Systems

To conclude of this section, we would like to see what types of company have family-friendly systems. In what follows we focus only on currently working sample points taken from the previous samples. Figure 2.5(i) shows the relationship between type of employment and the number of family-friendly systems at the workplace. For example, at workplaces of full-time workers, 19.9 per cent of workplaces do not have any systems, 63.7

Table 2.8   Estimate for female labor participation by probit

	Parameter estimate	Standard error	t-statistic	Marginal effect
Constant	2.662	0.822	3.239***	0.805
Housing loan	0.049	0.115	0.425	0.015
Children under 6	−0.932	0.127	−7.338***	−0.282
Family member who needs nursing	−0.294	0.285	−1.030	−0.089
Living with mother(s)	0.282	0.138	2.046**	0.085
Education I	−0.139	0.156	−0.891	−0.042
Education II	0.113	0.133	0.844	0.034
City	0.236	0.115	−2.051**	−0.071
Husband's income	−0.286	0.129	−2.211**	−0.086
Three or more systems	0.564	0.268	2.099**	0.170
One or two systems	0.003	0.117	0.028	0.001
Log likelihood	−345.841			
N	644			
# of currently working	458			

Notes:
** Significant at the 5% level.
*** Significant at the 1% level.

Source: Authors' calculation.

per cent have one or two systems, and 16.4 per cent have three or more systems. This graph tells us that part-time workers' and dispatched workers'[16] workplaces do not carry many family-friendly systems, at least for part-time workers.

Figure 2.5(ii) shows the relationship between types of company and the number of family-friendly systems. This indicates that public workplaces are better equipped with family-friendly systems than private workplaces. It is striking that 62.1 per cent of private workplaces do not carry family-friendly systems.

Figure 2.5(iii) shows the relationship between the size of company and the number of family-friendly systems. Workplaces with fewer than 99 employees are significantly ill-equipped with family-friendly systems. This fact is somewhat in line with the survey conducted by the Japan Institute of Labour (2001) which reported that companies with more than 1000 employees were attaching more importance to family-friendly systems.

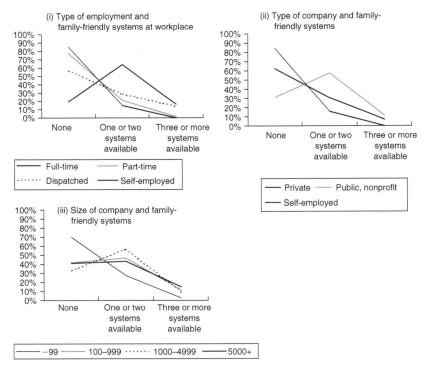

(i) Type of employment and family-friendly systems at workplace

Full-time — Part-time
Dispatched — Self-employed

(ii) Type of company and family-friendly systems

Private — Public, nonprofit
Self-employed

(iii) Size of company and family-friendly systems

−99 — 100–999 ⋯⋯ 1000–4999 — 5000+

Source: Our survey in August 2001.

Figure 2.5   Frequency distributions

5.   CONCLUSION

We have tried to analyze the factors affecting labor force participation of females and the elderly, which are important issues in view of the approaching ageing society, by using original survey data, and have considered what government, firms and employees should do to cope with problems caused by rapid ageing of the population.

We have examined the conditions necessary for the labor supply of the elderly with diversified work intentions in section 2. To work full-time for as long as possible is one of the ideal ways of working for the elderly. It is necessary for them to develop their skills by work-related education/training programs; however, present programs are not effective for this. Government and firms have to set some criteria for working qualifications to reduce the information asymmetry and to enrich the education/training programs so that they are of mutual benefit to firms and the elderly. Policy rules to prohibit age discrimination in employment, such as a mandatory retirement system, are also necessary for the elderly who are skilled. In addition, participating in the programs need time and funds. Requesting firms to guarantee their elderly employees participation in the programs, along with supporting them to adjust their workload, reducing their working hours, and paying their training expenses, are all required policies to promote long-term employment of the elderly who are willing to work. We should also note that ability, health conditions, and willingness to work of the elderly are diversified. Japanese firms should make an effort to offer a variety of work opportunities to meet their needs. It is necessary to create a more positive image of flexible working by establishing fair evaluation systems of various types of elderly workers, in order to increase the numbers of flexible workers.

In section 3, we confirmed that females' income-adjusting behavior (and thus a reduction in their labor participation) is more common when their husband's income is higher. Current tax and social security systems not only yield an unintended effect on income distribution, but also prevent certain numbers of females from working. Also, it is worth mentioning that even if workplaces introduce systems that allow females to work more flexibly, such systems may be reducing female labor participation under the current tax and social security systems, which are certainly dated. Future changes in policy promoting female labor have to take this effect into account.

In section 4, we confirmed that family-friendly systems promote labor participation of married women (with children) if systems are better prepared and publicized. Even under current Child-Care Leave Law, its effect is quite limited unless there are more complementary family-friendly systems at workplaces. Under the current economic situation in Japan, it might be difficult for employers to introduce family-friendly systems now, but firms (in particular, smaller firms) still need to be made aware that they will suffer from a shortage of human resources in the near future, unless they introduce such systems. Also considering the fact that there are significant numbers of females who choose to work part-time, the current Child-Care Leave Law might have to be updated, as the current law does not apply to short-term workers.

Finally, according to the empirical results that we have obtained in this chapter, we propose the following policy recommendations, to prevent Japan from suffering an undesirable labor shortage in the future.

- Enhance work-related education/training programs, so that the elderly who are willing to work can acquire skills, as the existing programs are often intended only for unskilled workers. Setting some criteria for working qualifications by firms and government is also necessary for the program to be effective.

- Prohibit age discrimination in employment, so that the elderly who are skilled can work for as long as possible.
- Support the elderly by adjusting their workload, reducing their working hours, and paying their training expenses, so that they can easily participate in the training/education programs.
- Establish work conditions to meet the diversified needs of the elderly to enable them to work more flexibly. In addition, negative images of flexible working must be changed by setting up fair evaluation systems.
- When changing tax and social security systems, the government should take into account their complementary/secondary effects so that such changes do not unduly suppress female labor participation.
- The current Child-Care Leave Law definitely needs complementary systems, that is, family-friendly systems at the workplace, in order for the law to be more effective. Considering the current economic situation in Japan, the government should promote the introduction of family-friendly systems at the workplace. Firms should also be aware that they could possibly attract a high-quality female labor force by introducing such systems.

Overall, the government should focus not only on the labor shortage in terms of quantity, but also consider labor market policies that promote a high-quality labor force which is currently suppressed directly or indirectly by existing economic and social systems. In particular, as we discussed in this chapter, the elderly who have accumulated significant professional skills because of longer working experience, and females, who are exhibiting higher educational attainment than before, should not only compensate the shortage in the labor force, but also increase labor productivity.

NOTES

1. We would like to thank Prof. Koichi Hamada of Yale University, Prof. Toshiaki Tachibanaki of Kyoto University, Dr Robert Dekle of University of Southern California, Mr Hiromi Kato and Dr Mitsuo Hosen of the Economic and Social Research Institute, and other participants at 'Collaboration projects on studying economic and social systems in the 21st Century' funded by the Economic and Social Research Institute, Cabinet Office, Japan. And we are indebted to an anonymous referee for valuable suggestions. The views expressed here are those of the authors and not necessarily those of Mitsubishi Research Institute, Inc. or of ESRI.
2. Genda (2003) discusses the fact that extending employment for the old is likely to reduce new job opportunities, particularly for young workers. Japan Institute for Labour Policy

and Training (2003) shows that the EU countries with a low youth unemployment rate have a high employment rate for elderly.

3. We chose 520 samples from municipalities with a population of more than 300 000, 260 samples from municipalities between 100 000–300 000, 520 samples from municipalities with less than 100 000 in each age group by using the 1995 Census.

4. The questionnaire asked 'If you were to consider working after the age of 60, how would you describe your state of health?'

5. The corresponding question is 'Have you received work-related education/training in the past outside of your workplace?'

6. The question is, 'If you do have work experience, did your work consist of specialized/ professional functions or did your work consist of more general/basic functions?' Two options: 1. I held a position that involved handling specific matters revolving around the field I specialized in; and 2. I held a position that involved handling a variety of functions related to various fields.

7. Temporarily transferring jobs from one company to another within the same group does not count.

8. The questionnaire asked 'If you want to work over the age of 60, how many hours on average do you want to work in a week?'.

9. We adopted pension eligibility and non-wage income dummies in our 2001 study, Sakai and Asaoka (2001), but they were statistically insignificant in the labor participation decision.

10. This is a standard labor supply model originally developed by Heckman (1979). Seike and Shimada (1994) adopted this procedure using the data for 55–69 year-olds from the Employment Status Survey of the Elderly by the Japanese Ministry of Labor in 1980 and 1983.

11. Income–leisure preference and income from non-labor sources, such as pension benefits, are the main explanatory variables for the reservation wage.

12. Age and health conditions are also thought to be explanatory variables for the market wage. Other explanatory variables are: education attainment, retirement experience, being a specialist, and so on.

13. The dependent variable for this function is the natural logarithm of the person's average hourly earnings, made by dividing annual salary by working hours, in August 2001.

14. We should note that the data obtained from our questionnaire, such as the numbers of hours worked and wages, are observed only for persons who are actually working. This means that there is a problem of sample selectivity bias in estimating the labor supply and market wage functions. Heckman (1979, 1980) has suggested adding an estimate of the inverse Mill's ratio as a regressor. The estimation problems are especially serious in the analysis of the labor supply behavior of married women, since a large part of this group will not be working (Mroz, 1987). Another alternative procedure for handling this sample selectivity issue has been suggested by Olsen (1980). Maddala (1983) gives a detailed explanation on the selectivity models.

15. That is, temporary, part-time, or contract employee.

16. 'Dispatched workers' here means workers employed and dispatched by temporary labor agencies.

REFERENCES

Abe, Y. and F. Ohtake (1995), 'Part-time labor supply and tax and social security system', *Kikan Shakai Hosho Kenkyu*, **31**(2) (in Japanese).

Genda, Y. (2003), 'Who really lost jobs in Japan? Youth employment in an aging Japanese society', in Seiritsu Ogura, Toshiaki Tachibanaki and David A. Wise (eds), *Markets and Firm Benefit Policies in Japan and the United States*, University of Chicago Press, pp. 103–33.

Greene, W.H. (1993), *Econometric Analysis*, 2nd edn, Prentice Hall.

Heckman, J.J. (1979), 'Sample selection bias as a specification error', *Econometrica*, **47**(1), January, pp. 153–62.

Heckman, J.J. (1980), 'Sample selection bias as a specification error', in James P. Smith (ed.), *Female Labor Supply*, Princeton, NJ: Princeton University Press, pp. 206–48.

Higuchi, Y. (1994), 'Empirical analysis of maternity leave system', in Social Development Research Institute (ed.), *Modern Family and Social Security*, Ch.9. (in Japanese).

Higuchi, Y. (1995), 'Economic consequences of advantageous treatments of housewives', in T. Hatta and N. Yashiro (eds), *Economic Analysis of Policies Protecting the Weak*, Nihon Keizai Shimbunsha. (in Japanese).

Higuchi, Y. (2001), *Economics of Employment and Unemployment*, Nihon Keizai Simbunsha. (in Japanese).

Japan Institute for Labour Policy and Training (2003), *Lecture transcript of JIL Labour Policy Forum*, No. 11. (in Japanese).

Japan Institute of Labour (2001), 'Survey on family-friendly systems'.

Kohara, M. (2001), 'Do nonworking housewives represent wealthy households?', *Nihon Rodo Kenkyu Zasshi* No.493, pp. 15–29 (in Japanese).

Maddala, G.S. (1983), *Limited Dependent and Qualitative Variables in Econometrics*, Cambridge University Press.

Maeda, N. (2000), 'Working style compatible with child-raising and policy needs', *Kikan Shakai Hosho kenkyu*, **36**(3) (in Japanese).

Mroz, T.A. (1987), 'The sensitivity of an empirical model of married women's hours of work to economic and statistical assumptions', *Econometrica*, **55**(4), July, pp. 765–99.

Olsen, R.J. (1980), 'A least squares correction for selectivity bias', *Econometrica*, **48**(7), November, pp. 1815–20.

Sakai, H. and H. Asaoka (2001), 'Factors affecting labor force participation in Japan: empirical study of labor supply of females and the elderly', mimeo.

Seike, A. and H. Shimada (1994), 'Social security benefits and labor supply of the elderly in Japan', in Yukio Noguchi and David A. Wise (eds), *Aging in the United States and Japan*, University of Chicago Press, pp. 43–62.

Shigeno, Y. and Y. Ohkusa (1998), 'Effects of maternity leave system on female marriage and continuation of working', *Nihon Rodo Kenkyu Zasshi* No.9, pp. 39–49.

APPENDIX

Table 2A.1 Descriptive statistics for section 2

	Mean	Std dev.	Max	Min	# of obs.	pos obs.
Dependent variables						
LFP	0.698	0.459	1	0	1017	710
Wage	−1.215	0.601	0.899	−2.973	700	–
Hours	119.356	91.167	312	0	1017	–
Preferred working age	2.952	0.937	6	1	991	–
Work flexibility	2.788	1.148	5	1	937	–
Work hours	2.742	0.849	4	1	943	–
Independent variables						
Age	56.868	6.816	64	50	1017	–
Health condition	0.343	0.475	1	0	1017	349
Education attainment	0.282	0.450	1	0	1017	287
Work-related education/training	0.252	0.434	1	0	1017	256
Specialist/generalist	0.522	0.500	1	0	1017	531
Manager	0.395	0.489	1	0	1017	402
Full-time employee	0.771	0.420	1	0	1017	784
Retirement experience	0.227	0.419	1	0	1017	231
Changing jobs	0.280	0.449	1	0	1017	285
Double income	0.445	0.497	1	0	1017	453
Pension payments	7.738	12.935	50	0	1017	–
Housing loans	0.287	0.453	1	0	1017	292
Gender	0.718	0.450	1	0	1017	730
Company size	0.269	0.444	1	0	1017	274
City/town	0.285	0.452	1	0	1017	290
Flexible work	0.236	0.425	1	0	1017	240
Amount of money one needs other than pension*	14.415	7.587	30	0	1017	–
Work old	0.764	0.425	1	0	1017	777

Note: * in 10 000 yen.

Source: Our survey in August 2001.

Table 2A.2   Descriptive statistics for section 3

	Mean	Std dev.	Max	Min	# of obs.	pos obs.
Variables used in estimation						
Income-adjusting	0.283	0.451	1	0	467	132
Housing loan	0.450	0.498	1	0	467	210
Self-employed	0.122	0.328	1	0	467	57
Self-employed (husband)	0.094	0.292	1	0	467	44
Education I	0.244	0.430	1	0	467	114
Education II	0.456	0.499	1	0	467	213
Spouse's allowance	0.499	0.501	1	0	467	233
System to telecommute	0.024	0.152	1	0	467	11
Flex-time system	0.047	0.212	1	0	467	22
City	0.358	0.480	1	0	467	167
Husband's income[1]	634.0	350.8	3250	200	467	–
Variables not used in estimation						
Age	40.3	5.7	58.0	22.0	463	–
Length of service[2]	8.7	7.7	34.0	0.0	466	–
Income[1]	256.4	226.7	1250	70	464	–
Hours worked per week	34.0	13.3	90	1	467	–
Hourly wage[3]	1440.9	1298.5	15625	0	467	–
Household income[1]	891.4	455.7	4500	335.5	464	–

Notes:
1. In 10000 yen.
2. In number of years worked at the current workplace.
3. In yen.

Source: Our survey in August 2001.

Table 2A.3   Descriptive statistics for section 4

	Mean	Std dev.	Max	Min	# of obs.	pos obs.
Variables used in estimation						
Currently working	0.711	0.455	1	0	644	458
Housing loan	0.464	0.499	1	0	644	299
Children under 6 years old	0.290	0.454	1	0	644	187
Family member who needs nursing	0.040	0.197	1	0	644	26
Living with mother (s)	0.280	0.449	1	0	644	180
Education I	0.248	0.432	1	0	644	160
Education II	0.447	0.497	1	0	644	288
City	0.384	0.486	1	0	644	247
Husband's income[1]	652.6	372.2	3250	200	644	–
Number of systems at workplace	0.741	0.981	5	0	644	–
Three or more systems at workplace	0.061	0.238	1	0	644	39
One or two systems at workplace	0.382	0.486	1	0	644	246
Variables not used in estimation						
Age	40.2	5.8	65	22	640	–
Length of service[2]	8.6	7.6	34	0	457	–
Income[1]	237.3	218.5	1250	70	454	–
Holiday system for child-rearing, giving birth to a child	0.393	0.488	1	0	644	253
Holiday system for nursing	0.160	0.366	1	0	644	103
System to telecommute	0.019	0.135	1	0	644	12
Re-employment system	0.057	0.233	1	0	644	37
Child-care facility at workplace	0.034	0.182	1	0	644	22
Flex-time system	0.043	0.204	1	0	644	28
Compensation for child-care	0.034	0.182	1	0	644	22

Note: See the note to Table 2.A2.

Source: Our survey in August 2001.

3. Labor force ageing and economic growth in Japan*

Masaya Sakuragawa and Tatsuji Makino

1. INTRODUCTION

In Japan the population will age rapidly over the first half of the twenty-first century. Fertility has declined over the past quarter century, reaching less than 1.4 in the 1990s, while mortality at older ages is greatly improved in the same decade. The share of the Japanese population that is 65 or over is expected to rise from 11 to 19 per cent over the next two decades.

Cutler et al. (1990) simulate the level of per capita consumption in Japan, finding that it is smaller by 15.2 per cent in 2050 than the level that would have been possible in the absence of the demographic shock.[1]

How should we evaluate their results? Cutler et al. make simulations using the standard growth model with exogenous technological progress.[2] Two points are to be noted. First, physical capital deepening is inherent in the standard growth model. It follows that an advance in the ageing population can raise per-worker income through this channel. On the other hand, recent developments in the growth literature have provided empirical evidence showing that not only physical capital but also human capital is an important driving force for long-run economic growth. Importantly, whereas physical capital is diluted as the population grows, human capital is never diluted due to the non-rivalrous property of human capital. This suggests that to the extent that human capital matters in the growth process, the effect of capital deepening may be weakened.

Secondly, in the standard growth model technological progress is independent of demographic factors. Indeed, whether an advance in the ageing population will promote or deter technological progress is an open question. Some demographers argue that the slower labor force growth or the advance in the ageing of the labor force may adversely affect productivity. Simon (1981) argues that a decline in population growth deters the pace of technological progress because the slowdown of population growth shrinks markets for capital goods, making innovation less profitable due to fixed costs. Alfred Sauvy, the French demographer, is afraid that in a 'matured'

57

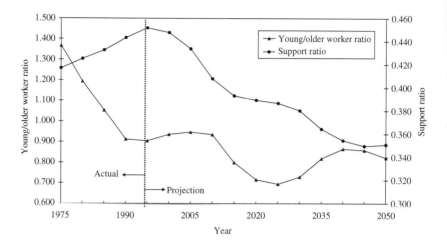

Figure 3.1   Young/older worker ratio and support ratio

society with an ageing population and a smaller proportion of younger people, there is less incentive to invest in human capital that embodies new skills and technology, while the society exploits the benefits of knowledge and human capital that have been accumulated by older people.[3]

Figure 3.1 plots the predictions of the young/older worker ratio defined by the number of workers aged 20–39 divided by those aged 40–65.[4] It peaks at 1.55 in 1964, beginning to decline afterwards, and dipping below unity at the start of the 1980s. Following the possible decline in the future total fertility rate, we suggest that the young/older worker ratio will decline even further over the coming decades. Figure 3.1 also depicts the support ratio, defined by the ratio of the working population relative to the total population.

The main idea that we advocate in this chapter is that the demographic distribution in the labor market influences wage profiles, is an incentive for accumulating human capital, and eventually growth and consumption. When the working population is increasing, more younger workers are combined with fewer older workers in production, which tends to make the wage profile steeper due to the standard decreasing return to each input. On the other hand, when the working population decreases, the reverse mechanism tends to hold, making the wage profile flat.

We present a human-capital-based growth model in which human capitals embodied in people of different generations are imperfect substitutes as inputs in production.[5, 6] A decreased competition among young workers, typically driven by the decline in fertility, tends to increase returns to young human capital relative to returns to older human capital. This arises from the property of standard decreasing returns. The flatter wage profile increases the opportunity cost of investing in human capital when young, which in turn eventually discourages the long-run growth of per capita income. To the extent that human capital of different ages are imperfect substitutes, the demographic distribution in the labor market influences the accumulation of human capital and, as a result, economic growth.

We simulate how the coming demographic change affects the level of consumption in Japan using the model presented in this chapter.[7] By simulation, we capture not only the demographic transition effect but also the adverse growth effect, both of which tend to decrease the per capita consumption level. The main findings are as follows. In response to the coming advance of the ageing population, the level of per capita consumption declines by 19.1 per cent through the decline in the support ratio and by 11.5 per cent through the adverse growth effect, and in total by 30.6 per cent in 2055. Alternatively, if we simulate the Japanese economy using the standard growth model, we find that the level of per worker consumption rises by 7.5 per cent through the effect of capital deepening, and so the level of per capita consumption declines only by 13.2 per cent. The level of per capita consumption is overvalued by 7.5 per cent + 11.5 per cent = 19.0 per cent when the standard model is used.

This chapter is organized as follows. In section 2 we set up the model. In section 3 we solve the equilibrium. In section 4 we conduct simulations.

2. THE MODEL

We present an overlapping-generations economy with altruistic parents in which human capital is the engine of growth. The economy consists of agents who live for two periods and sufficiently large numbers of firms that produce a single good competitively. The production process requires physical capital and two types of workers, skilled and unskilled. Two types of workers perform different tasks: skilled workers engage in management, and unskilled workers work as laborers. As argued below, young agents are identified with unskilled workers, and older agents with skilled workers.

Agents are endowed with one unit of productive time in both the first and the second period of life. They consume in both periods of life.

In the first period of life, each individual receives a bequest from his/her parent and decides how much time to allocate between work in the labor market and accumulation of human capital for him/herself. Note that agents in the same generation are identical except for the level of bequests that they receive from their parents. In the second period of life, an individual supplies one unit of time in the labor market, consumes, and leaves a bequest to his offspring.

At the beginning of the second period of life, each parent gives birth to $1+n_{t+1}$ children. We call the generation that appears at period t, 'generation t'. Letting N_t denote the size of generation t and $1 + n_{t+1} = (N_{t+1}/N_t)$ denote the population growth rate, the total number of labor employed at period t, denoted L_t, is $N_t + N_{t-1}$. Then the share of young workers to the total labor is $(1 + n_t)/(2 + n_t)$, while the share of older workers is $1/(2 + n_t)$. Finally, the evolution of the total labor is given as $(L_{t+1}/L_t) = ((2 + n_{t+1})(1 + n_t))/(2 + n_t)$.

Letting V_t denote the utility of an agent born at period t, V_t depends positively not only on own consumption when young and old, c_t^y and c_{t+1}^o but also on the welfare of each of his/her offspring given by V_{t+1}:

$$V_t = \log c_t^y + \theta \log c_{t+1}^o + \rho(1 + n_{t+1})V_{t+1}, \quad 0 < \rho(1 + n_{t+1}) < 1, \quad (3.1)$$

where ρ is an intergenerational discount factor and θ is a subjective discount factor.

Now we formulate the technology of human capital accumulation. Suppose that a young agent of generation t is endowed with an amount of human capital given by h_t^y. Then an amount of human capital that this agent will have in the subsequent period is

$$h_{t+1}^o = H(u_t)h_t^y, \quad (3.2)$$

where $u_t \in [0,1]$ is the fraction of productive time devoted to the accumulation of human capital and $H(.)$ is an increasing, concave and continuously twice differentiable function; $H(.)$ satisfies $\lim_{u_t \to 0} H'(u_t) = +\infty$, $\lim_{u_t \to 1} H'(u_t) = 0$, and $H(0) = 1$. Equation (3.2) implies that the growth rate of human capital of a person is an increasing and concave function of investment in human capital. The feature of decreasing returns to human capital captures the commonly accepted view that people accumulate human capital rapidly in their teens, fairly rapidly in their twenties, but less rapidly in their thirties.[8]

Assume that the average stock of human capital accumulated by the previous generation has positive intergenerational externalities on the level of human capital of the succeeding generation. In particular, assume that younger agents inherit a portion of the average human capital of elder agents, that is,

$$h_{t+1}^y = (1 - \delta)\bar{h}_{t+1}^o : \quad 0 \le \delta \le 1, \quad (3.3)$$

where $\bar{h}^o_{t+1}$ is the average stock of human capital of older agents at period $t+1$. Note that the initial level of human capital is given by h^o_0. Children are brought up in a better educational environment in countries where adults have a higher average education level. A wealth of literature on the human-capital-based growth model assumes some kind of intergenerational exter-nality of human capital. The parameter δ captures the extent of imperfect inheritance of human capital, which we set to be zero in order to simplify the analysis.

A single good can be produced, consumed and accumulated as physical capital. We assume that all firms are identical and the production in period t requires three inputs: physical capital saved by individuals of generation $t-1$, human capital of young workers of generation t, and human capital of elder workers of generation $t-1$. Under the constant-returns-to-scale technology, the aggregate production function is represented as

$$Y_t = A K_t^\alpha [(1 - u_t) N_t h_t^y]^\beta [N_{t-1} h_t^o]^{1-\alpha-\beta}, \qquad (3.4)$$

where Y_t is the output of the single good, K_t is the aggregate physical capital stock, $(1 - u_t) N_t h_t^y$ and $N_{t-1} h_t^o$ are the aggregate efficient unit of time sup-plied by young and older workers, respectively, and A is an exogenous tech-nological parameter.

A crucial feature of (3.4) is that human capital of unskilled young workers and skilled older workers are 'imperfect substitutes'. The formula-tion in (3.4) means that after accumulating human capital through school-ing, young agents work as laborers during the remaining first period of life. Older workers possess higher levels of experience and skill, but lower levels of physical stamina. Even highly educated young workers have to learn the specific skills required for actual production through on-the-job training by older workers.[9] Physical capital fully depreciates after one period. Compet-itive firms choose three different kinds of capital so as to maximize the current profit, taking factor prices as given.

3. THE EQUILIBRIUM IN THE BALANCED GROWTH PATH

In this section we characterize an equilibrium of this economy. In particu-lar, we investigate the uniqueness and the stability of a balanced growth path.

Under the assumption that individuals are identical within generations, we will obtain $\bar{h}^o_t = h^o_t$ in equilibrium. From this and (3.3), we obtain $h_t^y = h_t^o$ for any t. Together with this, the firm's profit maximization yields

$$1 + r_t = \alpha A \left(\frac{k_t}{h_t^o} \right)^{\alpha - 1} (1 - u_t)^\beta (1 + n_t)^\beta (2 + n_t)^{\alpha - 1}, \tag{3.5}$$

$$w_t^y = \beta A \left(\frac{k_t}{h_t^o} \right)^\alpha (1 - u_t)^{\beta - 1} (1 + n_t)^{\beta - 1} (2 + n_t)^\alpha, \tag{3.6}$$

$$w_t^o = (1 - \alpha - \beta) A \left(\frac{k_t}{h_t^o} \right)^\alpha (1 - u_t)^\beta (1 + n_t)^\beta (2 + n_t)^\alpha. \tag{3.7}$$

Note that r_t is the real interest rate, and w_t^y and w_t^o are wage rates of labor supplied by young and older workers, respectively. Note that $k_t \equiv K_t / N_t$ is the physical capital per young agent of generation t.

Finally we study the behavior of individuals. Each young agent of generation t receives a bequest from his/her parent, and earns the labor income by supplying $1 - u_t$ units of time in the labor market. The budget constraint of a young individual in period t is

$$w_t^y (1 - u_t) h_t^y + b_t = s_t + c_t^y, \tag{3.8}$$

where $w_t^y (1 - u_t) h_t^y$ denotes the labor income earned, b_t is the bequest that he/she receives from his/her parent, and s_t is the saved income. When this agent is matured, he/she earns the labor income and the interest income from his/her savings. These earnings are distributed between consumption and physical bequest to his/her offspring. Thus, the budget constraint of an old individual in period $t + 1$ is

$$(1 + r_{t+1}) s_t + w_{t+1}^o h_{t+1}^o = c_{t+1}^o + (1 + n_{t+1}) b_{t+1}, \tag{3.9}$$

where $w_{t+1}^o h_{t+1}^o$ denotes labor income earned when he/she is old.

The problem of an individual is to choose s_t, u_t and b_{t+1} in order to maximize the utility (3.1), subject to (3.2), (3.8), (3.9), and taking the predetermined variables h_t^y, b_t, and factor prices as given. Keep in mind that agents solve the problem not by taking into account the relation $h_t^y = h_t^o$. We obtain the following first-order conditions that are sufficient for optimality:

$$\frac{c_{t+1}^o}{c_t^y} = \theta (1 + r_{t+1}), \tag{3.10}$$

$$\frac{c_{t+1}^o}{c_{t+1}^y} = \frac{\theta}{\rho}, \tag{3.11}$$

$$\frac{c_{t+1}^o}{c_t^y} = \theta \frac{w_{t+1}^o}{w_t^y} H'(u_t). \tag{3.12}$$

From (3.10) and (3.11), we obtain

$$c_{t+1}^y = \rho(1 + r_{t+1})c_t^y. \tag{3.12a}$$

From (3.10) and (3.12), we obtain

$$(1 + r_{t+1})w_t^y = w_{t+1}^o H'(u_t). \tag{3.13}$$

The L.H.S. is the marginal cost of spending extra time on investment in human capital, and the R.H.S. is the marginal benefit of that extra time. Importantly, the cost is measured in terms of the wage rate of young workers, while the benefit is in terms of the wage rate of older workers. A change in the ratio of the two wage rates or the 'wage profile' w_{t+1}^o/w_t^y tends to affect investment in human capital significantly.

Letting $c_t = (N_{t-1}c_t^o + N_t c_t^y)/L_t$ denote the per-total-worker consumption, we obtain

$$\frac{c_{t+1}}{c_t} = \left(\frac{1}{2 + n_{t+1}}\right)\left(\frac{2 + n_t}{1 + n_t}\right)(1 + n_t)\left(\frac{\theta/\rho + (1 + n_{t+1})}{\theta/\rho + (1 + n_t)}\right)\left(\frac{c_{t+1}^y}{c_t^y}\right). \tag{3.14}$$

Assuming that $\theta = \rho$, we obtain $c_{t+1}/c_t = c_{t+1}^y/c_t^y$, so (3.12a) reduces to

$$\frac{c_{t+1}}{c_t} = \rho(1 + r_{t+1}). \tag{3.15}$$

The equilibrium in the goods market implies that investment equals savings: $K_{t+1} = N_t S_t$. It is useful to rewrite this condition as

$$K_{t+1} = Y_t - (N_{t-1}c_t^o + N_t c_t^y). \tag{3.16}$$

A competitive equilibrium must satisfy optimality conditions of firms, (3.5), (3.6), (3.7), those of households, (3.14), (3.15), the equations of the evolution of human capital (3.2), (3.3), and the good–market–clearing condition (3.16), with the consistency condition $\bar{h}_t^o = h_t^o$, at every period. An equilibrium in the decentralized economy evolves according to the following four-dimensional system with four variables $\{k_t, h_t, c_t, u_t\}$:

$$\frac{k_{t+1}}{k_t} = A\frac{(2+n_t)^\alpha}{2+n_{t+1}}(1+n_t)^{\beta-1}\left(\frac{k_t}{h_t}\right)^{\alpha-1}(1-u_t)^\beta - \frac{2+n_t}{(2+n_{t+1})(1+n_t)}\frac{c_t}{k_t},$$

$$(3.17)$$

$$\frac{c_{t+1}}{c_t} = \rho\alpha A\left(\frac{k_{t+1}}{h_{t+1}}\right)^{\alpha-1}(1-u_{t+1})^\beta(1+n_{t+1})^\beta(2+n_{t+1})^{\alpha-1}, \qquad (3.18)$$

$$\frac{k_{t+1}}{h_{t+1}} = \frac{\alpha\beta A}{(1-\alpha-\beta)H'(u_t)}\left(\frac{k_t}{h_t}\right)^\alpha(1-u_t)^{\beta-1}\frac{(1+n_t)^{\beta-1}(2+n_t)^\alpha}{2+n_{t+1}}, \qquad (3.19)$$

and

$$\frac{h_{t+1}}{h_t} = H(u_t), \qquad (3.20)$$

where we use new variable $h_t \equiv h_t^y = h_t^o$.

By defining new variables $X \equiv k/h$, we can reduce the system (3.17)–(3.20) to the two-dimensional system with two variables $\{X_t, u_t\}$:

$$X_{t+1} = \frac{\alpha\beta A}{(1-\alpha-\beta)H'(u_t)}X_t^\alpha(1-u_t)^{\beta-1}\frac{(1+n_t)^{\beta-1}(2+n_t)^\alpha}{2+n_{t+1}}, \quad (3.21)$$

and

$$u_t = \phi(u_{t+1}; n_t, n_{t+1}), \qquad (3.22)$$

where (3.22) is derived implicitly from

$$1 - \frac{\alpha\beta H(u_{t+1})}{(1-\alpha-\beta)H'(u_{t+1})(1-u_{t+1})}$$

$$= \rho\alpha\frac{(2+n_{t+1})(1+n_t)}{2+n_t}\left\{\frac{(1-\alpha-\beta)H'(u_t)(1-u_t)}{\alpha\beta H(u_t)} - 1\right\}. \qquad (3.23)$$

The reformulating of the dynamical system will greatly simplify the analysis. Here we characterize a balanced-growth path of this economy. In a balanced-growth path k_t, h_t and c_t grow at constant rates. We define these rates of growth as μ_k, μ_h, and μ_c, respectively. From (3.20), in the balanced-growth path, μ_t has to be constant. Since μ_c is constant, k_t/h_t has to be constant from (3.18) and the fact that u_t has to be constant. Thus we obtain $\mu_k = \mu_h$. Finally, c_t/k_t has to be constant from (3.17) so that we obtain $\mu_k = \mu_c$. Therefore, in a balanced-growth path, we obtain $\mu_k = \mu_h = \mu_c$.

We establish the existence and the uniqueness of a balanced-growth path. Substituting $u_{t+1} = u_t = u$ and $n_{t+1} = n_t = n$ into (3.23) and rearranging the terms, we obtain

$$1 - \frac{\alpha\beta H(u)}{(1 - \alpha - \beta)H'(u)(1 - u)} = \rho\alpha(1 + n)\left\{\frac{(1 - \alpha - \beta)H'(u)(1 - u)}{\alpha\beta H(u)} - 1\right\}.$$

(3.24)

Defining $\lambda(u) \equiv H(u)/\{(1 - u)H'(u)\}$, (3.24) reduces to

$$\lambda(u) = \frac{\rho(1 - \alpha - \beta)(1 + n)}{\beta}.$$

(3.25)

Note that the L.H.S. of (3.25) is increasing, with $\lim_{u \to 0} \lambda(u) = 0$ and $\lim_{u \to 1} \lambda(u) = \infty$, while the R.H.S. is constant given n so that there exists a unique u in the interval $(0, 1)$ satisfying (3.25). By incorporating u derived this way into (3.21), we obtain the unique value $X (= X_{t+1} = X_t)$.

Proposition 1: There is a unique balanced-growth path.

In the balanced-growth path, per capita output, per capita consumption, physical capital, and human capital grow at the same rate $H(u)$, which implies that the growth rate of the economy is positively linked to investment in human capital as in many human-capital based growth theories (for example Lucas, 1988).

Our main concern in this chapter is to study a causal link between the labor market ageing and per capita income growth. Suppose that there is a once-and-for-all decline in the population growth rate. The following result is immediate from (3.25).

Proposition 2: An advance of the labor force ageing, captured by a decrease in the population growth rate n, leads to a reduction in investment in human capital and as a result deters economic growth.

A rise in the ratio of skilled older workers to unskilled young workers, driven by a decline in the population growth rate, provides a less competitive environment among young workers, leading to a rise in the wage rate of the young relative to that of the older workers. Young people find it beneficial to invest less in human capital, which eventually discourages per capita income growth. From (3.6) and (3.7), we obtain the 'wage profile' as

$$w^o/w^y = (1 - \alpha - \beta)(1 + n)(1 - u)/\beta. \qquad (3.26)$$

An advance in the labor force ageing, possibly combined with a decline in the population growth, tends to make the wage profile less steep, which induces people to invest less in human capital. It turns out that an increase in the size of a generation or a cohort increases competition among people of that generation or cohort, driving down the wage rate and forcing them to make more effort to acquire skills to earn higher salaries in the future. In an aged society with large numbers of older people, young people tend to be 'myopic', in the sense that they do not find it beneficial to invest in themselves.

The implication about the relationship between population growth and economic growth is contrary to the prediction of the conventional neo-classical growth theory saying that an increase in the population growth will reduce the capital–labor ratio and eventually the per capita output. Srinivasan and Robinson (1997, p. 1268) argue for the positive correlation by assuming that the growth of per capita human capital is an increasing function of the growth of the aggregate employment. Our model can be interpreted to provide one micro-foundation behind their setting. Sala-i-Martin (1996) develops a theoretical mechanism behind which labor market ageing reduces the economy-wide average human capital, eventually deterring growth by assuming that human capital depreciates as workers get older. Our analysis provides an alternative channel between labor market ageing and growth.[10]

4. SIMULATION

In this section we conduct simulations to see how the path of consumption will evolve in response to the possible dramatic ageing of the population. We make simulations using the model developed in the previous section. We expect that the simulated result will differ from the one simulated from the standard growth model with exogenous technological change for two reasons. First, the positive effect of capital deepening emerges in the standard model while it does not in ours. Second, the adverse growth effect emerges in ours while it does not in the standard model.

We examine the following experiment. Given that the economy is initially at the steady state in 1995, we assume that people alive in 1995 face an unanticipated demographic shock involving a drop of the young/older worker ratio (or the gross population growth rate).

To begin with, we have to find parameter values that describe the steady state before the demographic change. First, we take the interval of one period to be 20 years and so choose the subjective discount rate as $\rho = (0.98)^{20} = 0.668$. Second, we have to select the share parameters of the production function. We choose the physical capital share as $\alpha = 0.333$ following the standard manner. We regard young workers as workers aged 20–39, and older workers as workers aged 40–59. In order to select β, we calculate the share of the wages of workers aged 20–39 in the total wage bill of workers aged 20–59. We obtain the value of β by multiplying this value with the labor share $1 - \alpha = 0.667$. We obtain $\beta = 0.297$ and $1 - \alpha - \beta = 0.370$.

Third, we choose the values of the young/older worker ratio and the support ratio used for simulation. As initial values in 1995, we set the young/older worker ratio and the support ratio to be 1.073 and 0.434. We obtain these two values by averaging values over the 1975–1995 period. For the future values, we use the projected data constructed by the National Institute of Population and Social Security Research and set the values to be 0.800 and 0.393 in 2015, 0.819 and 0.364 in 2035, and 0.822 and 0.351 in 2055. We assume that the values in 2055 go through from that period on.

Finally, we specify the $H(u)$ function as $H(u) = 1 + \mu u^{\lambda}$ and choose the pair (μ, λ) to be consistent with the empirical observation. We choose parameters to be consistent with the fact that the average annual growth rate of per-worker income over the 1975–1995 period is 2.43 per cent.[11] We set the exogenous technological parameter A arbitrarily and choose $A = 1$. The list of parameter values chosen is as follows.

α	β	$1 - \alpha - \beta$	$1 + n$	u	λ	μ	ρ	A
0.333	0.297	0.370	1.073	0.198	0.715	2	0.668	1

In conducting simulations, we extend the aggregate production function as

$$Y_t = A K_t^{\alpha} \left\{ \frac{\beta}{1-\alpha} [(1 - u_t) h_t^y N_t]^{1-\sigma} + \frac{1-\alpha-\beta}{1-\alpha} [h_t^o N_{t-1}]^{1-\sigma} \right\}^{\frac{1-\alpha}{1-\sigma}}, \quad \sigma \geq 0.$$

$$(3.27)$$

where $1 - \sigma$ represents the elasticity of substitution between young and older human capital. Note that when $\sigma \to 1$, this production function reduces to the Cobb–Douglas case developed in the previous analysis. Additionally, note that when $\sigma \to 0$, this production function reduces to the standard human-capital-based growth model where young and older workers are perfect substitutes (for example Lucas, 1988).

Table 3.1   Annual growth rate of per-worker consumption

Year	Sigma			
	0	0.5	1	1.5
1995	2.43	2.43	2.43	2.43
2015	2.43	2.46	2.43	2.33
2035	2.43	2.22	2.10	1.76
2055	2.43	2.15	2.01	1.62
2075	2.43	2.14	1.99	1.57
2095	2.43	2.13	1.98	1.56
2115	2.43	2.13	1.98	1.56
2135	2.43	2.13	1.98	1.55
2155	2.43	2.13	1.98	1.55
2175	2.43	2.13	1.98	1.55
2195	2.43	2.13	1.98	1.55

With the production function given by (4–1), we finally derive

$$\frac{\beta H(u^*)}{\rho H'(u^*)} = (1+n)^{\sigma}(1-\alpha-\beta)(1-u^*)^{\sigma}. \qquad (3.28)$$

We obtain two remarkable features. One is reasonable. When σ approaches $0, u^*$ is independent of n. The positive link between population and economic growth through the labor market channel disappears when young and older workers are perfect substitutes as assumed in the standard human-capital-based growth models. The other is surprising. When $\sigma \neq 0$ holds, u^* is always increasing in n irrespective of the sign of the cross-partial derivative. Proposition 2 still holds so long as young and old human capital are *not* perfect substitutes, including the case of perfect complements as a polar case.

Proposition 3: Suppose that the production function takes the quasi-CES form as given by (3.27) and two types of workers are imperfect substitutes. Then an advance of ageing in the labor force captured by a decrease in n deters economic growth through a decrease in investment in human capital.

Table 3.1 depicts the simulated paths of the annual growth rate of per-worker consumption. This table depicts the results for three different values of σ's; $\sigma = 0.5$; $\sigma = 1$; and $\sigma = 1.5$. As σ increases, young and older human capital are less substitutable with each other, and the effect of the adverse

Table 3.2 *Per capita consumption level relative to the no-demographic-change case*

Year	Sigma			
	0	0.5	1	1.5
1995	1.000	1.000	1.000	1.000
2015	0.907	0.911	0.906	0.889
2035	0.840	0.808	0.785	0.720
2055	0.809	0.736	0.694	0.589
2075	0.809	0.693	0.635	0.496
2095	0.809	0.653	0.580	0.416
2115	0.809	0.614	0.529	0.349
2135	0.809	0.578	0.483	0.293
2155	0.809	0.543	0.441	0.246
2175	0.809	0.511	0.402	0.206
2195	0.809	0.481	0.367	0.173

growth effect is expected to be greater. Table 3.2 shows that as σ increases, the growth rate of per-worker consumption declines. For example, when $\sigma = 0.5$, the long-run growth rate declines to 2.13 per cent, and when $\sigma = 1$, it declines to 1.98 per cent. When $\sigma = 0$, it is 2.43 per cent and, as predicted by Proposition 3, remains unchanged in the face of any demographic change.

Table 3.2 depicts the level of per capita consumption. Note that the value is depicted as the relative value compared to the level of consumption if there were no demographic change. Column 1 depicts the case for $\sigma = 0$. At 2055, the level of per capita consumption is smaller by 19.1 per cent. The decline of the level of consumption arises entirely from the change in the support ratio. Column 3 depicts the case for $\sigma = 1$. At 2055 it is smaller by 30.6 per cent, greater by 11.5 per cent than the case for $\sigma = 0$. The difference of 11.5 per cent is attributed to the adverse growth effect.

We finally compare these results with those simulated from the standard growth model with exogenous technological change. In response to the decline in the population growth rate, simulation results based on the standard theory are expected to exhibit the greater level of per-worker consumption because the positive effect of capital deepening is combined and the adverse growth effect does not emerge. We regard the value of 2055 as the steady-state value because we observe the values of 2055 to be almost the same as the steady-state values by many experiments.

Table 3.3 lists the results. The level of per-worker consumption rises by 7.5 per cent at the new steady state, while the level of per capita

Table 3.3   Result of the standard growth model

Young/older Worker Ratio: 1.073 → 0.822			
Per effective worker consumption			
Initial steady state	New steady state		
0.282	0.303	→	+7.5%
Relative per-capita consumption level to no-demographic-change case			
0.868	→		−13.2%

consumption declines by 13.2 per cent. The former positive effect is attributed to the capital deepening effect, and the latter negative effect implies that the effect of the change in the support ratio is dominant. It follows that the decline in the support ratio reduces per capita consumption, which declines by 20.7 per cent.

Simulation results of both models are comparable with each other because the amounts of the decline in the consumption stemming from the decline in the support ratio are fairly close. Therefore, we may argue that the level of per capita consumption in 2055 in the standard model is overvalued by 7.5% + 11.5% = 19.0% if the actual economy could be better described in the model presented in this chapter.

Cutler et al. (1990) calculate that in 2050 the level of per capita consumption of the Japanese economy is lower by 15.2 per cent than the one that would have been possible in the absence of the demographic shock.[12] If the adverse growth effect arising from the labor force ageing is taken into account, the decline in the level of per capita consumption is even greater.

NOTES

*   We are greatful to Koichi Hamada, Hiroyuki Hashimoto, Yuichi Morita, Fumio Ohtake, Hideki Toya, Akira Yagi and participants of the International Forum of Millennium Projects held in Tokyo and Osaka.
1.   Cutler et al. (1990) simulate the US economy using the Solow model, showing that in response to the coming demographic change consumption initially rises, but finally declines to the new steady state because the increase in dependency overtakes the capital deepening effects of the slowing labor force growth.
2.   Other literature in this field also conducts simulations by employing this model, including Kato (1998).
3.   Sauvy reveals that 'such a society [with ageing population] would hold a society of old people, living in old houses, ruminating about old ideas'. He attributed the slow technological progress in nineteenth century France to conservatism and ageing. He says, 'Under the influence of population aging, the French government and Parliament subsidized the Navy's sailing ships while other countries were adopting steam-powered craft.'

4. Table 3.1 is constructed based on the data of the National Institute of Population and Social Security Research.
5. In practice, the cohort of the baby boom generation has lower lifetime earnings relative to other cohorts both in the United States and Japan, as would be roughly consistent with this argument. Inoki and Ohtake (1997) found that there were cohort effects in the Japanese labor market.
6. Chari and Hopenhayn (1991), Fershtman, Murphy, and Weiss (1996), and Kremer and Thomson (1998) construct growth models allowing for complementarity between different vintages of human capital. Kremer and Thomson construct a model in which human capital of young and older workers are complementary inputs in production in order to explain slow convergence toward the steady-state income between countries. Chari and Hopenhayn develop a model allowing for complementarity between experienced and inexperienced workers in order to explain the empirically observed gradual diffusion of technology.
7. In arguing the ageing problem, much literature focuses on the burden of an increasing ratio of retired to working generations. See, for example, Cutler et al. (1990), Ehrlich and Lui (1990), and Meijdam and Verbon (1997). Ehrlich and Lui (1990) develop a model in which an increase in longevity promotes growth through interdependence within the family. Weil (1997) presents a survey on the economics of ageing, but he does not fully relate ageing to economic growth. On the other hand, surprisingly little of the existing research highlights the role of demographic distribution in the working population as a possible determinant of economic growth. Sala-i-Martin (1996) is an exception that relates ageing in the labor force to growth, showing that an advance in ageing of the workforce reduces economy-wide average human capital and discourages per capita income growth.
8. Empirical estimates of human capital production function indicate that the returns to private inputs are diminishing (Heckman, 1976 and Haley, 1976).
9. Empirical evidence supports the view that human capital of young and of older workers are imperfect substitutes. Murphy and Welch (1992) find that workers of similar age and education tend to be substitutes, while they are complements for much older or more educated workers. Welch (1979) estimates that a 10 per cent increase in cohort size reduced wages of college graduates by 9 per cent and of high school students by 4 per cent on entry into the labor market. Freeman (1979) finds that such a model could explain the differential change in the relative wages of younger and older workers over the period in which the baby boom cohort entered the labor market.
10. Jones (1998) constructs a R&D-based growth model in which a more populous economy leads to a richer economy by focusing on the non-rivalrous nature of ideas. The economic implication can be reconciled with that of the R&D-based growth model in its spirit. New ideas, inventions and new methods for improving productivity could be increased in a society where the young are so vigorous that they devote more resources to investing in themselves.
11. For $\sigma = 0.5, 1, 1.5$, the chosen pair (μ, λ) is $(2, 0.790)$, $(2, 0.715)$, $(2.5, 0.929)$, respectively.
12. Cutler et al. (1990) simulate the US economy using the Solow model, showing that in response to the coming demographic change consumption initially rises, but finally declines to the new steady state because the increase in dependency overtakes the capital deepening effects of the slowing labor force growth.

BIBLIOGRAPHY

Barro, Robert J. (1991), 'Economic growth in a cross section of countries', *Quarterly Journal of Economics*, **106**, 407–43.
Barro, Robert J. and Jong-Wha Lee (1994), 'Data set for a panel of 138 countries', mimeo.

Barro, Robert J. and Jong-Wha Lee (1996), 'International measures of schooling years and schooling quality', *American Economic Review*, **86**(2), 218–23.

Becker, Gary S. and Robert J. Barro (1988), 'A reformulation of the economic theory of fertility', *Quarterly Journal of Economics*, **103**, 1–25.

Becker, Gary S., Kevin M. Murphy and Robert Tamura (1990), 'Human capital, fertility, and economic growth', *Journal of Political Economy*, **98**, S12–37.

Benhabib, Jess and Mark M. Spiegel (1994), 'The role of human capital in economic development: evidence from aggregate cross-country data', *Journal of Monetary Economics*, **34**,143–73.

Bloom, David E. and Jeffrey G. Williamson (1997), 'Demographic transitions and economic miracles in emerging Asia', NBER Working Paper No. 6268.

Brander, James A. and Steve Dowrick (1994), 'The role of fertility and population in economic growth: empirical results from aggregate cross-national data', *Journal of Population Economics*, **7**, 1–25.

Caballc, Jordi and M.S. Santos (1993), 'On endogenous growth with physical and human capital', *Journal of Political Economy*, **101**, 1042–67.

Chari, V.V. and Hugo Hopenhayn (1991), 'Vintage human capital, growth, and the diffusion of new technology', *Journal of Political Economy*, **99**, 1142–65.

Ciccone, A. and R.E. Hall (1996), 'Productivity and the density of economic activity', *American Economic Review*, **86**(1), 54–70.

Cutler, D.M., J.M. Poterba, L.M. Sheiner and L.M. Summers (1990), 'An aging society: opportunity or challenge?', *Brooking Papers on Economic Activity*, **1**, 1–73.

Ehrlich, Isaac. and Francis T. Lui (1990), 'Intergenerational trade, longevity, and economic growth', *Journal of Political Economy*, **99**, 1029–59.

Fershtman, C., K.M. Murphy and Y. Weiss (1996), 'Social states, education, and growth', *Journal of Political Economy*, **104**, 108–32.

Freeman, R. (1979), 'The effects of demographic factors on age-earnings profiles', *Journal of Human Resources*, **14**, 289–318.

Galor O. and H. Zang (1997), 'Fertility, income distribution, and economic growth: theory and cross-country evidence', *Japan and the World Economy*, **9**, 197–229.

Glaeser, E.L., J.A. Scheinkman and A. Shleifer (1995), 'Economic growth in a cross-section of cities', *Journal of Monetary Economics*, **36**, 117–43.

Glaeser, E.L., H.D. Kallal, J.A. Scheinkman and A. Shleifer (1992), 'Growth in Cities', *Journal of Political Economy*, **100**(6), 1126–52.

Haley, W. (1976), 'Estimation of the earning profile from optimal human capital accumulation', *Econometrica*, **44**, 1223–38.

Hanushek, Eric A. and Dongwook Kim (1995), 'Schooling, labor force quality, and economic growth', NBER Working Paper No. 5399.

Hashimoto, H. and H. Toya (1998), 'Skills of labor forces and economic growth: cross-country evidence', mimeo.

Heckman, J. (1976), 'A life-cycle model of earnings, learning, and consumption', *Journal of Political Economy*, **84**, S11–S44.

Inoki, T. and F. Ohtake (1997), 'Rodo shijyo Ni Okeru Sedai Koka', in *Gendai Makuro Keizai Bunseki-Tenkanki No Nihonkeizai*, Todai-Shuppankai.

Jones, Charles I. (1998), 'Population and ideas: a theory of endogenous growth', Manuscript, Stanford University.

Kato, R. (1998), 'Transition to an aging Japan: public pension, savings, and capital taxation', *Journal of the Japanese International Economics*, **12**, 204–31.

Kremer, Michael. (1993), 'Population growth and technological change: one million BC to 1990', *Quarterly Journal of Economics*, **108**, 681–716.

Kremer, Michael and Jim Thompson (1998), 'Why isn't convergence instantaneous? Young workers, old workers, and gradual adjustment', *Journal of Economic Growth*, **3**, 5–28.

Kuznets, Simon. (1960), 'Population change and aggregate output', in NBER, *Demographic and Economic Change in Developed Countries*, Princeton University Press.

Levine, Ross and David Renelt (1992), 'A sensitivity analysis of cross-country growth regressions', *American Economic Review*, **82**, 942–63.

Lucas, Robert E., Jr (1988), 'On the mechanics of development planning', *Journal of Monetary Economics*, **22**, 3–42.

Mankiw, N. Gregory, David Romer and David N. Weil (1992), 'A contribution to the empirics of economic growth', *Quarterly Journal of Economics*, **107**, 407–37.

Meijdam, L. and H.A.A. Verbon (1997), 'Aging and public pensions in an overlapping generations model', *Oxford Economic Papers*, **49**, 29–42.

Murphy, K.M. and F. Welch (1992), 'The structure of wages', *Quarterly Journal of Economics*, **102**, 285–326.

Raut, L.K. and T.N. Srinivasan (1994), 'The dynamics of endogenous growth', *Economic Theory*, **4**, 777–90.

Sala-i-Martin, Xavier. (1996), 'A positive theory of social security', *Journal of Economic Growth*, **1**, 277–304.

Simon, Julian (1977), *The Economics of Population Growth*, Princeton University Press.

Simon, Julian (1981), *The Ultimate Resource*, Princeton University Press.

Solow, Robert M. (1956), 'A contribution to the theory of economic growth', *Quarterly Journal of Economics*, **70**(1), 65–94.

Srinivasan, T.N. and James A. Robinson (1997), 'Long-term consequences of population growth: technological change, natural resources, and the environment', in M.R. Rozenzweig and O. Stark (eds), *Handbook of Population and Family Economics*, North-Holland.

Weil. D.N. (1997), 'The economics of population aging', in M.R. Rozenzweig and O. Stark (eds), *Handbook of Population and Family Economics*, North-Holland.

Welch, F. (1979), 'Effect of corhort size on earnings: the baby boom babies' financial bust', *Journal of Political Economy*, **87**, 565–97.

White, H. (1980), 'A heteroskedasticity-consistent covariance matrix and a direct test for heteroskasticity', *Econometrica*, **48**, 721–46.

Williamson, J.G. (1997), 'Growth, distribution and demography: some lessons from history', NBER Working Paper No. 6244.

APPENDIX

Table 3A.1　Actual, projected young/old labor force ratio and support ratio

	Young/older worker ratio	Support ratio
1975	1.367	0.417
1980	1.194	0.425
1985	1.053	0.433
1990	0.913	0.443
1995	0.905	0.452
2000	0.936	0.448
2005	0.947	0.434
2010	0.935	0.408
2015	0.800	0.393
2020	0.716	0.389
2025	0.694	0.387
2030	0.729	0.380
2035	0.819	0.364
2040	0.866	0.355
2045	0.859	0.350
2050	0.823	0.351

Notes:
Young: 20–39, Old: 40–59.
Labor force participation rate: Young: 0.777, Old: 0.817 (Actual 1995 value).

Table 3A.2　Actual, projected young/old labor force ratio and support ratio

Year	Young/old labor force ratio	Support ratio
1975–95 average	1.073	0.434
2015	0.800	0.393
2035	0.819	0.364
2055	0.823	0.351

Notes:
Young: 20–39, Old: 40–59.
Labor force participation rate: Young: 0.777, Old: 0.817 (Actual 1995 value).
Used 2050 projected value as 2055 value.

4. Ageing and elderly care in an open economy

Koichi Hamada and Lakshmi K. Raut[1]

In order to go astray into the mountain sooner, I destroyed myself my teeth by rocks to look older. (Shichiro Fukasawa, *Narayamabushi-ko* (Elegy for the Old: The Tune of Narayama, 1968))

We are told, in the future, two of young people have to take care of one old person. (Sawako Ariyoshi, *The Twilight Years*, 1972)

You have begot me, bred me, lov'd me. I return those duties back as are right fit. (William Shakespeare, *King Lear*, Cordelia: Act 1, Scene 1, 95)[2]

1. INTRODUCTION

Care of the elderly presents a difficult challenge to the developed countries where the population is rapidly ageing. Costs of medical care of the elderly will grow more than proportionally as the ageing proceeds. To nurse the elderly, human labor services are essential and cannot easily be substituted by machines or tools. The medical cost and labor cost of elderly care can have strong macroeconomic effects on household savings and current account balances of an ageing economy such as Japan with rising life expectancy and a falling fertility rate. We present a prototype model of overlapping generations to study these macroeconomic effects under different assumptions about the substitutability of the present consumption of goods and the future consumption of nursing services, and about the substitutability of machines and human nurses in the elderly nursing sector. The model will shed light on the policy debate on whether to import foreign labor services or to invest capital abroad from the perspectives of elderly care in an ageing open economy.

More specifically, the chapter is driven by three motivations. First, as is illustrated in the opening extracts, caring for the elderly poses serious problems in society. According to *The Illustrated White Paper for the Elderly* (Miura, 1999), in 2000 about 17.2 per cent of the population in Japan consisted of people over 65 years old, and 7.0 per cent consisted of people over 75 years old. There are about four people in the active age group of 15 to 64 years are for every elderly person aged 65 years or over. In 2025, it is expected that more than 27.4 per cent of Japan's population will consist of elderly people aged 65 or more, and about 11.9 per cent of the population will be at least 75 years old. There will be about 2.5 people in the active population for every elderly person aged 65 or more and about 5 persons in the active population for every elderly person aged 75 or over. This trend goes to an extreme by the year 2050: slightly less than a third (32.3 per cent) of the population will be over 65 years old, and almost one fifth (18.8 per cent) of the population will be over 75 years old. That means there will be about 1.7 people in the active population for every elderly person aged 65 or more, and that about 3 people in the active population for every elderly person aged 75 or over.

Less conspicuous but similar patterns can be depicted in many developed countries. For instance, in the year 2025, the proportions of the population over 65 years of age are expected to be 18.8 per cent in the United States, 21.2 per cent in Great Britain, 23.4 per cent in Germany, 21.7 per cent in France and 24.3 per cent in Sweden (Miura, 1999). This means that the ageing pattern in Japan is not an isolated problem case. The ageing trend is being seen all over the world.

The second motivation for this chapter is the rising cost of elderly care. The cost of nursing as a proportion of national income is increasing more rapidly than the proportionate increase in the elderly population. Nursing requires human care which is difficult to substitute by medical instruments and robots. Thus the ageing of the population will necessitate a larger proportion of the labor force to be engaged in the elderly care sector.

Of course, not everyone older than 65 needs active care from others. As ageing progresses, however, more and more people will require intensive care. For instance, while only 2.5 per cent of people between the age of 65 and 69 need care either at home, in nursing facilities or in hospitals, the ratio of people who need such care climbs rapidly for older age groups, namely to 4.3 per cent for the age group 70–74, 8.0 per cent for the age group 75–79, 16.8 per cent for the age group 80–84, and as high as 35.3 per cent for the age group 85 or over. According to the Ministry of Welfare (1995), out of 850 000 households who needed elderly care, about 5.6 per cent are single households, about 16.9 per cent are households consisting of couples, and about 56 per cent are households consisting of three generations, namely, the adults, their parents and their children.

In 1995, the Ministry of Welfare of Japan surveyed households with recently deceased family members to shed light on the caring arrangements of the dying family members. The findings of the survey are striking: about

66.8 per cent of such care was provided by direct family members, about 5.5 per cent of care was provided by other relatives, and about 16.4 per cent by professionals in the hospitals and clinics. The average age of caring family members and relatives was 60.4 years. About 30 per cent of those who took care of the old often resigned from jobs or took leave of absence. The majority of them were under heavy stress, and a substantial fraction of them were unable to have sufficient sleep or to leave the house.

Thus, although the average length of time during which old people must be nursed might not be too long, the anxiety of people in Japan over nursing expenses during old age has been tremendous and has significant macroeconomic consequences. Because of such strong anxieties over health and nursing care expenses, older people often refrain from consuming enough, which aggravates recession and deflation in Japan. There are some studies on these issues in the US. Alan Garber (1994) made a careful investigation of the rapid increase in costs and the uncertainty about the medical care of aged persons. He emphasized the need for alleviating the anxiety of the elderly and their family members and for better saving behavior to meet resource needs.

Incidentally, a few studies examined the link between rising elderly health care expenditures and the ageing pattern in the US. Fuchs (1990) notes that the health sector's share in GDP in the United States rose from under 4 per cent to more than 11 per cent in the 1980s. He attributed this to price factor – prices of medical services grew by 1.6 per cent per annum, much faster than other prices – and to quantity factor – the growth in the quantity of health care consumption was 0.9 per cent faster per annum than the other factors. He found that the speed of ageing, wage growth, technological change in the medical sector, and human factors like moral hazards were significant determinants of this rapid rise in the health care costs in the US. On the other hand, taking into account the effects of income, productivity and distribution of income on medical expenses, Karatzas (2000) finds that ageing has little to do with the medical costs. This is contrary to the common sense view.

The problem of rising medical expenditure is also present in Japan. Japan spent 21.5 billion yen on health care services in 1955. In 1995 this figure rose to 28.5 trillion yen. In the United States, however, the national expenditure on health care grew from 27 billion dollars in 1960 to 698 billion dollars in 1990. Sato (2001) puts Japanese medical expenditure in an international perspective. She points out that medical care as a proportion of GDP is as high as 14 per cent in the United States, but it is low, at the rate of 7.2 per cent in Japan. She classifies the causes of rising medical costs as follows: (1) the demand side factors such as better access to care, more use of care and the ageing population; (2) the supply side factors such as technological advances and moral hazards; and (3) the higher price of medical care.

Summing up, we note that for the intensive care of old people, human labor is essential and cannot easily be substituted by capital equipment. While technological progress in gerontology is greatly needed to find cheaper ways to provide for care of the elderly, its outcome at present is uncertain. In the meantime, the cost of caring for the elderly is rising steeply and it is hard to substitute nurses with robots and machines. Our second motivation in this chapter is to find alternative means of financing the elderly care expenses once the economy is open to exporting capital to and importing labor services from foreign countries.

The third motivation of this chapter is to examine theoretically the often-made claim that Japanese people saved too much and accumulated too great a balance of payments surplus because they had to spend a large amount when the population suddenly ages. The state of the debate involving Noguchi (1990), Horioka (1991, 1992), and EPA (1991) on the effect of ageing on the balance of payments of Japan is excellently summarized by Yashiro and Sato-Oishi (1997). An informal but lucid explanation is given by Lincoln (1993). A theoretical analysis incorporating ageing and care will shed light on this open-economy issue. It will be shown that, depending on the elasticity of substitution between the present consumption of goods and future consumption of nursing services, an ageing of the population may exhibit an increase in its saving rate.

We will also find conditions that support the claim by Goto (1998) that since trade and capital movements tend to equate with factor prices, migration is redundant for the adjustment. We show that this holds if the adjustment costs for capital movements and for international labor movements are not taken into account, and if the production function of the foreign country is identical to the home country.

In this chapter, we will construct a simple, prototype model of overlapping generations in which a person works when young and consumes elderly and nursing care during old age. The model may seem too simple, but it clarifies the basic nature of the nursing problem of the aged. We show that the individuals with utility functions that limit substitution between the present consumption of goods and the future consumption of nursing services will be forced to save more during their working years. The decline of the labor growth rate implies a decrease in the transformation possibility from present consumption to the nursing care in the next period. We also argue that when the nursing services cannot be substituted by capital expenditures, it is desirable to import foreign labor services as well as to encourage outflow of capital. We also show that in spite of the extreme emphasis on the need for nursing care during old age in our model, the neoclassical property of the overlapping generation model is kept intact.

The rest of the chapter is organized as follows. In section 2, we set out our theoretical apparatus, and examine the theoretical issues. In section 3 we use the theoretical apparatus of section 2 to address the policy issues that we mentioned above.

2. THEORETICAL APPARATUS

The welfare of the elderly depends on the level of care. Elderly care includes medical care and nursing services. The welfare of an individual in a society depends also on their material well-being during their lifetime. In this chapter we consider only nursing services during old age, and we identify all material well-being with consumption of an aggregate good during the first period. More specifically, we assume an overlapping generations economy in which each agent lives for two periods – young and old. Each adult is endowed with 1 unit of labor that he/she supplies to the labor market inelastically and earns wage rate w_t out of which he/she consumes c_t and saves s_t. In the second period, he/she retires, and consumes nursing services n_{t+1}. Let the agent of the tth generation have the lifetime utility $u(c_t) + v(n_{t+1})$, where $u(c_t)$ is the present utility of the tth generation defined on the present consumption of goods and $v(n_{t+1})$ is the utility derived from the nursing service n_{t+1} which we assume as hours of nursing time and provided by the future generation. The consumption good is the numeraire and the total available time of a young person is normalized to 1.

Household's Choice Problem

The choice problem of an adult of tth generation is: maximize: $u(c_t, \ell_t) + v(n_{t+1})$ subject to

$$c_t + \frac{w_{t+1} n_{t+1}}{1 + r_{t+1}} \le w_t \tag{4.1}$$

Note that $s_t = w_t - c_t$. Denote by $\rho_{t+1} = w_{t+1}/(1 + r_{t+1})$ the wage–rental ratio in period $t+1$. The optimal solution for s_t and n_{t+1} depend on the wage rate w_t and the wage–rental rate ρ_{t+1} in period $t+1$. We denote the optimal solution by

$$s_t = s(w_t, \rho_{t+1}), \quad \text{and} \quad n_{t+1} = n(w_t, \rho_{t+1}) \tag{4.2}$$

Suppose there is a drop in fertility rate in period t. To examine the effect of this fertility decline on savings, consumption of nursing services and the welfare of various generations, notice that the effect in our set-up is percolated through the income w_t and the price of the nursing services ρ_{t+1} for any generation t. The agents take these as given. In a closed economy, the effect of fertility decline in period t will affect the wage rate w_{t+1} and the rental rate $1+r_{t+1}$ and hence the wage–rental ratio ρ_{t+1} but the wage rate w_t will be unaffected. Let us assume that a fertility decline in period t increases the wage rate w_{t+1} and decreases the interest rate r_{t+1}, and thus increases the wage–rental rate ρ_{t+1} (we shall show that this will be the case in most situations). As shown in Figure 4.1a, this will shift inward the budget line of a representative adult of period t (the dotted budget line with a slope of $-1/\rho'_{t+1}$. We use x' to denote the variable x after the demographic shock, and x to denote the variable before the demographic shock in Figure 4.1). The effect on savings and consumption of nursing services will depend on the income and substitution effects, but there will be a fall in the welfare level of generation t.

Could the outflow of capital or the immigration of labor improve the welfare of generation t? Either of the two will lower the wage–rental ratio ρ_{t+1} and hence will improve welfare of generation t and can even attain a higher level of autarky welfare level than the level that the representative adult of generation t would have achieved if there were no drop in fertility.

The welfare effects on the future generations are more complicated to determine since there is a wealth effect from the fertility decline because generation $t+1$ will have a higher wage rate w_{t+1}, which shifts his budget

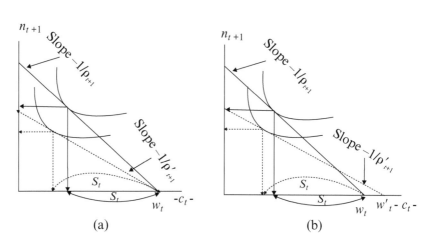

(a)   (b)

Figure 4.1

constraint along the consumption axis as shown by the dotted lines in Figure 4.1b. In this case we cannot even determine the welfare effect. To determine these effects we shall consider the constant elasticity of substitution (CES) utility function, which assumes constant inter-temporal rate of substitution, beginning with the case of the Cobb–Douglas utility function, that is, with the unit elasticity of substitution case. To that end, we describe the autarky equilibrium.

Autarky Equilibrium

Let L_t be the number of young agents in period t. We assume that population is growing exogenously at the rate of g, that is, $L_{t+1} = (1+g)L_t$. Denote by $\hat{L}_{t+1}$ the labor in the productive sector. Then in equilibrium we must have,

$$\hat{L}_{t+1} = L_{t+1} - n_{t+1}L_t = \left[1 - \frac{n_{t+1}}{1+g}\right]L_{t+1}. \tag{4.3}$$

Denote by e_t the fraction of labor in the productive sector in period t. It then follows from the above that

$$e_{t+1} = \frac{\hat{L}_{t+1}}{L_{t+1}} = 1 - \frac{n_{t+1}}{1+g} \tag{4.4}$$

Assume that capital fully depreciates in one period and it takes one period to gestate. This also means that rental rate and interest rate are identical. The aggregate capital K_{t+1} in period $t+1$ is given by

$$K_{t+1} = L_t s_t \tag{4.5}$$

We assume that the nursing sector does not require any capital. The productive sector uses capital and labor to produce output using a constant return to scale production function $Y_t = F(K_t, \hat{L}_t)$. Denote the capital–labor ratio in the productive sector in period $t+1$ by $\hat{k}_{t+1} = K_{t+1}/\hat{L}_{t+1}$. Utilizing (4.3) and (4.5) we have,

$$\hat{k}_{t+1} = \frac{s_t}{(1+g) - n_{t+1}} \tag{4.6}$$

In autarky, the competitive wage rate and interest rate between period t and $t+1$ are determined in the productive sector as follows

$$1 + r_t = f'(\hat{k}_t) \tag{4.7}$$

$$w_t = f(\hat{k}_t) - \hat{k}_t \cdot f'(\hat{k}_t) \equiv \omega(\hat{k}_t) \tag{4.8}$$

where, $f(k) \equiv F(k, 1)$. We assume that production function is concave. Notice that the wage rental rate $\rho_t(\hat{k}_t) = (f(\hat{k}_t) - \hat{k}_t f'(\hat{k}_t))/f'(\hat{k}_t)$, which as a function of $\hat{k}_t$ is an increasing function.[3] Substituting (4.7), (4.8) and (4.2) in (4.6), we have the following non-linear difference equation in the capital–labor ratio $\hat{k}_t$ of the productive sector.

$$\hat{k}_{t+1} = \frac{s(w_t, \rho_{t+1})}{(1 + g) - n(w_t, \rho_{t+1})} \equiv \varphi(\hat{k}_t, \hat{k}_{t+1}) \tag{4.9}$$

for an appropriately defined function φ. Equation (4.9) provides the fundamental difference equation of our growth model. Once we obtain $\{\hat{k}_t\}_0^\infty$ we can derive all other equilibrium quantities. Thus the dynamic properties of our economy could be studied from the properties of (4.9).

The implicitly defined second order difference equation in (4.9) is, however, hard to study. We shall consider two examples to study the dynamic properties of our economy when there is exogenous shock in the fertility rate: one with Cobb–Douglas utility and production functions, and the other with constant elasticity of substitution (CES) utility function and Cobb–Douglas production function.

Cobb–Douglas Economy

Assume Cobb–Douglas utility function $u(c_t) = \alpha \ln c_t$ and $v(n_{t+1}) = (1 - \alpha)\ln n_{t+1}$, $\alpha > 0$. Assume Cobb–Douglas production function as $f(k) = k^\theta, 0 < \theta < 1$. We then have the following optimal solutions:

$$c_t = \alpha w_t$$

$$n_{t+1} = (1 - \alpha)(1 + r_{t+1})\frac{w_t}{w_{t+1}} \tag{4.10}$$

Thus we have

$$s_t = (1 - \alpha)w_t \tag{4.11}$$

Notice that a rise in wage rate in the next period only due to a fall in the fertility rate in this period will have no effect on consumption and savings in this period, but the demand for nursing services will fall to the level such that the share of current income spent on nursing will remain constant. However, if both w_t and w_{t+1} change due to a constant fertility decline over time which started in the past, there will be an increase in savings. The effect on demand for nursing services will depend on how the ratio of the wage rates w_t / w_{t+1} and the interest rate r_{t+1} are affected by such fertility decline. To that end, we study the difference equation (4.9) which for this specific economy becomes,

$$\hat{k}_{t+1} = \frac{(1-\alpha)}{(1+g)} \hat{k}_t^\theta, \quad \hat{k}_0 \quad \text{given}, \quad t \ge 0. \tag{4.12}$$

The above is a first order difference equation in the capital–labor ratio which has a stable steady-state given by

$$\hat{k}* = \left[\frac{(1-\alpha)}{(1+g)} \right]^{\frac{1}{1-\theta}} \tag{4.13}$$

and the phase diagram is as shown in Figure 4.2. It is clear from the phase diagram that if there is a constant fertility decline beginning in time period t, the capital–labor ratio in all subsequent periods will be higher than the levels without the fertility decline,[4] and hence the economy will have higher wage rates w_{t+1}, w_{t+2} ... and higher wage rental rates ρ_{t+1}, ρ_{t+2} ...

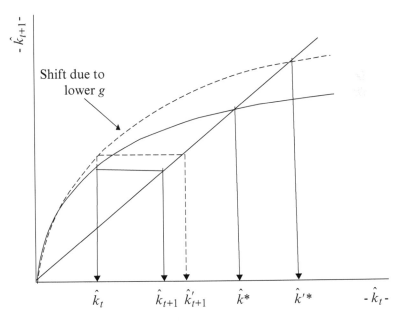

Figure 4.2   Phase diagram before and after fertility decline

compared to the rates when there was no fertility decline. We now examine the general equilibrium effect of fertility decline on other variables.

From equation (4.4) it follows that

$$e_t = 1 - \frac{(1-\alpha)(1+r_t)w_{t-1}/w_t}{1+g}$$

$$= 1 - \frac{(1-\alpha)}{1+g} \cdot \frac{\theta}{1-\theta} \cdot \frac{\omega(\hat{k}_{t-1})}{\hat{k}_t}$$

$$= 1 - \theta \qquad (4.14)$$

The last equality follows after substituting equation (4.12) in the denominator in the previous step and then simplifying. Thus in this economy the fraction of labor in the nursing sector is independent of the population growth rate in all periods.

From the second line of equation (4.10) we have

$$n_{t+1} = (1-\alpha)w_t/\rho_{t+1}$$

$$= (1-\alpha)\theta\hat{k}_t^\theta/\hat{k}_{t+1}$$

$$= \theta(1+g) \qquad (4.15)$$

In the above, we derived the last equality after substituting $\hat{k}_{t+1}$ from equation (4.12) and then simplifying. It is clear from (4.15) that all generations will have the same level of consumption of nursing services, the level of which becomes lower, the lower is the population growth rate.

Since wage rates in all future periods are higher, it follows that there will be higher savings due to a fall in fertility rate. The savings rate, defined as s_t/w_t will, however, remain unaffected by a drop in fertility.

Constant Elasticity of Substitution Economy

We consider now a more general CES utility function to shed light on the effect of fertility decline on savings rate and other variables. We assume the following forms for the CES utility function:

$$u(c_t) = \frac{c_t^{1-\sigma}}{1-\sigma}, \quad \text{and} \quad v(n_{t+1}) = \frac{n_{t+1}^{1-\sigma}}{1-\sigma}, \quad \sigma > 0, \sigma \neq 1. \qquad (4.16)$$

After algebraic manipulations, we have the optimal solution for n_{t+1} and s_t as follows:

$$n_{t+1} = \frac{w_t}{\rho_{t+1} + \rho_{t+1}^{1/\sigma}} \tag{4.17}$$

and

$$s_t = \rho_{t+1} n_{t+1}$$

$$= \frac{w_t}{1 + \rho_{t+1}^{1/\sigma - 1}} \tag{4.18}$$

Notice that in this case the effect on savings rate of generation t from a constant fertility decline over time beginning in time period t depends on whether $\sigma > 1$ or $\sigma < 1$. We know that an increase in interest rate has a negative income effect and a positive substitution effect on savings and the net effect depends on which effect is dominant. It is well known that when $\sigma > 1$, the income effect dominates the substitution effect and the net effect of an increase in interest rate on savings is negative. The opposite is the case when $\sigma < 1$. The empirical estimates of σ in macroeconomics and public finance literature vary anywhere from 1 to 4 for the US during the post world war period. Assuming similar estimates hold for Japan, we can see that a decline in fertility rate will increase the savings rate s_t/w_t. The economic interpretation of this result is that the households save more so that they can afford more costly nursing services when they become old.

Substituting the first part of equation (4.18) in equation (4.6) we have,

$$\hat{k}_{t+1} = \frac{\rho_{t+1}}{(1+g)/n_{t+1} - 1} \tag{4.19}$$

For the Cobb–Douglas production function we have, $\rho_{t+1} = ((1 - \theta)/\theta) \cdot \hat{k}_{t+1}$. Substituting this in equation (4.19) we have

$$n_{t+1} = \theta(1 + g). \tag{4.20}$$

Thus, the equilibrium consumption of nursing services does not depend on elasticity of substitution, σ, and its level is constant over time. The equilibrium consumption of nursing services is, however, lower if there is a decline in the fertility rate g. From equation (4.4) it also follows that

$$e_t = 1 - \theta \tag{4.21}$$

Substituting equation (4.17) in equation (4.20) and after simplification, we have the following non-linear difference equation for $\hat{k}_t$,

$$\left[\frac{1-\theta}{\theta}\right]^{(1-\sigma)/\sigma} \hat{k}_{t+1}^{1/\sigma} + \hat{k}_{t+1} = \frac{1}{(1+g)}\hat{k}_t^{\theta} \qquad (4.22)$$

The above defines implicitly $\hat{k}_{t+1}$ as a function of $\hat{k}_t$. This is an increasing function of $\hat{k}_t$ and its derivative at $\hat{k}_t = 0$ is ∞. It will have a phase diagram similar to the one shown in Figure 4.2. Thus the dynamic properties of this model will be similar to those of a standard neoclassical growth model.

3. FOREIGN CAPITAL INVESTMENT AND INTERNATIONAL LABOR MIGRATION

If this country is opened to the world market, then certainly immigration from abroad will help the welfare of the country as long as the foreign technology and population growth rate are initially identical to those in the home country. This proposition can be seen easily by looking at the wage-rental frontiers of the two countries. The wage-rental frontier of a country depicts the relationship between the present wage rate and the rate of return to savings for the future. Initially, the foreign wage-rental frontier is given. The home country's wage-rental frontier shrinks downward because the same amount of saving will be less effective in obtaining care in the future. Therefore, the inflow of foreign workers will recover the labor growth rate and improve the consumption possibility of the home country. In the simplest case assume that the foreign country is a large country, so that its wage-rental frontier does not change because of migration of its labor to the other country. Then it is clear that the home country can enjoy the same welfare level as the foreign country.

Incidentally, in Kageyu spa of the (mid-mainland) Nagano prefecture in Japan, there were 21 nurses (or carers) from Brazil in the year 2000. Before World War II, many Japanese migrated to Brazil and their descendants still speak Japanese. Probably because of that, Brazilian citizens are under less strict regulations for immigration into Japan. Patients as well as the aged in Japan welcome these carers from abroad.

According to the Asahi Newspaper (14 January, 2000), the Japanese Government started a debate on whether foreigners should be admitted to provide nursing services. In the year 2025, the numbers of elderly who will require intensive care will increase to 5.2 million from the present level of 2.8 million. Presently there are only 170 000 in-home carers, but Japan will need more than a million nurses including their administrative support in the future. There are different opinions about letting immigrants provide this service. For instance, the nursing service organizations are hardly welcoming such a policy. Some economists admit that this trend is inevitable. The aged and the patients often say that they are happier to be taken care of by kind foreigners than by busy natives.

On the other hand, we could achieve the same goal by exporting capital. Instead of accumulating capital in the home country where the rate of return will be lower because of a fall in the labor force due to a fall in the fertility level and decreasing utility from nursing, the home country can invest capital abroad, earning a higher rate of return, and pay for the nursing care in the next period utilizing the higher returns from foreign investment. This provides a theoretical explanation for the commonly made observation that the Japanese save a large percentage of their income in order to consume in old age. This analysis is also consistent with the claim by Goto (1998) that Japan can avoid the social problems involved with immigrant workers by trading with foreign countries first and then investing capital in foreign countries.

We live, however, in a world where technological levels differ from one part of the world to the other. There are two conceivable cases. One case is where the labor force in Northern countries possesses a higher level of human capital, so that a worker in the North is as effective as, say, two workers in the rest of the world. Then if the production function in terms of the effective labor unit is identical, the neoclassical theory of capital movements and migration hold true. A worker in the South will have a wage rate equal to only half of the wage rate in the North after migration.

On the other hand, suppose instead that the technological level of the North is higher than that in the South. If the two regions have the same shape for production isoquants in terms of capital and labor, and if the levels of total factor productivity between the two regions are different, what will the pattern of international factor movements be? The exodus of capital from the North to the South is not the solution in this situation. The flow of both capital and labor from the South to the North will enhance world welfare.[5] This would mean that there will be a higher concentration of production in the North. But after a while there will be congestion in the North, especially when the northern country is geographically small, such as Japan or a Europen country. To see this formally we consider a variation of the congestion model of Raut and Srinivasan (1994). Assume that population density affects total factor productivity of inputs. Assume further that very high population density has a negative effect on total factor productivity level due to congestion. More precisely, we assume that the output per unit of labor in the productive sector of the North is given by

$$y^N = A^N(L_t)f(\hat{k}_t) \tag{4.23}$$

where $A^N(L_t)$ denotes the total factor productivity level as a function of population density in period t. Assume that the South does not have a congestion effect on productivity and assume its output per unit of labor in the production sector is represented by the same production function as described in the previous section. Suppose that at a very high level of L_t, the total factor productivity level $A^N(L_t)$ becomes less than 1. Then it is clear that the wage rate in the North $w_t^N = A^N(L_t)[f(\hat{k}_t) - \hat{k}_t f'(\hat{k}_t)]$ will be higher than that in the South initially. There will be labor migration to the North up to the point when the congestion effect of labor makes the productivity level $A^N(L_t)$ in the North less than or equal to 1. After that there will be no more labor mobility to the North.

4. CONCLUDING REMARKS

In order to focus on the problem associated with the caring of the aged, we have built an overlapping generation model that takes full account of the nursing cost of an economy facing rapid ageing. Rapid ageing presents a challenge to society because the present generation will face a less favorable trade-off in transforming the saving into nursing services when it becomes old. If the elasticity of substitution between the present consumption and the future nursing consumption is less than unity, the saving of the current generation will be increased.

In such a case the increased saving may find an outlet to foreign markets. We found that immigration and capital outflow are alternative remedies to a country's rapid ageing problems.

Needless to say, the ageing and nursing problems also have much wider dimensions, such as ethical, sociological and medical aspects. Transportation costs for migration and foreign investments also vary depending on the situation. The Gastarbeiter (guest workers) issues in Europe pose social problems of adjustment even a generation afterwards. The 'hollowing out' of capital exports presents another serious problem to the home country. Conclusions given in this chapter should be qualified in the light of these elements if they are to be applied to policy-making.

NOTES

1. Lakshmi Raut is an Economist at the Social Security Administration (SSA). This chapter was prepared prior to his joining SSA and the analyses and conclusions expressed are those of the authors and not necessarily those of the organizations with which they are affiliated.
2. Literature describes the depth of emotion attached to caring for an ageing generation, which is often a hard and sublime duty for mankind. In medieval villages in the highlands

of Japan, a legend told of old people who sacrificed themselves by straying into the mountains to spare the young from caring for them and to save food for them. Fukasawa writes that a woman even prepared herself for this sacrifice by destroying her own still young teeth so that she would look old. In the best-selling novel about modern Japan, Sawako Ariyoshi describes a process of how a middle class family was disrupted by an elderly man who was losing his memory as well as control of his physical faculties. A housewife had to give up her full-time job to become a part-timer so that she could take care of her elderly father-in-law. In Shakespeare's classic drama, one sees a prototype of generational conflicts and even implicit strategic negotiations.

3. To see this, note that $\rho_t'() = - [f''(k_t)f(k_t)]/[f'(k_t)]^2$, which is positive for the concave production function.
4. In the figure we used x' to denote the variable x after the fertility shock.
5. See Raut (2007) for further discussions.

BIBLIOGRAPHY

Ariyoshi, Sawako (1972), *Kokotsunohito*, (*The Twilight Years*, translated by Mildred Tahara, 1987), Tokyo: Kodansha.
Economic Planning Agency (EPA) (1991), '2010 Nen heno Sangyo Santaku' (Japan in the year 2010), Tokyo: Government Printing Office.
Fuchs, Victor (1990), 'The health sector's share of the gross national product', *Science*, New Series, **247**(4942).
Fukasawa, Shichiro (1968), *Fukasawa Shichiro Senshu*, Tokyo.
Garber, Alan M. (1989), 'Long-term care, wealth, and health of the disabled elderly living in the community', Chapter 9 in D.A. Wise (ed.), *The Economics of Aging*, Chicago: NBER.
Garber, Alan M. (1994), 'Financing health care for elderly Americans', Chapter 7 in Y. Noguchi and D.A. Wise (eds), *Aging in the United States and Japan: Economic Trends*, NBER Conference Report, Chicago: University of Chicago Press.
Goto, J. (1998), 'The impact of migrant workers on the Japanese economy: trickle vs. flood', *Japan and the World Economy*, **10**, 63–83.
Horioka, Charles Yuji (1991), 'The determinants of Japan's savings rate: the impact of the age structure of the population and other factors', *Economic Studies Quarterly*, **42**(3), 237–53.
Horioka, Charles Yuji (1992), 'Future trends in Japan's savings rate, and the implications thereof for Japan's external imbalance', *Japan and the World Economy*, **3**(4), 307–30.
Hurd, M.D. and N. Yoshino (1997), *The Economic Effects of Ageing in the United States and Japan*, Chicago: NBER.
Karatzas, George (2000), 'On the determination of the US aggregate health care expenditure', *Applied Economics*, **32**(9).
Lincoln, E. (1993), *Japan's New Global Rule*, Washington DC: Brookings Institution.
Ministry of Welfare of Japan (1995, 2000), *Basic Survey of National Life*, Tokyo.
Miura, Fumio (ed.) (1999), *Illustrated White Paper for the Elderly, 1999*, Tokyo: National Social Welfare Association.
Noguchi Yukio (1990), 'Jinko Kozo to Chochiku/Toshi: Kakkoku Hikaku ni yoru Bunseki' (The age structure of the population and saving/investment: An analysis

based on cross country comparisons), *Financial Review* (Institute of Fiscal and Monetary Policy, Ministry of Finance), **17** (August), 39–50.

Noguchi Y. and D.A. Wise (eds) (1994), *Aging in the United States and Japan: Economic Trends*, NBER Conference Report, Chicago: University of Chicago Press.

OECD (1987), *The Future of Migration*, Paris: OECD.

Raut, L.K. (2007), 'Immigration vs. foreign investment to ease the ageing problems of an ageing open economy', Chapter 5, this volume.

Raut, L.K. and T.N. Srinivasan (1994), 'Dynamics of endogenous growth', *Economic Theory*, **4**, 777–90.

Sato, Yoko (2001), 'Comparative analysis of health care costs in Japan and the United States: a simulation of productivity and savings behavior', *Japan and the World Economy*, **13**, 429–54.

Stahl, C. (1982), 'International labour migration and international development', International Employment Working Paper (No.1), Geneva.

Todaro, M.P. (1986), 'International migration, domestic unemployment, and urbanization: a three-sector model', Center for Policy Studies Working Papers, (No.124).

Wise, D.A. (ed.) (1989), *The Economics of Ageing*, Chicago: NBER.

Yashiro, N. and A. Sato-Oishi (1997), 'Population aging and the saving investment balance in Japan', in M. Hurd and N. Yoshino (eds), *The Economic Effects of Aging in the United States and Japan*, Chicago: NBER.

5. Immigration vs. foreign investment to ease the ageing problems of an ageing open economy[1,2]

Lakshmi K. Raut

1. INTRODUCTION

In this chapter I formulate an overlapping generations model of the world economy with two regions that vary in ageing pattern: one region consists of Japan and other OECD countries with high life expectancy, low fertility rate and high labor productivity, and the other region consists of the developing countries with low life expectancy, high fertility rate and low labor productivity. It is often argued that the ageing pattern of Japan and other OECD countries would have led to dynamic inefficiency or capital over-accumulation in the absence of their pay-as-you-go social security systems. The ageing in the OECD countries also led to the insolvency of their public pension systems. Calibrating the above model, I examine these issues and also the policy issue of when to invest capital from OECD countries in developing countries and when to import labor from developing countries to cope with the ageing problem of OECD countries. I then use cross-country aggregate data to empirically examine why not much capital flows from OECD countries into less developed countries, and draw policy conclusions.

In the past century the world has witnessed an unprecedented pattern of demographic transitions. Japan and other OECD countries have achieved very high life expectancies and very low total fertility rates. For instance, the life expectancy at birth in Japan increased from 64 years in the 1950s to 83 years in the late 1990s, and the total fertility rate dropped from 2.75 in the 1950s to 1.43 in the late 1990s, which is well below the replacement total fertility rate of 2. Other OECD countries have had similar experiences. The ageing pattern of the OECD countries has led to serious financing problems for their publicly provided social security and health care programs. The potential support ratio in Japan, defined as the number of persons aged 15–64 per person aged 65 or older, has fallen from 12.06 in 1950 to

3.99 in 2000, and the United Nations (UN) projects it to drop to 1.71 by the year 2050 (see United Nations, 2000 for details).

Japan and most other OECD countries have very generous publicly provided old-age pension programs, which transfer a large amount of resources from the young to the old, and they also have generous publicly provided health care systems. In Japan, while a higher life expectancy and a lower fertility rate might have led to a higher savings rate and a current account surplus, the same ageing process also led to economic problems involving a higher demand for labor services in the elderly care sector (see Sato, 2001 for some estimates) and to heavier tax burdens on the younger generation to provide for the promised pension benefits of the old. For instance, social security benefits as a percentage of national income totaled 17 per cent in 1995 (9 per cent in pensions, 6 per cent in medical care and 2 per cent in welfare) and are expected to rise to 33.5 per cent in 2025 (16 per cent in pension, 13 per cent in medical care, and 4.5 per cent in welfare). The above pattern of demographic transitions also has significant consequences on future population size. The United Nations (2000) projects that in the absence of immigration, the total population of Japan will decline from its current level of 127 million to 105 million in 2050.

In contrast, the contemporary developing countries have much higher fertility rates and much lower life expectancies, and thus much higher potential support ratios. Most developing countries do not have a formal publicly provided social security program or a health care system that covers the majority of their population.

Policy makers around the world have been debating on ways to cope with the 'ageing' problems of the OECD countries. The problems are threefold: first, there is a shortage of resources to provide for the consumption of the elderly, including their medical expenditures; second, there is also a shortage of labor services to provide for elderly care; third, because individuals expect longer retirements and higher elderly care costs, they save a higher percentage of their incomes, which in a closed economy can lead to dynamic inefficiency, that is, an excessively high amount of capital formation compared to a socially optimal level. Some of the highly debated and highly recommended policy suggestions include reforming the pay-as-you-go social security program, such as by reducing benefits, gradually increasing the retirement age, and partially privatizing social security by introducing personal savings accounts. The long-term solution to the problems of ageing in OECD countries, however, inevitably requires tweaking the age structure either by increasing fertility rates or by increasing immigration of foreign workers so that the potential support ratio is reasonably high. Since it is impossible to increase the fertility rate of

OECD countries, the United Nations (2000) and other practitioners recommend that Japan and other OECD countries should seriously consider 'replacement migration' as a way to increase population size and the potential support ratio. It estimates that Japan will require approximately 312 000 immigrants each year to keep the population size constant, and approximately 10 million to keep the potential support ratio constant. The optimal population size for Japan, however, is not obvious because the concept of optimal population is a highly controversial issue in the economics literature.

Immigration of labor is one plausible solution to ageing problems. Investment of capital in developing countries is another plausible solution. The main rationale for this is that the demographic mismatch of OECD and developing countries would generally mean a higher rate of return from capital invested in a developing country. Thus, by investing part of its capital in developing countries or by allowing immigration of labor from developing countries, Japan could remove its dynamic inefficiency in capital over accumulation. Furthermore, Japan could use the gains from foreign capital incomes or payroll taxes of the immigrant guest workers to finance its publicly provided social security program. Even a cursory look at the foreign investment and immigration statistics of Japan would tell us that Japan has very little foreign investment in the less developed countries and very few immigrant workers.

In this chapter, I formulate an overlapping generations model to study the following policy issues surrounding Japan's ageing problems:

- Out of the two options of foreign investment in developing countries and immigration of labor from developing countries, which is a better policy option from the perspective of the ageing problem in Japan?
- Why, contrary to the prediction of the neoclassical theory, does so little capital flow from Japan into less developed countries?

Section 2 describes a few stylized facts about Japan. In section 3, the basic theoretical framework is detailed. In section 4, I first briefly discuss the economic arguments from the international economics literature on the choice between foreign investment and immigration, and then I use the calibrated model to shed further light on the choice between the two from the public finance perspectives of the ageing problems in Japan. In section 5, I carry out a cross-country regression analysis to examine empirically the significant determinants of foreign capital flows to less developed countries.

2.   A FEW STYLIZED FACTS ABOUT JAPAN

Figure 5.1 depicts the population pyramid of Japan in 1950 and how it has changed in the past 50 years to the current age structure in 2001, and how it is expected to change in another 50 years as a result of the steady decline in fertility rate and increase in life expectancy. In the 1950s, 100 adults took care of only 8 elderly people, currently 100 adults take care of 26 elderly persons, and in another 50 years 100 adults will have to take care of 67 elderly persons. This will cause the labor force of the productive sector to dwindle. Figure 5.2 compares Japan's scenario with other OECD countries and India. It is clear that in 1950, while all other OECD countries had much higher proportions of elderly population than Japan, by the year 2000 Japan began to surpass all other OECD countries. This was due to the fact that while other OECD countries experienced their demographic transitions (low mortality and fertility rates) slowly over a longer period of time, Japan had a very rapid demographic transition.

Figures 5.3–5.5 show some of the effects of Japan's demographic transitions on the resource and labor requirements for elderly care. Figure 5.3 shows that while in the early 1980s only 10 per cent of national income went towards pensions and medical care, by the year 2000 the share went up to more than 20 per cent of national income. Figures 5.4 and 5.5 show that there are sharp increases in the demand for female and homecare nurses in the late 1990s. It is clear from these trends that, in another 50 years, a

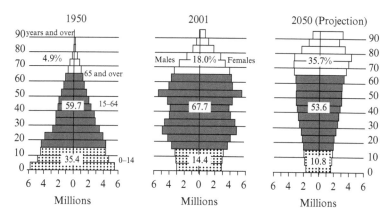

Source: Statistics Bureau, Ministry of Public Management, Home Affairs, Posts and Telecommunications; Ministry of Health, Labour and Welfare.

Figure 5.1   Changes in population pyramid

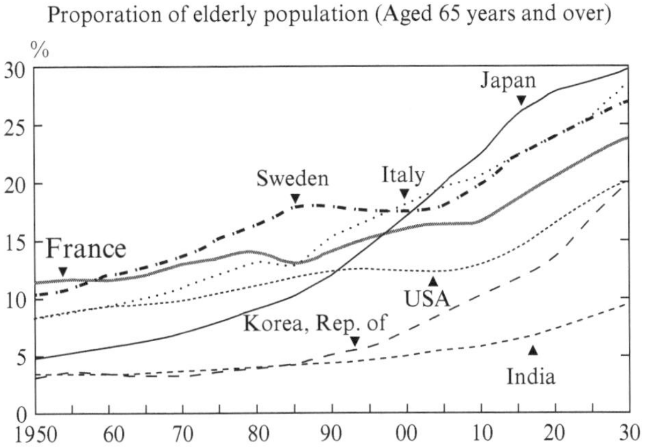

Proporation of elderly population (Aged 65 years and over)

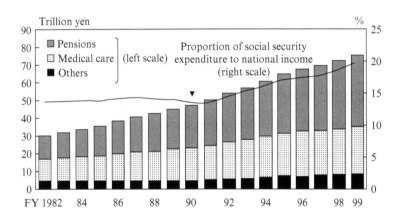

Source: United Nations; Statistics Bureau, Ministry of Public Management, Home Affairs, Posts and Telecommunications; Ministry of Health, Labour and Welfare.

Figure 5.2   Comparison of Japan's ageing population with other countries

Source: Ministry of Health, Labour and Welfare.

Figure 5.3   Trend in social security and medical care expenditures

significantly high proportion of national income and the labor force need to be devoted to the elderly care sector.

Another important development in Japan has been its persistent current account surpluses over the past several years (see Figure 5.6). In other words, Japan persistently invested abroad more than foreigners invested in Japan. The International Investment Position (IIP) is defined as a stock

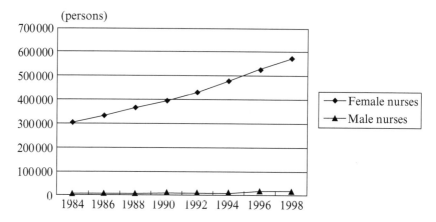

Source: Summary of Vital Statistics, The Statistics and Information Department, Minister's Secretariat, Ministry of Health and Welfare.

Figure 5.4 *Demand for nurses during 1984–1998*

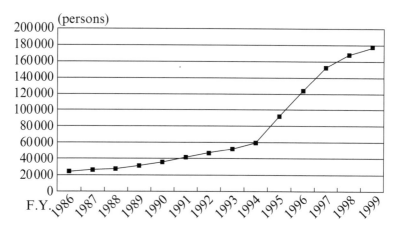

Source: Summary of Vital Statistics, The Statistics and Information Department, Minister's Secretariat, Ministry of Health and Welfare.

Figure 5.5 *The demand for home care nurses during 1986–1999*

variable consisting of the capital and financial accounts plus the reserve assets in the balance of payments. Table 5.1 shows the investment position and the composition of Japan's foreign investment in the second half of the 1990s. From the table it is clear that Japan's stock of foreign assets, which went down a bit during the Asian crisis years, has been growing over a long

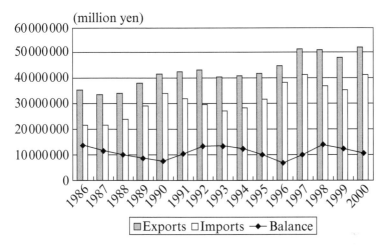

Figure 5.6   Japan's current account surplus during 1986–2000

Table 5.1   International investment position of Japan (asset in billion Yen)

End of year	Assets					
	Total	1. Direct investment	2. Portfolio investment			3. Other investments
			Total	(1) Equity securities	(2) Debt securities	
1995	270 738	24 520	88 257	15 040	73 217	139 129
1996	307 703	29 999	108 711	17 968	90 743	143 751
1997	355 731	35 334	117 821	20 632	97 188	173 884
1998	345 132	31 216	122 719	24 205	98 515	166 335
1999	307 989	25 425	127 426	29 161	98 265	125 740
2000	346 099	31 993	143 420	30 130	113 290	129 208

Source: The Bank of Japan.

period of time at a high positive rate. Table 5.1 also shows the stocks of the three components of total foreign assets: (1) direct foreign investment, which is 9.25 per cent of total assets, (2) portfolio foreign investment, which is 41.44 per cent of total assets, and (3) other investments, which comprise 37.33 per cent of total stock of foreign assets at the end of year 2000.

Two sources of private capital flows – direct foreign investment and portfolio foreign investment – have grown substantially over the past several years. Where did most of these investments go? From Table 5.2 it is clear

Table 5.2   Percentage distribution of Japan's foreign direct investment

FY	1989	1990	1991	1992	1993	1994	1995	1996	1997	1998	1999	2000
North America	50.35	47.84	45.31	42.81	42.37	43.27	45.18	47.94	39.63	26.86	37.14	25.26
Latin America	7.74	6.33	8.00	7.95	9.37	12.85	7.55	9.26	11.74	15.86	11.15	10.77
Asia	12.18	12.38	14.26	18.77	18.48	23.56	24.05	24.19	22.57	16.02	10.74	12.21
Europe	21.84	25.11	22.57	20.71	22.17	15.24	16.71	15.35	20.76	34.38	38.69	50.24
Rest of the World	7.90	8.33	9.87	9.76	7.60	5.08	6.52	3.26	5.30	6.88	2.28	1.52

Source: The Bank of Japan.

that much of the Japanese direct foreign investments went to Europe and to the US, and very little went to less developed countries. Furthermore, even among developing countries, much of Japanese foreign investment went to East Asia.

3. THE BASIC FRAMEWORK

I consider a simple overlapping generations (OLG) model in which agents live for two periods, adult and old. To incorporate variations in life expectancy among countries, and to keep the analysis analytically manageable, I assume that agents survive the first period with probability one, and survive the second period with probability π, $0 < \pi \leq 1$. A period in our model would typically mean about 40 years. Assuming that adulthood, that is, period 1 of the life cycle in our model, starts at age 20, the life expectancy in our model is then given by $60 + 40\pi$. I assume that Japan has a much higher π than a representative developing country. While gender does not play any role in this chapter, I will address everyone here as he instead of she or (s)he.

Denote by c_t^t and c_{t+1}^t respectively the consumption in period t and $t+1$ of an adult of period t. I further assume that when an agent survives to be old, he does not work and he needs a fixed γ hours of nursing services, $0 < \gamma < 1$. For simplicity of exposition, I assume that it is a fixed constant and not a choice variable.[3] A young worker has one unit of labor which he supplies inelastically either to the nursing/medical sector or to the production sector.

Let w_t be the wage rate in period t. A young worker earns w_t, pays social security taxes $\tau_t w_t$ and chooses to consume c_t^t and to save s_t. His savings are immediately put into an annuity market which promises to pay $1 + \rho_t$ for each unit of annuity until the agent dies.

The resolution of uncertainty and the savings decisions happen in the following order: first the agent decides on his savings, which he immediately puts in the annuity market. Then the uncertainty about his death is resolved. If he survives, he receives $(1 + \rho_t)s_t$ when he is old. If he dies, he receives nothing. I assume the existence of an annuity market as a modeling simplification. Other more realistic institutions could be introduced at the cost of extra complications. The agent's expected utility function is given by

$$E(U^t) = u(c_t^t) + \beta\pi u(c_{t+1}^t), \tag{5.1}$$

He maximizes (5.1) subject to the following budget constraints:

$$c_t^t + s_t = (1 - \tau_t)w_t \tag{5.2}$$

and

$$c_{t+1}^t + \gamma w_{t+1} = (1 + \rho_{t+1})s_t + B_{t+1}, \tag{5.3}$$

where B_{t+1} is the old age security benefits he receives in his old age. Optimal savings s_t depends on the wage rates w_t and w_{t+1}, on the rate of returns from capital ρ_{t+1}, on the social security benefits B_{t+1} and on the survival probability π.

I assume that Japan has a defined benefits pay-as-you-go public pension program with the replacement rate μ, which means that a worker is promised by the social security administration to be paid a fraction μ of his adult age wage earnings when he retires. For the less developed countries, I assume that there is no formal social security program. The old age pension-related intergenerational transfers from young to old are, however, performed within the family. More specifically, I assume that an adult of generation t transfers a fraction $a_t, 0 < a_t < 1$, of his wage earnings to his elderly parents. The fraction a_t is determined by social norms.[4] Informal transfers are generally lower than the formal transfers, and thus, the economies with an informal system of old age transfers experience higher fertility rates. I will not make fertility endogenous, but assume that it is higher in less developed countries than in Japan and other OECD countries. Assume that the population is growing exogenously at the rate of n, that is, $(1 + n)$ is the fertility rate. Assume that the private annuity markets are actuarially fair. Denote the interest rate between period t and $t+1$ by r_{t+1}. Then the following holds for Japan,

$$B_{t+1} = \mu w_t = (1 + n)\tau_{t+1} w_{t+1}/\pi \tag{5.4J}$$

and the following for the less developed countries (LDCs),

$$B_{t+1} = (1 + n)a_{t+1} w_{t+1}/\pi. \tag{5.4L}$$

Notice that equation (5.4J) for Japan implies that the social security tax rate is given by $\tau_{t+1} = \mu\pi/((1 + n)(1 + g_{t+1}))$, where $1 + g_{t+1} = w_{t+1}/w_t$ is the growth in wages between periods t and $t+1$. This implies that when fertility rate, $1+n$, goes down as in Japan, unless it maintains a high growth rate in productivity, g_{t+1}, the social security tax rate will be very high to provide the promised replacement rate μ. Notice also that the actuarially fair tax rate τ_{t+1} becomes higher, the higher is the life expectancy, that is, the higher is the survival probability π in our case. Thus, two critical elements of Japan's social security problems are the drop in fertility rate $1+n$, and the increase in life expectancy or survival probability π. We have assumed π and n to be exogenously given and fixed over time. An immediate policy implication for the ageing crisis is that Japan must maintain a high growth rate of productivity and increase its fertility rate in order to keep the social security tax rate within a viable limit. Higher wage growth also has an effect on savings s_t, because it increases the cost of nursing $\gamma\omega_{t+1}$ relative to ω_t.

The assumption about an actuarially fair annuity market implies the following:

$$(1 + \rho_{t+1})s_t\pi_t L_t = (1 + r_{t+1})L_t s_t \Rightarrow 1 + \rho_{t+1} = \frac{1 + r_{t+1}}{\pi} \quad (5.5)$$

3.1 Household Decisions

A representative adult of time period t maximizes his expected utility function (5.1) subject to budget constraints, (5.2) and (5.3).

From the budget set, it can be seen that an increase in π has income and substitution effects. Furthermore, the marginal rate of substitution of the expected utility function is also affected by π. I consider the Cobb–Douglas[5] utility function, $u(c) = \ln c$, to derive the optimal solution explicitly. The optimal savings of a representative agent is given by

$$s_t = (1 - a_t)w_t - \frac{1}{1 + \beta\pi}\left[(1 - a_t)w_t + \frac{\pi}{(1 + r_{t+1})} \cdot (B_{t+1} - \gamma w_{t+1})\right]$$

Substituting the value of B_{t+1} from equation (5.4L) in the above expression, one has the following:

$$s_t = \frac{\beta\pi}{1 + \beta\pi}(1 - a_t)w_t - \frac{[(1 + n)a_{t+1} - \pi\gamma]w_{t+1}}{(1 + \beta\pi)(1 + r_{t+1})}$$

$$= w_t\left[\frac{\beta\pi}{1 + \beta\pi}(1 - a_t) - \frac{[(1 + n)a_{t+1} - \pi\gamma](1 + g_{t+1})}{(1 + \beta\pi)(1 + r_{t+1})}\right]. \quad (5.6)$$

It is clear from the above that the household savings rate is higher for an economy that has a higher survival probability π or a higher need for nursing services γ; an economy with a lower fertility rate also has a higher savings rate; furthermore, an economy that transfers a higher amount of resources from the young to the old, (that is, has a higher value for a_{t+1}), has a lower savings rate. In deriving these properties I assumed that w_{t+1} and r_{t+1} remained constant as a result of changes in the above parameters.

3.2 Autarky Equilibrium

Assume that all the economies use a common neoclassical constant returns
to scale technology in production of GDP which uses capital and labor as
inputs. Assume that the production of GDP is represented by the following production function,

$$Y_t = A_t F(K_t, b_t L_t), \tag{5.7}$$

where A_t represents factor neutral productivity level. I assume it to depend
on infrastructure and other social factors that affect the productivity of
both capital and labor equally. The variable b_t denotes the efficiency level
of a unit of labor in period t. I assume that b_t grows over time at the rate of
φ per period, and this growth rate depends on the average education level
of the workforce of an economy. Notice that the difference in the level of
b_t for Japan and a representative LDC determines the wage differences of
the two economies, and the difference in the level of A_t determines the
difference in interest rates between the countries in the free world capital
market equilibrium. In this section, however, I assume that $A_t \equiv 1$ for all
t and for all countries.

Denote by $\hat{x}_t$ the variable x_t in efficiency unit, that is, $\hat{x}_t = x_t/b_t$. Let
$\hat{y}_t = f(\hat{k}_t)$ be the output per unit of labor in efficiency unit when the
capital–labor ratio in efficiency unit is $\hat{k}_t$.

I assume that capital lasts for one period and savings take one period to
gestate before they become capital. The annuity firm invests all its receipts
$L_t s_t$, in the capital market. Thus the next period's capital stock is given by
$K_{t+1} = L_t s_t$. The labor in the productive sector is then given by

$$\overline{L}_{t+1} = (1+n)L_t - \pi\gamma L_t. \tag{5.8}$$

The second term in the above represents labor needed to meet nursing/
medical care of the surviving elderly.

Note that the capital–labor ratio in efficiency unit $\hat{k}_{t+1}$ in period $t+1$ is
then given by

$$\hat{k}_{t+1} = \frac{K_{t+1}}{b_{t+1}\overline{L}_{t+1}} = \frac{s_t}{b_{t+1}[(1+n) - \pi\gamma]}. \tag{5.9}$$

Under the assumption that all markets are competitive, it follows that

$$\hat{w}_t = f(\hat{k}_t) - \hat{k}_t f'(\hat{k}_t) \equiv \omega(\hat{k}_t), \tag{5.10}$$

and

$$1 + r_t = f'(\hat{k}_t). \tag{5.11}$$

I denote the solution of equation (5.11) for $\hat{k}_{t+1}$ as a function of r_{t+1} by $\hat{k}_{t+1} = \kappa(r_{t+1})$, which determines the demand for capital per unit of efficiency labor, and it can be shown easily that it is a standard downward-sloping curve as shown in Figure 5.7.

The supply of capital–labor ratio in efficiency unit can be easily derived by substituting equation (5.6) in equation (5.9). I have shown the supply curves for Japan and a representative LDC in Figure 5.7.

To study the equilibrium dynamics of the closed economy, I derive the fundamental difference equation of the economy in terms of capital–labor ratio in efficiency unit. Note that from equation (5.9), it follows that $s_t = [(1+n) - \pi\gamma]\hat{k}_{t+1}b_{t+1}$. Substituting this in the first part of equation (5.6), one has

$$[(1+n) - \pi\gamma]\hat{k}_{t+1} = \frac{\beta\pi}{1+\beta\pi}(1 - a_t)\frac{\omega(\hat{k}_t)}{1+\phi} - \frac{[(1+n)a_{t+1} - \pi\gamma]R(\hat{k}_{t+1})}{1+\beta\pi},$$

$$\tag{5.12}$$

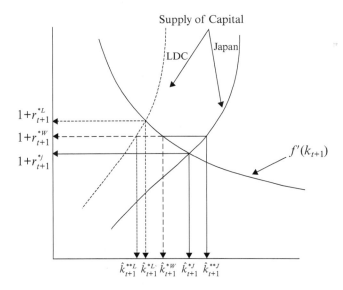

Figure 5.7 *Determination of world interest rate and the direction of capital flow*

where $R(\hat{k}) = [f(\hat{k}) - \hat{k}f'(\hat{k})]/f'(\hat{k})$, the efficiency wage–rental ratio as a function of capital–labor ratio in efficiency unit. Equation (5.12) implicitly defines a first order non-linear difference equation $\hat{k}_t$. For the Cobb–Douglas production function, the above provides an explicit first order difference equation as follows:

$$\hat{k}_{t+1} = \frac{\beta\pi(1 - a_t)\sigma(1 - \sigma)}{(1 + \phi)[((1 + n) - \pi\gamma)(1 + \beta\pi)\sigma + ((1 + n)a_{t+1} - \pi\gamma)(1 - \sigma)]} \cdot \hat{k}_t^{\sigma}.$$

(5.13)

The above difference equation exhibits the same type of phase diagram as in a standard neoclassical growth model. I assume that a_t is constant over time. Under this assumption, it is clear that the autarky equilibrium dynamics of the capital–labor ratio in efficiency unit has the same type of phase diagram as the neoclassical growth model. For the above Cobb–Douglas case, the explicit solution for the steady-state capital–labor ratio in efficiency unit, $\hat{k}^*$, is given by

$$\hat{k}^* = \left[\frac{\beta\pi(1 - a)\sigma(1 - \sigma)}{(1 + \phi)[((1 + n) - \pi\gamma)(1 + \beta\pi)\sigma + ((1 + n)a - \pi\gamma)(1 - \sigma)]} \right]^{\frac{1}{1 - \sigma}}.$$

(5.14)

It follows from equation (5.14) that the lower the population growth rate n, or the higher the life expectancy π, or the higher the social security transfers rate a, the higher is the balanced growth capital–labor ratio in efficiency unit $\hat{k}^*$ and the higher is the growth in capital–labor ratio in efficiency unit. Thus Japan, expecting a higher life-expectancy and a lower fertility rate, saved relatively more than a representative less developed country, even after countering the opposite effect of social security on savings. Since in each period the autarky interest rate in Japan is lower than in developing countries, there would be a drive for capital to flow from Japan to developing countries. See Figure 5.7 for details.

3.3 Predicted Savings Rate in the Calibrated Model

There has been a long-standing controversy over Japan's high savings rate. Most studies find the Japanese household savings rate to be around 12 per cent (see, for instance, Horioka, 1997), and the Japanese national savings rate to be a little less than 30 per cent in the 1980s. Some argue that these savings figures are too high compared to other OECD countries, and that the savings rate would be much smaller when depreciation and government expenditures are properly taken into account; see, for instance, Hayashi (1986, 1989). I use our highly aggregative model to compute the predicted household savings rates and national savings rates for Japan and the representative developing country after calibrating the model as follows:

I first assume that $\gamma = 0$. As I pointed out earlier, I take each of adulthood and old-age periods to be 40 years, and the young-age period to be 20 years. Taking Japan's life expectancy to be 80 years, and noting that life expectancy in our model is given by $60 + 40\pi$, I calibrate π for Japan to be $\pi = 0.5$. I assume the average annual growth rate of labor productivity to be 2.5 per cent. I take the annual rate of time preference ρ to be 0.0075 which yields the discount factor in the utility function $\beta = 1/(1 + \rho)^{40} = 0.7416$.

The two-tier social security program in Japan does not have an explicit replacement rule. But the benefits are estimated to be equivalent to a replacement ratio of around 70 per cent (see Horlacher, undated). So I take $\mu = 0.70$. Furthermore, I take the annual growth rate of population to be 0.1 per cent and the non-social security related payroll tax rate to be 15 per cent. Given parameters μ, φ, π and n, one can find a corresponding social security tax rate a from equation (5.4J). For the above parameter values, assuming the economy is in the stationary state, the model predicts the household savings rate of Japan to be 9.91 per cent, and assuming σ in the Cobb–Douglas production function to be 0.33, the model predicts the domestic savings rate to be 30.19 per cent.

It is unrealistic to have $\gamma = 0$. To be more realistic and to examine the effect of elderly care on savings behavior, I assume that an elderly person requires on average an hour of nursing services a day, which is about 5 per cent of the 18-hour day of an adult, that is $\gamma = 0.05$. The calibrated model predicts the stationary state household savings rate in Japan to be 11.35 per cent and the domestic savings rate to be 34.39 per cent. The calibrated model gives us a capital–labor ratio in efficiency unit of 0.0487, yielding an annual interest rate of 2.3 per cent. I take these parameter values to calibrate the Japanese economy in the rest of the chapter.

For the representative developing country, I take the parameter values to be the same as the Japanese parameter values with the following exceptions. I take the non–social security payroll tax rate to be 5 per cent, the social security replacement rate to be 30 per cent, the life expectancy to be 65 years, and the annual population growth rate to be 2 per cent. The calibrated model of the representative developing country predicts its stationary state household savings rate to be 7.49 per cent, the domestic savings rate to be 22.71 per cent, capital labor ratio in efficiency unit to be 0.00493 and the annual interest rate to be 6.68 per cent.

Both for Japan and the representative developing country, the predicted values are close to the observed values. From these simulated results it appears that the savings rates are higher for economies that have higher life expectancies, and lower fertility rates.

3.4 Ageing and Dynamic Inefficiency

If workers expect to live longer, they will save a larger portion of their income to provide for their longer retirement years. Thus in an ageing economy private decisions guided by self-interests may lead to socially undesirable outcomes of over-accumulation of capital in the sense that the marginal product of capital falls below the growth rate of the economy. This is known in the economics literature as dynamic inefficiency. In such economies if everyone were forced to consume more and save less, all the agents could be made better-off (Samuelson, 1958; Diamond, 1965). In closed economy growth models, social security programs can be designed to remove dynamic inefficiency. In the context of global ageing there are, however, other ways to handle dynamic inefficiency. If part of the savings of the ageing economy is invested in a developing country, or some immigrant workers are brought in from developing countries, the capital–labor ratio of the ageing economy will fall and the dynamic inefficiency could be removed. Furthermore, the taxes from the migrant workers and the excess interest incomes earned from exported capital could be used to finance social security. Which of these two options is better? In this section I first derive the condition for dynamic inefficiency and then examine if the calibrated Japanese economy inherits dynamic inefficiency. In the next section, I examine the choice between these two policy options.

To derive conditions for dynamic inefficiency one solves the social planner's problem in the stationary state. The social planner decides how much of the per capita output should be allocated for capital formation and how the remaining output for consumption should be allocated between the young and the old in each period so that a representative individual attains the maximum welfare. More formally, the social planner's choices are c_y and c_o, the consumption level of a representative young and a representative old, and $\hat{k}$, the capital–labor ratio in efficiency unit of an economy in stationary state. Then the welfare level of a representative agent is $u(c_y, c_o)$ and the feasible choices satisfy the following equation:

$$L_t c_y + \pi L_{t-1} c_o + L_{t+1} b_{t+1} \hat{k} = b_t L_t F(\hat{k}, 1)$$

which, after algebraic manipulations becomes

$$\hat{c}_y + \frac{\pi}{1+n}\hat{c}_o = f(\hat{k}) - (1+n)(1+\phi)\hat{k}$$

Under the assumption that the utility function is homothetic, it is easily seen that the social planner's problem is broken down into two parts: The first problem is to choose the capital–labor ratio in efficiency unit $\hat{k}$ such that $f(\hat{k}) - (1+n)(1+\phi)\hat{k}$ is maximized and the second problem is to divide this maximum available consumption between old and young. The first order condition for the first problem is given by $f'(\hat{k}) = (1+n)(1+\phi)$, which is known as the *Golden rule* of capital accumulation. Is it possible that in ageing economies the private decisions may lead to excessive savings and hence too much capital–labor ratio in efficiency unit such the marginal product of capital $f'(\hat{k})$ is smaller than the growth of the economy $(1+n)(1+\phi)$, that is, the economy is *dynamically inefficient*? I investigate this using the calibrated models of Japan and the representative developing country.

For Japan, the stationary state capital–labor ratio in efficiency unit is $\hat{k}_J = 0.04868636004$. The marginal product of capital over the 40-year period is 2.50, which is less than the growth rate of the economy $(1+n_J)(1+\phi_J) = 2.79$. Thus the Japanese economy inherits dynamic inefficiency. For the representative developing country, the stationary state capital–labor ratio in efficiency unit is $\hat{k}_L = 0.004030703332$. The marginal product of capital over the 40-year period is 13.27, which is higher than the growth rate of the economy $(1+n_L)(1+\phi_L) = 5.93$. Thus the representative developing country does not exhibit dynamic inefficiency. I also found that if Japan had the population growth rate and life expectancy of the representative developing country, Japan would not have dynamic inefficiency. Thus we conclude that in the Japanese economy there is dynamic inefficiency and the dynamic inefficiency is the result of its ageing population.

4.   THE WORLD CAPITAL AND LABOR MARKETS

To analyze whether foreign investment or immigration of labor could remove the dynamic inefficiency of Japan and which of the two is a better choice from the point of view of social security financing, we need to examine the equilibrium in the world capital and labor markets. From equations (5.9) and (5.6) it is clear that Japan, with a higher π and a lower fertility rate n, will have a higher capital–labor ratio in autarky as compared to the rest of the world. In other words, Japan's autarky interest rate is lower and the wage rate is higher than the rest of the world.

Suppose the world interest rate between period t and $t+1$ is denoted by r_{t+1}^*. Let $w(r_{t+1}^*) \equiv \omega(\kappa(r_{t+1}^*))$ be the corresponding wage rate (in the wage-rental rate frontier). The current account balance CA_t in period t is the net change in the value of its net claims on the rest of the world, which in our case is the total export after domestic absorption. The capital account balance in the balance of payment statistics is the net sale of assets to foreigners. Each dollar surplus of current account is a dollar negative sale (that is, purchase) of foreign asset. In the one good case, which is used for both consumption and investment, exports of the good are the same as the investment abroad, that is, the payment for obtaining an equal amount of foreign asset, measured in the unit of the good. Thus, in the simple one good case, it is enough to work with the current account balance. The current account balance at time t in our framework is given by,

$$\frac{CA_t(r^*_{t+1})}{L_t} = \left[\frac{\beta\pi}{1+\beta\pi}(1-a_t)\hat{w}_t - \frac{[(1+n)a_{t+1} - \pi\gamma]\hat{\omega}(r^*_{t+1})}{(1+\beta\pi)(1+r^*_{t+1})} \right]$$

$$- (1+n)\hat{\kappa}(r^*_{t+1}) \tag{5.15}$$

It is clear from the above that the current account balance over a long period of time and hence the international investment position over a long period of time are affected by the demographic factors such as fertility rate and life expectancy.

The world equilibrium interest rate r^*_{t+1} between period t and $t+1$ is obtained by solving the following:

$$CA^J_t(r^*_{t+1}) + CA^L_t(r^*_{t+1}) = 0. \tag{5.16}$$

In the world equilibrium with free capital flows, capital would flow from Japan to the rest of the world. Figure 5.7 shows the potential amount of capital outflow in this period.

Note that under free capital mobility or free labor mobility or both, and under the assumption that there is no difference in technology or in infrastructure between countries, the capital–labor ratio in efficiency unit is going to be the same in all economies, and this common capital–labor ratio in efficiency unit in period $t+1$ is given by

$$\hat{k}_{t+1} = \frac{L^J_t \cdot s^J_t + L^L_t \cdot s^L_t}{\hat{L}^J_{t+1} + \hat{L}^L_{t+1}}. \tag{5.17}$$

After some algebraic manipulations (5.17) becomes,

$$\hat{k}_{t+1} = \frac{\hat{s}_t^J + \hat{\theta}_t \cdot \hat{s}_t^L}{(1 + \varphi^J)[(1 + n^J) - \pi^J \gamma] + \hat{\theta}_t \cdot (1 + \varphi^L)[(1 + n^L) - \pi^L \gamma]}, \quad (5.18)$$

where $\hat{\theta}_t = (b_t^L/b_t^J) \cdot (L_t^L/L_t^J)$. The first term in $\hat{\theta}_t$ also represents the ratio of wages between the representative LDC and Japan, and the second term represents the ratio of working population sizes of a representative LDC and Japan.

Substituting the values of $\hat{s}_t$ for Japan and the representative LDC from equation (5.6) in equation (5.18), and assuming Cobb–Douglas production function $f(k) = k^\sigma$, I derive the following first order difference equation for the world capital–labor ratio in efficiency unit,

$$\hat{k}_{t+1} = \frac{\left[\frac{\beta \pi^J}{1 + \beta \pi^J}(1 - a^J) + \hat{\theta}_t \frac{\beta \pi^L}{1 + \beta \pi^L}(1 - a^L) \right](1 - \sigma)}{\frac{[(1 + n^J)a^J - \gamma \pi^J](1 + \varphi^J)}{\sigma(1 + \beta \pi^J)/(1 + \beta \pi^J \sigma)} + \hat{\theta}_t \frac{[(1 + n^L)a^L - \gamma \pi^L](1 + \varphi^L)}{\sigma(1 + \beta \pi^L)/(1 + \beta \pi^L \sigma)}} \cdot \hat{k}_t^\sigma.$$

$$(5.19)$$

The dynamics of the world economy depends on the exogenous dynamics of $\hat{\theta}_t$, and demographics and productivity growth rates of the economies. If we assume that $\hat{\theta}_t$ is constant over time, then the dynamics of the world capital–labor ratio have the same standard properties as a neoclassical growth model.

It is not possible to determine the long-run behavior of the world economy without further assumptions about how the fertility rate and life expectancy in the developing country evolve over time. The crucial parameter is the dynamics of $\hat{\theta}_t$. For simplicity I assume that fertility and life expectancy in the representative developing country remains at its current level. Which means $\hat{\theta}_t$ tends to infinity; that is, in the long-run the world economy will converge to the autarky steady-state of the representative developing country. We use this assumption to carry out our policy analysis.

4.1 Immigration or Foreign Investment?

Before World War II, Japan had mostly out-migration of labor. After the war, and because of rapid demographic transitions, Japan faced labor shortages. To meet labor shortages Japan allowed limited immigration of foreign workers. The relative number of immigrant workers in Japan is, however, much lower than most OECD countries. There are many social and political factors that determine immigration policies. I will not go into the details in this chapter. I use the current model to examine if immigration is a better option vis-à-vis foreign capital investment to cope with ageing problems and to achieve economic efficiency.

Is it possible that a dynamically inefficient ageing economy can achieve dynamic efficiency and hence Pareto optimality if the economy opens up its capital account or its door to immigration?[6] It is clear from Figure 5.7 that Japan and other OECD countries will have a higher marginal product of capital once they invest abroad or allow immigration, and it is quite possible that the marginal product of capital as a result will become higher than the growth of the economy. Hence from an efficiency point of view, it is better for an ageing economy with over-accumulated capital to allow immigration or invest abroad. Both policies will, however, lead to the same efficiency gains and thus the efficiency criterion by itself cannot sort out which of the two is a better policy option.

In an extreme case, however, our model has an unambiguous prescription for immigration over foreign capital investment. With a lower population growth rate, and a higher life expectancy in Japan, there is a higher demand for labor in the elderly care sector. This will lead to a huge shift of labor from industries to health and the elderly care service sector. Consider the extreme case within our framework by supposing that $\gamma\pi L_t > (1+n)$ L_t, that is, the hours needed to nurse the surviving elderly are greater than the total hours available from the total young adult population. In this extreme case it is obvious that immigration of workers is essential.

Suppose that the labor shortage is not a serious problem. Which of the two options is better for Japan? A number of authors in the international economics literature studied this issue from a national advantage point of view. In a seminal paper, Ramaswamy (1968) considered a world with two countries, say Japan and a developing country, each producing a single good using identical technology, and two factors of production, capital and labor. He showed that a capital-rich country such as Japan can ensure a higher gross national income by optimally taxing its capital outflow or immigration of labor as compared to using a quota for capital outflow or labor inflow. These policies are better than allowing capital and labor to move freely and competitively across the two regions. Between the options of foreign investment with optimal taxation and import of foreign labor with discriminatory taxation of labor, he established that import of labor can produce a higher income for Japan and other OECD countries than foreign investment. The economic intuition behind this result is as follows: suppose Japan withdraws its foreign investment and the labor working on it from the less developed countries and invests in an isolated island in Japan. The capital–labor ratio in this island will remain the same as when this capital was invested in the less developed countries. Thus the income from this capital in the island after paying the imported labor their marginal product is going to be same as when this capital was invested in the developing country. If the capital and labor can now freely move between the island and the rest of Japan, there will be a uniform capital–labor ratio which is higher than the capital–labor ratio of the island and lower than the rest of the economy. This produces a higher level of income and a higher wage rate for the immigrants and a lower wage rate for the natives. If the foreign workers' wage gains are taxed away, Japan can ensure a higher income than that which it obtained from foreign investment.

Discriminatory payroll taxation of foreign workers is, however, problematic for most host countries. Furthermore, the well-being and income of which country – the host country or the country of origin – should be considered? Taking these issues into account, Bhagwati and Srinivasan (1983) further refined this line of research, again from the national advantage point of view. Bhagwati and Hamada (1982) extended this analysis to include brain-drain issues. This line of research, however, assumes that the OECD countries have a national monopoly in implementing the optimal discriminatory tax policies. Given that there are many OECD countries which will compete for the same investment opportunities in the developing countries and for the same pool of immigrant labor from the developing countries, it is reasonable to assume that the world capital and labor markets are competitive. It is then well-known that under the assumption that all countries share the same technology and have a common labor productivity, there is no particular advantage for a country to export capital or import labor. Either of the two policies, or any mixture of the two will lead to the same gain in income (Bhagwati and Srinivasan, 1983). Furthermore, either policy will also be able to remove the dynamic inefficiency problem that I mentioned earlier. However, I would like to argue that when labor productivity differs between OECD and developing countries, the two policies are not equivalent. Furthermore, these two policy options will differ from the point of view of the public social security finances.

To investigate this, I assume that A_t is identically equal to 1 in all periods for all economies and that both Japan and the representative LDC are in their stationary states. Let $\hat{w}_J$ and $\hat{w}_L$ be the steady-state wage rates of a unit of efficiency labor in Japan and in the representative developing country as given in equation (5.10). From the calibrated model I estimate these to be $\hat{w}_J = 0.2471$ and $\hat{w}_L = 0.1086$. To calculate b_t^J, the labor productivity level in Japan in period t, and b_t^L, the productivity level of labor in period t in the representative developing country, I take the current wage rate of Japan to be $w_t^J = \$14\,740$ and the current wage rate of the representative developing country to be $w_t^L = \$2010$. Note that in the stationary state we have $w_t^J = b_t^J \hat{w}_J$ and $w_t^L = b_t^L \hat{w}_L$ in period t. From these relationships, I estimate the current productivity level of a unit of labor to be $b_t^J = 59645.58$ in Japan and $b_t^L = 18507.41$ in the representative developing country. From these estimates it appears that a unit of labor in Japan is $b_t^J/b_t^L = 3.223$ times more productive than a unit of labor in the representative developing country.

I now examine whether foreign investment or immigration of labor is a better solution to the ageing problems in Japan. There are many effects of these policies, but I only look at the following partial equilibrium marginal analysis: consider the option that Japan invests k_t^J amount of capital in the representative developing country and taxes the gains in capital incomes $(r_L - r_J)k_t^J$. The alternative policy option is that Japan brings in a guest worker from the representative developing country to work on the capital k_t^J and collects the social security taxes. Which option is better from the point of view of financing of social security? The answer depends crucially on the productivity level of the immigrant worker. What would the productivity level of the immigrant labor be in Japan? For simplicity I contrast two cases: one, the productivity level of the immigrant labor is the same as in his home country and I interpret this as immigration of unskilled labor. Second, the productivity level of the immigrant labor is the same as the productivity level of the Japanese worker after the worker moves to Japan and I interpret this as immigration of skilled labor. There are, however, other interpretations that are consistent with these assumptions and furthermore, the productivity level of the immigrant worker could be anywhere between these two extremes. While the government also collects payroll taxes from the guest workers, I disregard this effect, assuming that the immigrant worker consumes public goods such as health care and education commensurate with his payroll tax contribution. I also assume that in the long run the developing countries dominate the world markets.

With respect to gains in income of each region of the world, two policies are equivalent under the first assumption, and the import of labor policy is better than the policy of foreign investment under the second assumption. With respect to public financing of social security for Japan, I will use the calibrated model to show that the foreign investment is a better policy option under the first assumption, and the import of labor is a better policy option under the second assumption.

From the calibrated model, I compute the current capital labor ratio to be $k_t^J = 2903.9262$. Over the 40-year period, the revenue from foreign investment of this much capital is \$31 278.46. The contribution to social security by an immigrant worker over the 40-year period is \$22 912.64 when the immigrant worker is an unskilled worker, and is \$73 842.74 when the immigrant worker is a skilled worker. Thus, if the immigrant worker's productivity level is close to or higher than the productivity level of a Japanese worker, the immigration of labor is a better option than foreign investment.

But on the other hand, if the immigrant worker's productivity level in Japan is close to the productivity level in the representative developing country, foreign investment is a better option than immigration of labor.

There are other considerations in the choice between the two options. Many economists have argued that investment abroad is preferred over immigration since immigrant workers may cause social tensions in a homogeneous population such as in Japan. It is important to note that investment abroad instead of immigration of workers also has side effects on Japanese workers. For instance, with more foreign capital outflow, many Japanese workers will lose their jobs or will be forced to accept lower wages and benefits. This can happen even to skilled workers in a similar way to what is currently happening to skilled workers in the US software and telecommunications industries, as more and more such jobs are outsourced to India and other developing countries.

While the model does not provide clear-cut guidance for the choice and since immigration policies are more difficult to implement politically and socially, the foreign investment option may win a slight edge. It is, however, important to keep in mind that the US economy does not have serious ageing problems because of its more liberal open door immigration policies. In the next section I turn to the empirical investigation of why, in that case, little capital from Japan and other OECD countries flows into developing countries.

5.   WHY TOO LITTLE CAPITAL FLOWS INTO LESS DEVELOPED COUNTRIES

From Figure 5.7 and the discussions in the previous section it is clear that the demographic mismatch between Japan and LDCs creates an environment in which Japan would benefit from investing in less developed countries. In section 2 we saw, however, that not much capital flows from Japan to LDCs. Why?

Could it be due to lack of demand in LDCs? Even though many developing countries had misgivings about foreign capital, because of their past colonial bad experiences or some other internal vested interests, in recent years most developing countries welcome foreign capital since foreign capital, if invested properly, enhances economic growth. Direct foreign investment is likely to have a greater impact on economic growth than portfolio foreign investment. To find empirical support for these claims, I carried out a cross-country regression analysis to estimate the effect of two types of foreign investments and a few other standard determinants on economic growth. Table 5.3 shows the parameter estimates for two sets of

Ageing and the labor market in Japan

Table 5.3   The determinants of growth in per capita income

Variables	Only LDCs	All countries
Intercept	2.420	3.043
	(2.05)	(3.09)
Direct Foreign Investment	1.123	0.527
	(4.03)	(2.83)
Private Capital Flow	−0.052	−0.015
	(1.20)	(0.49)
Savings Rate	0.0004	0.034
	(0.02)	(1.39)
Population Growth Rate	0.306	0.057
	(0.86)	(0.198)
Expenditure on Education	−0.711	−0.679
	(4.39)	(4.77)
Telecommunication	−0.005	0.001
	(0.77)	(0.30)
Per Capita Income	$0.4E-3$	$-0.8E-5$
	(1.76)	(0.38)
Voice Accountability	−0.311	−0.008
	(0.47)	(0.01)
Political Stability	0.038	−0.101
	(0.05)	(0.16)
Government Effectiveness	−0.109	−0.009
	(0.10)	(0.01)
Rule of Law	1.707	1.959
	(1.73)	(2.29)
Control of Corruption	2.236	1.433
	(1.76)	(1.34)
No. of Countries	96	111
R^2	0.2272	0.1887

Note: Absolute value of the t-statistic is in parenthesis under a parameter estimate.

countries – one set containing all LDCs with per capita income less than US$12 000 (measured in constant 1995 US dollars) in 1997 and the second set consisting of all countries, including the OECD countries. The estimates are based on the three-year averages of all the variables from 1988 to 1997. I had to drop the countries with inadequate data and ended up with 96 countries in the first group and 111 countries in the second group. As determinants of growth, I included direct foreign investment as a percentage of GDP and private capital flow as a percentage of GDP, together with the other standard determinants of economic growth such as savings rate, population growth rate and public spending on education as a percentage of GNP as a measure of investment in human capital. I also included among the determinants the number of telephone mainlines per 1000 population in each country as a measure of infrastructure.

It has been argued that governance plays a significant role in the growth process and in attracting foreign investment. There are many aspects of governance. The World Bank collected data on five aspects: (1) Voice Accountability (2) Political Stability (3) Government Effectiveness (4) Rule of Law and (5) Control of Corruption (see Kaufmann et al., 2002 for details on how these variables were created). Since the standard socioeconomic indicators that are generally used in cross-country growth regressions might be correlated with these governance variables, I modify these variables by purging out the effects of the standard socioeconomic indicators.

Table 5.3 reports the parameter estimates for both samples. From these estimates it appears that while direct foreign investment has a positive effect on income growth, the other form of private capital flow has no significant effect. A country, especially a less developed country, generally prefers direct foreign investment over the other forms of private capital flow since FDI brings along better technology and management of the host country, and since the risk of the return from capital investment is borne by the source country, whereas in the other forms of private capital flows the risk is borne by the host country, and furthermore the latter type of foreign investment introduces a greater risk of financial crisis.

Notice that out of the five aspects of governance, only the rule of law has a significant positive effect on growth in per capita income for both sets of countries, and the control of corruption has a positive effect on growth for less developed countries.

Based on our finding that foreign direct investment has a significant positive effect on growth of per capita income after controlling for other standard determinants of growth, one would expect that much of the private capital flows, especially direct foreign investment, would flow from Japan to less developed countries. But we saw in section 2 that the bulk of the Japanese FDI flew to other developed countries, and very little to less developed countries. The natural question, is then, what determines private foreign capital inflow of a host country?

The main determinants of any private investment are the rate of return and the riskiness of the investment. In the international context, there is also empirical evidence for home bias. We saw in section 3 that the rate of return in less developed countries would be higher than in Japan under the assumption that all countries share the same technology, infrastructure and technological capability. But in reality LDCs have poorer technology, infrastructure and technological capability than Japan and other OCED countries. I empirically examine the effects of these factors on foreign capital inflow of a country. Another important determinant of foreign investment is the risk perceived by the foreign investors. The main determinants of this type of risk are political instability, corruption and bad governance. I now examine how these factors affect foreign capital inflow into a host country.

There are several ways economists have looked for determinants of capital flows. For instance, Higgins (1998) used cross-country regression to examine how age structure affects savings, and the savings investment gap, that is, foreign capital inflow. Obstfeld and Rogoff (1996) employed a present value model of current account, Lane and Milesi-Ferretti (2001) used an error correction model (ECM) to empirically determine the nature of capital flows and some of the economic and demographic variables that are related to each other in the long-run. Murata (1998) used a survey of Japanese enterprises to determine statistically the most effective practices of the Japanese firms that lead to higher direct foreign investment of the Japanese multinationals.

I used the same two sets of sample countries mentioned earlier and ran regressions on the three-year averages during 1988–1997 to examine the determinants of direct foreign investments and other forms of private capital flows. The results are shown in Table 5.4. The theory of section 3 predicted that the higher is the population growth rate, the higher the amount of foreign capital flow would be into a country, and the opposite is the case with life expectancy. The parameter estimates, however, show that only the effect of population growth is significant and its sign is consistent with the prediction of the theory. The effect of life expectancy is, however, not significant in any of the regression estimates. The effects of other variables are discussed in the following subsections.

5.1   Corruption and Poor Governance in the Host LDC

I used five revised measures of governance after purging out the effects of other right-hand side variables that are listed in Table 5.4. Out of the five aspects of governance, only the control of corruption has a significant positive effect on direct foreign investment for both sets of countries. None of these variables has significant effect on private portfolio capital investment.

5.2   Low Human Capital Level of Less Developed Countries

Assume that there are no barriers to free capital movement, and that both Japan and the representative LDC have the same level of infrastructure capital, and normalize this common level of infrastructure capital to $A_t = 1$ in all periods. Assume that the representative LDC and Japan, however, differ in their level of human capital b_t. Japan with a much higher average

Table 5.4   *Regression estimates of the determinants of FDI and private capital flows*

Variables	Direct foreign investment		Private capital flows	
	Only LDCs	All countries	Only LDCs	All countries
Intercept	0.270	−0.203	−6.816	−4.227
	(0.34)	(0.20)	(1.34)	(0.66)
Population	0.035	0.209	1.219	0.823
Growth Rate	(0.37)	(1.92)	(2.03)	(1.18)
Life Expectancy	−0.001	−0.005	0.067	0.026
	(0.13)	(0.39)	(0.91)	(0.28)
Expenditure on	0.081	0.125	0.637	0.765
Education	(2.00)	(2.52)	(2.45)	(2.40)
Telecommunication	0.002	0.006	0.024	0.026
	(1.40)	(4.66)	(2.41)	(3.03)
Per Capita Income	0.7E–4	0.3E–4	0.2E–3	0.0003
	(1.33)	(1.46)	(0.62)	(1.91)
Voice Accountability	0.179	−0.014	1.677	1.150
	(1.06)	(0.07)	(1.56)	(0.86)
Political Stability	−0.079	−0.03	1.188	1.392
	(0.42)	(0.14)	(1.00)	(0.94)
Government	−0.026	0.174	0.653	2.514
Effectiveness	(0.09)	(0.50)	(0.36)	(1.13)
Rule of Law	−0.126	−0.420	−1.978	−2.891
	(0.50)	(1.37)	(1.23)	(1.48)
Control of	0.622	1.071	−2.134	−0.975
Corruption	(1.93)	(2.80)	(1.03)	(0.40)
No. of Countries	96	111	96	111
R^2	0.158	0.516	0.177	0.416

Note: Absolute value of the t-statistic is in parenthesis under a parameter estimate.

education level has a higher growth rate of b_t and thus a much higher level of human capital in all periods. As shown in the previous section, when capital moves freely, the interest rates and hence capital–labor ratio in efficiency units must equate between LDCs and Japan. If the human capital level of the representative LDC is very low relative to the human capital level of Japan, Japan will have a substantially high level of effective labor, and the capital will rather flow from the representative LDC to Japan in that case, or at least it will reduce Japanese capital flow into the representative LDC. In this case, the Japanese wage rate will also be substantially higher than that of the representative LDC. Thus, this explanation is also consistent with the observed wage differentials between Japan and LDCs. If this is the case, then the choice between immigration of workers and exporting capital is clear: it is beneficial to bring skilled workers, preferably temporary guest workers such as IT (Information Technology) specialists into Japan.

The parameter estimates show that the level of human capital has a positive effect on both types of capital flows for both sets of countries.

5.3   Poor Infrastructure in Less Developed Countries

In contrast to the previous two subsections, assume now that there is no difference in human capital level of Japan and the representative LDC, and without loss of generality normalize $b_t = 1$ for all t. Assume also that there are no barriers to capital flow, but the infrastructure capital stock A_t is low in the less developed country. Infrastructure in our set-up includes transportation systems, telecommunication systems, and legal systems to enforce contacts. It follows then that the autarky interest rate and the wage rate in the representative LDC will be lower than those in Japan. This is consistent with the pattern of capital flow we saw in section 2 and the observed wage differentials between LDCs and OECD countries.

I did not readily find a good measure of infrastructure in the World Development Indicators database of the World Bank. I used a simple measure, namely the variable telecommunication, which measures the telephone mainlines (per 1000 people). It appears that a better infrastructure of a host country attracts a higher level of foreign capital of both types.

In this case, what will the right kind of policy be for Japan's ageing problem? The policy prescription would be that instead of investing only in the manufacturing sector, as it has generally done so far, Japan should increase its capital flow into LDCs and allocate the investment funds appropriately between the manufacturing and the infrastructure sectors. This strategy can be shared with other official international investments or private investments from other countries. This strategy can produce a higher rate of return from foreign investment in LDCs than the existing low rate. Moreover, it will ease the resource requirements of the Japanese social security system. The populations of the less developed countries will benefit from such foreign investment. However, this kind of policy might be hard to implement since it involves another sovereign government.

NOTES

1. Lakshmi Raut is an Economist at the Social Security Administration (SSA). This chapter was prepared prior to his joining the SSA, and the analysis and conclusions expressed are those of the author and not necessarily those of the SSA.

2. Earlier drafts of this chapter were presented at the Third and Fourth International Forums of the Collaborative Projects, sponsored by the Economic and Social Research Institute, Cabinet Office, Ministry of Japan, and subsequently at the Population Association of America 2004 Annual Meeting, Boston, and at the conference on 'Improving Social Insurance Programs', University of Maryland, College Park, 13–14 September 2003. I am grateful to the participants and to the discussants of the forums and the conferences, and to an anonymous referee during the conference volume editorial process for many useful comments. I am especially grateful to Junichi Goto and Koichi Hamada for inviting me to collaborate on this project.
3. See Hamada and Raut (2007) for a model in which γ is a choice variable, and for its implications on ageing problems.
4. See Raut (1991), Raut and Srinivasan (1994), for details of this line of modeling and Raut (1995) for an extended model in which a_t is endogenized by introducing two-sided altruism in a similar overlapping generations framework.
5. Cobb–Douglas utility function implies unit elasticity of inter-temporal substitution.
6. I am grateful to an anonymous referee who suggested that I explore this issue.

REFERENCES

Bhagwati, J.N. and Koichi Hamada (1982), 'Tax policy in the presence of emigration', *Journal of Public Economics*, **18**(3), 291–317.

Bhagwati, J.N. and T.N. Srinivasan (1983), 'On the choice between capital and labor mobility', *Journal of International Economics*, **14**, 209–21.

Diamond, Peter (1965), 'National debt in neoclassical growth models', *American Economic Review*, **55**(5), 1126–50.

Hamada, Koichi and L.K. Raut (2007), 'Ageing and elderly care in an open economy', chapter 4, this volume.

Hayashi, Fumio (1986), 'Why is Japan's savings rate so apparently high' (mimeo).

Hayashi, Fumio (1989), 'Is Japan's savings rate high?', *Federal Reserve Bank of Minneapolis Quarterly Review*, **13**(2), 3–9.

Higgins, Mathew (1998), 'Demography, national savings and international capital flows', *International Economic Review*, **39**(2), 343–69.

Horioka, Charles Y. (1997), 'A cointegration analysis of the impact of the age structure of population on the household saving rate in Japan', *Review of Economics and Statistics*, **79**(3), 511–16.

Horlacher, David E. (undated), 'Ageing in Japan: causes and consequences, Part II: Economic Issues', Austria: IISA.

Kaufmann, Daniel, Aart Kraay and Pablo Zoido-Lobaton (2002), 'Governance matters II: Updated Indicators for 2000/01', World Bank Policy Research Department Working Paper.

Kotlikoff, L.J. (1996), 'Simulating the privatization of social security in general equilibrium', NBER, W5776.

Lane, Philip R. and Gian Maria Milesi-Ferretti (2001), 'Long-term capital movements', *NBER Macroeconomic Annual*.

Murata, Sujiro (1998), 'Japanese foreign direct investment in Asia: its impact on export expansion and technology acquisition of the host economies', (mimeo) Waseda University.

Obstfeld, M. and K. Rogoff (1996), *Foundations of International Macroeconomics*, Cambridge, MA: MIT Press.

120 *Ageing and the labor market in Japan*

Ramaswamy, V.K. (1968), 'International factor movements and the national advantage', *Economica*, **35**, 309–10.

Raut, L.K. (1991), 'Capital accumulation, income distribution, and endogenous fertility in an overlapping generations general equilibrium model', *Journal of Development Economics*, **34**(1/2).

Raut, L.K. (1995), 'Learning to perfect manipulation: implications for fertility, savings, and old-age social security', Discussion Paper, University of California, San Diego, http://ideas.repec.org/p/wpa/wuwpla/9705003.html.

Raut, L.K. and T.N. Srinivasan (1994), 'Dynamics of endogenous growth,' *Economic Theory*, **4**, 777–90.

Samuelson, Paul (1958), 'An exact consumption-loan model of interest with or without the social contrivance of money', *Journal of Political Economics*, **66**(6).

Sato, Yuko (2001), 'Comparative analysis of healthcare costs in Japan and the United States: a simulation of productivity and simulation behavior', *Japan and the World Economy*, **13**, 429–54.

United Nations (2000), 'Replacement migration: is it a solution to declining and ageing populations?', United Nations Population Division Department of Economic and Social Affairs, New York.

6. Ageing society and the choice of Japan: migration, FDI and trade liberalization

Junichi Goto

1. INTRODUCTION

As the Japanese population is rapidly ageing, it is expected that Japan will face a serious labor shortage in the near future. It is often pointed out that, in order to cope with such a labor shortage, Japan should open the door to international migration. It is also pointed out that the increased migration to Japan would also benefit sending countries through remittance and employment creation. However, as I wrote elsewhere (see Goto, 1993), in order to realize the same positive effects, there are various alternatives to international migration. For example, the increased labor participation of Japanese women would relieve the expected labor shortage. Further, instead of accepting huge numbers of workers migrating from abroad, Japan could utilize foreign labor *indirectly* by increasing outgoing FDI and/or by reducing trade restrictions on labor-intensive imports (that is, movement of 'money' and/or 'goods' rather than the movement of 'people'). In view of the above, in the present study, I will investigate, both theoretically and empirically, the merits and demerits of the international movements of labor, capital and goods, and their implications for the ageing society in Japan. I will investigate what kind of policy measure is most desirable for Japan and labor-sending countries.

In the next section, I will briefly examine the ageing issue in Japan. The Japanese population is rapidly ageing and the fertility rate is steadily declining. In view of this, it is widely argued that, in order to cope with a possible labor shortage in the near future, Japan should make every effort to raise the fertility rate now. However, as discussed in detail below, since the rapid ageing problem will continue only for 20 years or so in the early 21st century, and since it takes about 20 years before those born today can start working, I believe that an increase in the fertility rate now will increase, rather than decrease, the burden on the working population.

In section 3, the impact of migration on the host country and the home country is theoretically analyzed, because there are heated, and often emotional, debates on the desirable policies toward migration. Traditional economic theorists are generally in favor of migration, at least as far as the economic effect is concerned, because it involves the movement of labor from a labor abundant country to a labor scarce country. However, it is demonstrated that such a rosy picture depends on fairly restrictive assumptions, such as perfect competition, and that, when we relax some assumptions of the traditional theory, the admission of migrant workers can give (or is likely to give) adverse economic effects to the host country. In addition to the economic effect, some social effects of migration are also discussed, because migration involves the movement of workers as human beings, rather than the movement of labor as a production factor. In addition to the impact of migration on the host country like Japan, the impact on the home country will be discussed.

In section 4, the empirical analysis of migration is carried out, taking the relationship between Japan and seven countries/areas in East Asia (China, Indonesia, Korea, Malaysia, the Philippines, Thailand, and Taiwan province of China) as an example. In section 4, a simple $2 \times 2 \times 2$ CGE model is developed first, which incorporates migration, FDI and international trade. The model differs from a usual $2 \times 2 \times 2$ trade model in that it incorporates additional realities such as the existence of migration, FDI and trade barriers. Using the model, welfare impacts of migration, FDI and trade liberalization are calibrated and compared with each other. The simulation result suggests that, generally speaking, migration is inferior to trade liberalization as a means of increasing the welfare in both the host country and the home country.

In section 5, I will discuss some empirical issues on the relative benefit of various measures to cope with the possible labor shortage due to the ageing population in Japan. Based on a simple simulation result, it will be argued that, at least in aggregate, the decline in working-age population and the resulting increase in the burden on the working population can be compensated if various measures, such as utilization of female labor, are taken effectively.

Section 6 summarizes major findings of the paper and discusses some agenda for future research.

2. AGEING ISSUES IN JAPAN: OLD POPULATION RATIO VS. DEPENDENCY RATIO

Recently, the impact of ageing has been one of the most seriously discussed topics in Japan. The Japanese population is rapidly ageing and the fertility

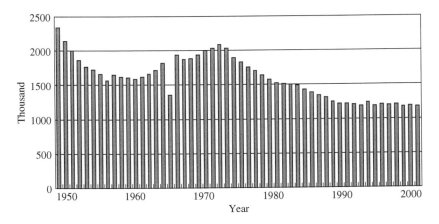

Figure 6.1   Number of births

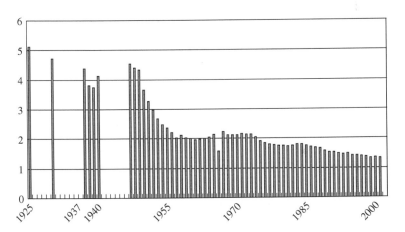

Figure 6.2   Long-term trend of total fertility rate

rate is steadily declining. Figures 6.1 and 6.2 show the number of births and the total fertility rate in Japan, respectively. The bar graph in Figure 6.1 shows the number of births (in thousands), and the bar graph in Figure 6.2 shows the long-term trend of the total fertility rate (in per cent). There are several periods that stand out on the graph: the first baby boom after the war, the sharp decline in the 1950s, the sudden drop in births in 1966 due to the superstition of the year of the special horse (*hinoeuma*), and the second baby boom.

Due to the decline in the fertility rate the ratio of the aged in the total population (the old population ratio) has been steadily increasing and is expected to increase dramatically in the next 20 years or so. Faced with the imminent arrival of an ageing society, it is widely argued that in order to cope with this rapid ageing the most important thing is to raise the fertility rate in Japan, which has been steadily declining as shown in Figure 6.2.

However, I believe that the present fear of this rapid ageing is a little exaggerated, because the economic burden should be properly judged by the ratio of the dependent population (that is, the ratio of the elderly *and young children* in the total population (dependency ratio) rather than by the ratio of the elderly in the total population (old population ratio). Obviously, newborns cannot work, and instead they have to be raised by parents and by society. I do not here investigate whether raising children requires more or fewer resources than caring for the elderly.

When we look carefully at the dependency ratio and the old population ratio, the two ratios give us very different impressions. First, as widely argued, the old population ratio in Japan is among the highest in the world. According to the United Nations, in the international ranking of the old population ratio, Japan is fourth out of 153 countries, after Italy, Greece and Sweden. However, when we look at the international ranking of the dependency ratio, Japan is 131st out of 153 countries. Very poor developing countries, such as Uganda, Congo and Yemen, are high in the ranking of the dependency ratio, where due to the high fertility rate many children are suffering from disease and malnutrition. In other words, contrary to popular belief, the current burden on the Japanese working population is fairly light in comparison with other countries.

Second, in Japan, the time trend of the dependency ratio shows a very different picture from the trend of the old population ratio. Figure 6.3 plots the old population ratio and the dependency ratio since 1950. The figure shows that the old population ratio in Japan has been steadily increasing from 4.9 per cent in 1950 to 17.2 per cent in 2000. The old population ratio is expected to increase to 25.2 per cent in 2020. In other words, one in every four Japanese will be over 65 years old in 2020. However, the dependency ratio, which represents the burden of the working population more correctly than the old population ratio as discussed above, shows a very different trend. Due to the dramatic decline in the fertility rate in the 1950s, the dependency ratio in Japan declined sharply from 40.3 per cent in 1950 to 31.0 per cent in 1970. In other words, while in 1950 six people had to support four people, in 1970 seven people had to support three people; thereby the burden to the Japanese working population was reduced very much during this period. Since then the dependency ratio has remained fairly constant for many years at around 30 per cent, and the dependency ratio in 2000 is still 31.9 per cent, which is about the same as that in 1970 (31.0 per cent). The dependency ratio is expected to rise rapidly in the early

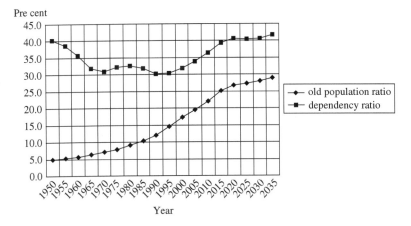

Figure 6.3   Old population ratio vs. dependency ratio

twenty-first century to become 40.5 per cent in 2020, and to remain constant after that. It should be noted that the dependency ratio in 2020 (40.5 per cent) is about the same as that in 1950 (40.3 per cent). In other words, Japan already experienced a long time ago the magnitude of the peak level of dependency ratio expected in the twenty-first century. Further, as discussed above, we should note that if the fertility rate is raised now, the dependency ratio in Japan in the early twenty-first will rise.

The sharp rise in the dependency ratio due to the decline in the working-age population does not necessarily cause a labor shortage or an increased burden on the Japanese economy. Various measures, such as increase in labor productivity and female participation, can mitigate (or even offset) the adverse effects in the ageing society, as discussed in detail in section 5 below.

3.   IMPACT OF MIGRATION: PROS AND CONS

(1)   The Economic Effect of Migration on the Host Country

(a)   Conventional wisdom: what does the textbook economics say about migration?

Traditional economic theorists usually consider that the overall effect of international migration is favorable to both home and host countries, because it involves a movement of labor from a labor abundant (and capital scarce) country to a labor scarce (and capital abundant) country, and therefore, it will increase productivity (and economic welfare) in both countries. For example, when some workers move from the Philippines (a labor abundant country) to Japan (a labor scarce country), the Japanese employers who have been suffering from unfilled vacancies can gain from hiring these workers and the Filipino workers can earn more than what they could earn in the Philippines. If these workers remit some part of their income earned in Japan to their home country, people left behind in the Philippines also benefit from the migration of their fellow Filipinos indirectly. Of course, there could be some conflict of interests among various economic agents in each country. For example, an inflow of Filipino workers may have a dampening effect on Japanese wages, and thereby the income of Japanese workers could decrease while the income of employers in Japan increases. But the *overall* effect is, they argue, positive in both countries. Thus, the movement of workers (or unemployed persons) from the home country to the host country would increase national incomes (and economic welfare) in both countries.

The economic reasoning for their argument for economic gain is summarized in Figure 6.4. In the figure, the horizontal axis plots the amount of labor supply, where the amounts of labor supply in country 1 (home country) and country 2 (host country) are measured from O_1 and O_2, respectively. The vertical axis plots the marginal productivity of labor (MPL), which is equal to the wage rate in the competitive equilibrium. The MPL of labor in country 1 (country 2) is expressed by line NE (by line AT).

Suppose that at the initial stage before migration the labor endowment in country 1 (home country) is O_1H and that in country 2 (host country) is O_2H, and therefore the labor supply in the two countries as a whole is O_1O_2. At this stage, the value of total production (that is, national income) of the sending home country is the area of the trapezoid $NGHO_1$, and the value of the national income of the receiving host country is the area of the trapezoid $AFHO_2$. In this pre-migration situation, the wage rate in the host country is BO_2, which is higher than that in the home country (SO_1). Such a wage gap between the two countries constitutes an incentive for the workers in country 1 to migrate to country 2.

Now, suppose that some workers in country 1 (the number of workers expressed by HK) migrate to country 2 in order to seek a higher wage there. In this post-migration situation, the amount of labor that can be mobilized for the production in country 2 is increased to O_2K, and that in country 1 is decreased to O_1K, because the labor HK moves from country 1 to country 2. Now, the value of goods produced in country 2 (Gross Domestic Product, GDP) increases to the area of trapezoid $AIKO_2$. But the area of rectangular DIKH is paid as wages to the workers from country 1, and the net gain of income of the host country's citizen is equal to the area of triangle FDI. While the GDP in country 1 is decreased to the area of trapezoid $NJKO_1$, the national income of the citizen of country 1 (the Gross

MPL,W

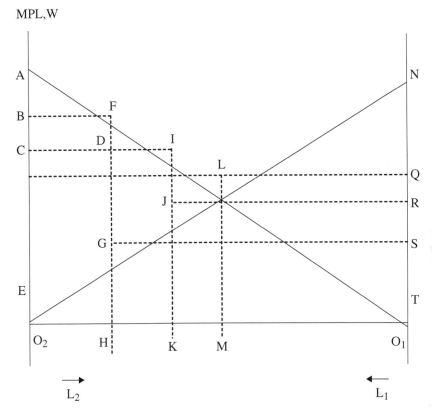

Figure 6.4   Economic effect of migration

National Product, GNP), which includes the income earned by the workers who are migrating to country 2, is increased to the area $NJIDHO_1$.[1] So, the net gain to Country 1 is equal to the area of the trapezoid DIJG. Needless to say, the national incomes in both countries keep increasing until the number of workers expressed by HM migrate to country 2.

Therefore, according to the traditional economic theory, international migration increases the national income (and economic welfare) of both sending and receiving countries. As shown in Figure 6.4, when HK of workers move from Country 1 to Country 2, the economic welfare of country 1 is increased by the area of the triangle FDI and that of country 2 is increased by the area of the trapezoid DIJG.[2] Based on such reasoning, traditional economists often argue that international migration gives economic gains to both countries, although both countries may incur some social costs as discussed below.

(b)   Economic effects under the new framework

However, the above rosy picture of international migration hinges upon various restrictive assumptions, such as perfect competition, constant returns to scale and so on. There are several studies demonstrating that the conclusion of the traditional framework breaks down when new realistic assumptions are introduced. For example, Schiff (1999) introduced the role of social capital, and Goto (1998) analyzed the impact of migration when trade barriers and non-traded goods exist. Both authors cast some doubts on the orthodox conclusions based on Figure 6.4, and pointed out that migration can (and is likely to) give adverse economic effect on receiving countries.

In this sub-section, I summarize the argument of Goto (1998) on the economic impact of migration of the host country: if we incorporate other realities such as the existence of trade restrictions and non-traded goods in the economy, the above simple argument collapses. The effect of immigration is not so simple as the conventional argument implies. Using a rigorous mathematical model, which incorporates additional realities mentioned above, it can be shown that the economic effect of immigration can be divided into a few sub-effects as follows:

(Effect of Immigration) = (Cheaper Foreign Labor Effect)

+ (Trade Barrier Effect)

+ (Non-tradable-Good Effect)

Although the formal proof is a little complicated, the underlying logic behind the above sub-effects is straightforward.[3]

(i)   Cheaper foreign labor effect   It is often the case that the wage rate in the host country becomes lower as more and more foreign workers are admitted. In other words, as the number of admitted migrant workers increases, the cost of hiring them becomes cheaper and cheaper because the increase in the number of foreign workers has a dampening effect on the level of the prevailing wage rate in the host country. So, the host country as a whole can benefit from the cheaper foreign labor. Needless to say, there would be conflict of interests between employers and workers in the host country, because workers, including native workers, would incur a loss from the decline in wage rate.

Figure 6.5 demonstrates an intuitive reasoning for this cheaper foreign labor effect. In the figure, ABEG shows the marginal value product of labor (MVPL) curve. Since the wage rate is equated with the MVPL in equilibrium, the equilibrium before the admission of foreign labor is B, where total domestic labor (OD) is employed with the wage rate of W^0. In this case, the

MVPL, W

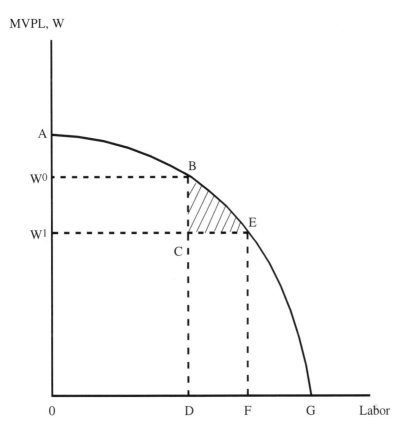

Figure 6.5   Cheaper foreign labor effect

total labor income is W^0ODB and the total capital income is AW^0B. If the foreign labor of DF is admitted to the country, the new equilibrium point moves to E, and the wage rate decreases to W^1. In this case, capital income increases to AW^1E, and total labor income accrued to the native workers and the income accrued to migrant workers become W^1ODC and CDFE, respectively. Thus, total income of domestic factors (capital and labor) is increased by the hatched area BCE. Note that the magnitude of the (positive) cheaper foreign labor effect increases, *ceteris paribus*, as the scale of the admission of migrant workers becomes larger.

(ii)   Trade barrier effect   Brecher and Diaz-Alejandro (1977) point out this effect in the context of international capital movement, but similar reasoning also holds for international movement of labor. Although the

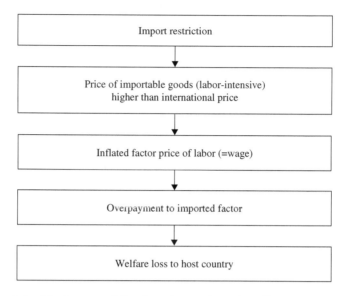

Figure 6.6   Mechanism of Brecher–Diaz-Alejandro effect

mechanism of this effect is a little complicated, intuitive discussion goes as follows. Suppose that Country 2 is imposing tariffs on labor-intensive importable goods, such as textiles and clothing. In this situation, the domestic price of the labor-intensive goods is higher than that of the goods in the international market due to the tariff, and therefore, the price of the factor intensively used for the production of the labor-intensive goods (that is, the wage rate) is inflated and higher than that under free trade. When the admitted migrant workers are paid this inflated wage rate, they are in some sense overpaid, and therefore the host country incurs economic loss. Figure 6.6 summarizes the mechanism of this effect.[4]

(iii)   Non-tradable-good effect   In the real world, the share of non-traded goods such as construction and services in total production is very high, although traditional economists have paid less attention to these goods. For example, the share of non-traded goods in total consumption in Japan is about 54 per cent. When we take into account the existence of the non-traded goods sector, additional insights into the economic effects of immigration can be obtained. In fact, two-thirds of the unskilled immigrants are employed in the non-traded goods sector in Japan, and the number of immigrants working in such sectors in the United States and Europe is also large. Due to the employment of immigrants, the price of non-traded goods is generally lower than otherwise. In other words, thanks to immigrant

workers, consumers can enjoy less expensive non-traded goods, for example, a cheaper maid service or street cleaning (*positive consumption effect*). On the other hand, the income of native workers in the non-tradable goods sector would be lowered by hiring cheaper immigrants in that sector (*negative income effect*).

(iv)   Overall economic effect under the new framework   Since some sub-effects are positive and others are negative, the next important question is whether the net effect of the above sub-effects is positive or negative. As shown in Goto (1998), the net economic effect of migration has a systematic relationship to the level of admitted migrant workers (L_f) and the magnitude of trade barrier (t). After some tedious algebra, it can be shown that the following two propositions hold:

(a)   The welfare declines by the initial inflow of migrant workers, but after a certain number of foreign workers are admitted the economic welfare turns to an increase;

(b)   The smaller the degree of trade barrier (t), the smaller the value of the threshold number L_f^1, at which the welfare level turns to be increased by the further admission of foreign workers. In other words, the less severe the trade barriers are, the more likely it is that the admission of a certain number of migrant workers can be welfare-improving.

Figure 6.7 summarizes the above two propositions. In the figure, the welfare level of the host country (U) is plotted on the vertical axis, while the number of admitted foreign workers is plotted on the horizontal axis. Curve I plots the welfare level as a function of admitted migrant workers when the magnitude of trade barriers is t_1 (higher t). The admission of migrant workers causes the welfare level of the host country to decrease first, but when the number of admitted foreign workers reaches $L_f^{1,I}$, the welfare level begins to increase, and exceeds the initial level when the number of admitted foreign workers exceeds $L_f^{2,I}$. In other words, the admission of a small number (or *trickle*) of migrant workers produces a negative effect on the host country while a large number (or *flood*) produces a positive impact on the host country. This finding implies that when migrant workers are admitted, the admission quota should be large if it is to produce a positive welfare impact in the host country. Curve II plots the welfare level when the magnitude of trade barriers decreases to t_2 due to, for example, a successful implementation of the Uruguay Round agreement. The curve shifts upward and leftward, and therefore the trough of the curve also shifts leftward and upward. In other words, a smaller number of migrant workers can be welfare-improving.

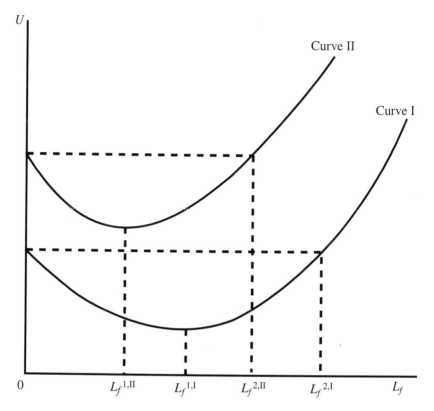

Figure 6.7   Migrant workers and host country's welfare

Although proofs of the above propositions require a cumbersome manipulation of the equilibrium conditions of the model, a rough argument is that when the level of the admission of migrant workers is relatively small the negative 'trade barrier effect' dominates, while the positive 'cheaper foreign labor effect' becomes dominant as the number of migrant workers increases, and that the magnitude of the negative trade barrier effect is larger when the trade barrier is stronger.[5]

(2)   The Social Effect of Migration in the Host Country

(a)   Diversiflcation and internationalization

Since international migration involves the international movement of human beings as a whole, it brings about various social effects in addition to the economic effects discussed above. For example, suppose that a Japanese university in Tokyo hires an Indonesian mathematics professor.

Although the job description of the Indonesian professor is probably to teach and carry out research into mathematics, his contribution to the university, and perhaps to Japanese society, is much more than that. His colleagues at the university in Japan can learn from him the economic and social situation in Indonesia and ASEAN countries as well as mathematics, and listening to the Indonesian fellow professor will widen their perspective. These interactions between Japan and Indonesia would enhance mutual understanding between the two countries. In economic jargon, such an effect is called (positive) externality.

(b) Possible burden on the fiscal expenditure in the host country

Since migrant workers pay taxes and receive various social services from the government of the host country, they have various effects on public finance in the host country. On the one hand, the existence of these migrant workers increases the revenue of the government, because they pay income taxes, consumption tax, property taxes and so on, and if they are enrolled in the social security system in the host country, they contribute to the social security system, too. On the other hand, this increases the expenditure of the government, because they receive various social services from the government of the host country, for example, education for their children, medical services, and a pension.

The Japanese government has published an estimate of fiscal cost and benefit to the host government (both central and local government) for three different stages of admission of migrant workers (see Table 6.1). While the host government benefits from migrant workers in Stage 1 (when only single youths are admitted) because their tax payment exceeds the social services they receive; in Stage 2 (with spouse) and Stage 3 (with spouse and two children), the fiscal cost of the social expenditure far exceeds the tax revenues. When half a million migrant workers are admitted, the net cost to the government in Stage 3 exceeds one trillion yen (or about 8 billion dollars).

(c) Possible increase in crime

It is sometimes argued that the admission of migrant workers may increase crime in the host country. Since Japan is a relatively homogeneous society and enjoys a very low crime rate, some Japanese argue that the migrant workers may cause the level of crime to increase in their safe country. Their logic behind such a fear is very simplistic and is something like this: most large US cities like Los Angeles and New York are filled with migrant workers, and the crime situation there is extremely serious, and therefore, there must be some correlation (and causality) between migration and crime. Therefore, an increase in migrant workers in Japan would make Japan a more dangerous country.

Table 6.1   Social cost of migrant workers (billion yen)

	Stage 1	Stage 2	Stage 3
Receipt			
Central government	181.1	93.1	77.5
Local government	0.0	38.3	28.2
Social security	145.5	180.2	193.2
Total	**326.6**	**311.6**	**298.9**
Expenditure			
Central government	12.8	77.8	353.8
Local government	15.5	486.1	901.5
Social security	52.3	89.1	158.1
Total	**80.6**	**653.0**	**1413.4**
Net			
Central government	168.3	15.3	−276.3
Local government	−15.5	−447.8	−873.3
Social security	93.2	91.1	35.1
Total	**246.0**	**−341.4**	**−1114.5**

Notes:
Stage 1: Single
Stage 2: Married
Stage 3: Married, two children.

Source: Japanese Ministry of Labor.

However, in my view, such a claim is not substantiated at all. There is no scientific evidence that connects a high crime rate with migrant workers. On the contrary, some studies suggest that, as far as the first generation is concerned, migrant workers commit fewer crimes than natives in the host country. That is probably because newly migrated workers have higher motivation toward success in the new country, and because the effective penalty for committing a crime is far more severe for migrant workers than for the native workers. (that is, only migrant workers face possible deportation from the rich host country to a poor home country!)

(d)   Continuation of '3-D' jobs

In many cases, migrant workers are employed in jobs whose working conditions are less favorable than other jobs. In Japan, such jobs are often referred to as '3-D jobs', that is, 'dangerous', 'dirty' and 'demanding' jobs. Since nobody prefers such 3-D jobs to other more comfortable jobs, employers of 3-D jobs often experience unfilled vacancies. The existence of such

Table 6.2   The ratio of remittances to exports earnings (%)

	1980	1983	1986	1988
Bangladesh	26.6	73.0	61.4	57.1
India	36.3	27.2	25.0	21.4
Pakistan	67.5	94.3	79.7	44.6
Philippines	3.6	3.6	3.4	5.5
Sri Lanka	14.6	27.9	28.0	24.1
Thailand	5.9	13.4	12.2	n.a.

Source: The World Bank and the United Nations Statistics.

unfilled vacancies may encourage employers to make working conditions there more favorable (for example, better wages, safer workplace). However, if such 3-D vacancies are easily filled by migrant workers, the incentive for employers to achieve better working conditions will disappear. In other words, the hiring of migrant workers, who are willing to take jobs under the 3-D working conditions because even the 3-D jobs there are better than regular jobs in their home country, may cause the 3-D jobs in the host country to persist in the long run.

(3)   The Effect of Emigration on the Sending Country

What is the impact of emigration on the sending country? In what follows, the benefits and costs of *emigration* will be briefly discussed to supplement the above analysis. I will concentrate on four effects of emigration: (a) remittance and income creation; (b) alleviation of domestic unemployment; (c) transfer of knowledge and skills; and (d) the brain drain.

(a)   Remittance and income creation
Needless to say, most migrant workers emigrate in an attempt to make more money in foreign countries than they can make in their home countries. It is often argued that such higher income benefits not only individual migrant workers but also their sending countries as a whole. Since poor sending countries are often suffering from prolonged balance of payment problems, the remittance from emigrant workers is an important source of foreign exchange receipt for these countries. In fact, the size of remittances for some Asian developing countries is remarkable. Table 6.2 shows the ratio of remittances to total exports in selected Asian sending countries in the 1980s, when many workers from these countries migrated to the Middle East. For example, in 1983, when the number of Asian emigrations to the Middle East was the highest, the ratios of remittances to total export

earnings of Bangladesh and Pakistan were as high as 73 per cent and 94 per cent, respectively. While the ratio has declined after that due to the return of emigrant workers from the Middle East, the remittance was still a very important source of foreign exchange earnings in these countries. But, as is often pointed out, the flow of remittances is often unstable. When the host country is in recession, migrant workers are often the first to be fired, and therefore, in recession years, when sending countries particularly need foreign exchange receipts, the remittances tend to decrease. Further, it is often the case that, as more and more migrant workers decide to stay in the host country longer than initially expected and decide to invite families to join them, the remittances begin to decline. Moreover, the remittance may not necessarily help sending countries improve their balance of payment. The marginal propensity to consumption (especially consumption of imported luxury goods) out of remittance income is believed to be very high.

(b)   Alleviation of domestic unemployment

Can emigration of labor alleviate serious unemployment problems in sending countries? In many Asian sending countries, there exists an enormous unemployment (and under-employment) problem in the rural agricultural sector and the urban informal sector. Some argue that Japan should admit migrant workers from Asian LDCs in order to relieve unemployment problems in these countries. But it seems rather questionable whether emigration to Japan relieves unemployment problems in Asian LDCs to a greater extent. As Todaro (1986) rigorously showed using his three sector model, while labor emigration may contribute to the relief of *overall* domestic unemployment, this favorable effect may be offset by a costly rise in urban unemployment caused by increased rural–urban migration. In other words, urban unemployment gets worse because more and more of the rural population move to an urban sector in the hope of further emigrating to Japan. Furthermore, the number of unemployed in Asian sending countries is too large to be relieved by emigration to Japan. Probably, in order to relieve unemployment, creation of employment opportunities in these sending countries through foreign direct investment and/or increase of exports would be more important than emigration.

(c)   Transfer of knowledge and skills

As is well known, technology transfer has been one of the most important issues in economic development. In a similar vein, it is often argued that emigration contributes to the economic development and modernization of sending LDCs through the introduction of new knowledge and skills

Table 6.3 Acquisition of skills by emigrant workers (%)

Acquired through employment in the host country	13.6
Acquired through official training	13.3
No skill acquired	67.8
Acquired through books	4.4
Other	1.0
Total	**100.0**

Source: The Government of the Philippines.

brought back by returned migrant workers. But, a survey by the Philippine Government (see Table 6.3) suggests that this alleged benefit is questionable. According to the survey, two-thirds of migrant workers, which includes both skilled and unskilled, said that they acquired no skills. A mere 13.6 per cent of migrants said that they acquired skills through employment in the host country. In view of this, it seems unlikely that unskilled migrant workers in Japan acquire skills through their employment. Probably, a formal training program would be much more useful than migration, in order to introduce new skills and knowledge to developing countries.

(d) The brain drain
Economists have long pointed out that emigration causes a 'brain drain' from sending LDCs. Since good skilled labor emigrates in the hope of receiving higher pay in the developed country, sending LDCs often suffer from the lack of essential professional workers, such as doctors and nurses. It should be noted that even unskilled migrant workers in Japan often have a very high level of education. Since the wage rate for an unskilled worker such as a construction worker in Japan is often higher than the wage rate for a skilled worker such as a doctor or nurse in LDCs, people with higher education also come to Japan to take an unskilled job. According to the survey by the *Nikkeijin Kyokai*, more than 90 per cent of migrant workers have high school education (42 per cent have college education), although almost all of them take unskilled jobs in Japan. In other words, those who would work as skilled workers such as teachers and doctors in their home country come to work in Japan as unskilled workers, simply because the wage rate of unskilled workers in Japan is generally higher than that of skilled workers in their home country. Although it may economically benefit the migrant workers themselves, it is clearly a misallocation of labor, and causes a substantial loss to those left behind in the sending country.

4.   MIGRATION, FOREIGN DIRECT INVESTMENT, AND TRADE LIBERALIZATION

In the above section, I have summarized various costs and benefits of inter-national migration. Since migration implies an international movement of human beings (workers) rather than a factor of production (labor), it causes a myriad of effects, both economic and social, to both receiving and sending countries. This complicated nature of migration is one of the reasons why everyone has a different opinion about the policy toward inter-national migration and why a consensus on immigration policy has been too difficult to reach. Moreover, it should be noted that various economic effects of migration mentioned above, for example, income creation and employment creation can be brought about by other measures such as foreign direct investment and international trade. For example, a Tokyo-based Japanese company that currently hires migrant workers from, say, China, can move the production plant to China and hire workers there. Similarly, instead of importing labor from countries in East Asia, Japan can import *labor-intensive products* from them through international trade.

In view of the above, a simply CGE model will be developed below to empirically analyze the impact of migration in a wider perspective, incorporating migration, foreign direct investment and international trade. While the model is so general that it can be applied to many different situations in many different countries, in what follows, I will calibrate the model, as an illustrative simulation for Japan as a labor-importing country and seven countries/areas in East Asia (China, Indonesia, Korea, Malaysia, the Philippines, Thailand, and Taiwan province of China) as labor-exporting countries. By calibrating the model, I will examine the relative effectiveness of migration, FDI and trade liberalization as means of enhancing economic welfare in Japan and developing countries in East Asia.

(1)   The Model

In the general model, the world consists of two countries (or two groups of countries). Country *A* (*B*) is relatively capital (labor) abundant, and there-fore, Country *A* (*B*) is a potential importer of labor (capital) and exporter of capital (labor). Also, country *A* (*B*) tends to export capital-intensive (labor-intensive) goods, while importing labor-intensive (capital-intensive) goods. The outline of the $2\times2\times2$ model is given below.

(Country A: capital-abundant)
Consumers in country *A* are characterized by the following social utility function.

$$U_A = C_{1A}^{\alpha} C_{2A}^{1-\alpha}, \quad 0 < \alpha < 1 \tag{6.1}$$

where U_A is social utility of consumers in country A and C_{1A} and C_{2A} are the amount of consumption of good 1 and good 2, respectively, in country A. Good 1 is more capital-intensive than good 2. Hence, in a regular situation, country A exports good 1 and imports good 2. Consumers maximize social utility function (6.1) subject to the budget constraint (6.2).

$$P_{1A}C_{1A} + P_{2A}C_{2A} = Y_A \tag{6.2}$$

where P_{1A} and P_{2A} are, respectively, domestic (i.e., tariff-inclusive) prices of good 1 and good 2 in country A, and Y_A is the national income of country A. From the above utility maximization problem, the following two demand functions are obtained.

$$C_{1A} = \alpha Y_A / P_{1A} \tag{6.3}$$

and

$$C_{2A} = (1 - \alpha) Y_A / P_{2A} \tag{6.4}$$

The producers of good 1 sector maximize the profit function (6.5) subject to the production function (6.6).

$$\pi_{1A} = P_{1A}Q_{1A} - r_A k_{1A} - w_A l_{1A} \tag{6.5}$$

$$Q_{1A} = k_{1A}^{\alpha} l_{1A}^{1-\alpha} \tag{6.6}$$

where π_{1A}, Q_{1A}, k_{1A}, and l_{1A} are, respectively, profit, amount of production, capital input, and labor input, in the good 1 sector of country A. r_A and w_A are rental rate of capital and wage rate of labor, respectively.

Solving the profit maximization problem, the following equilibrium conditions are obtained.

$$r_A = P_{1A} a k_{1A}^{a-1} l_{1A}^{1-a} \tag{6.7}$$

$$w_A = P_{1A}(1 - a) k_{1A}^{a} l_{1A}^{-a} \tag{6.8}$$

Note that equations (6.7) and (6.8) show that factor prices are equal to their marginal value product in equilibrium.

Similarly, the production of good 2 in country A is characterized by the following four equations, which correspond to equations (6.5), (6.6), (6.7) and (6.8) for good 1 production.

$$\pi_{2A} = P_{2A}Q_{2A} - r_A k_{2A} - w_A l_{2A} \tag{6.9}$$

$$Q_{2A} = k_{2A}^b l_{2A}^{1-b} \tag{6.10}$$

$$r_A = P_{2A} b k_{2A}^{b-1} l_{2A}^{1-b} \tag{6.11}$$

$$w_A = P_{2A}(1-b) k_{2A}^b l_{2A}^{-b} \tag{6.12}$$

Note that I am assuming that good 1 is more capital-intensive than good 2, or assuming $a > b$.

Domestic labor supply is assumed to be given, that is, there is no wage–leisure trade-off. So, the sum of labor input in two sectors is equal to the sum of the domestic labor supply (L_A) and the number of migrant workers (L_F) in country A.[6]

$$l_{1A} + l_{2A} = L_A + L_F \tag{6.13}$$

Similarly, the amount of capital input in two sectors is equal to the domestic capital supply (K_A) less the amount of outgoing FDI from country A into country B (K_F).

$$k_{1A} + k_{2A} = K_A - K_F \tag{6.14}$$

Since the tariff revenue accrued to the government is assumed to be distributed to domestic consumers in a lump-sum fashion, and since there is no profit in equilibrium, the national income (GNP rather than GDP), which does not include the income accrued to the imported factor but does include the income accrued to the exported factor which is employed in the foreign country, is as follows.

$$r_A(K_A - K_F) + r_B K_F + w_A L_A + P_{2A}(t_A/(1+t_A))(C_{2A} - Q_{2A}) = Y_A \tag{6.15}$$

where t_A is the tariff rate imposed on the imported goods by country A. Note that, since we are dealing with an interior solution here, capital-abundant (or labor-scarce) country A is importing labor-intensive good 2.

(Country B: labor-abundant)
Consumers in country B are characterized by the following social utility function.

$$U_B = C_{1B}^\alpha C_{2B}^{1-\alpha}, \quad 0 < \alpha < 1 \tag{6.16}$$

where U_B is the social utility of consumers in country B and C_{1B} and C_{2B} are the amount of consumption of good 1 and good 2, respectively, in country B. Since, good 1 is more capital-intensive than good 2, in a regular situation, country B exports good 2 and imports good 1. Consumers maximize the social utility function (6.16) subject to the budget constraint (6.17).

$$P_{1B}C_{1B} + P_{2B}C_{2B} = Y_B \tag{6.17}$$

where P_{1B} and P_{2B} are, respectively, domestic (that is, tariff-inclusive) prices of good 1 and good 2 in country B, and Y_B is the national income of country B.

From the above utility maximization problem, the following two demand functions are obtained.

$$C_{1B} = \alpha Y_B / P_{1B} \tag{6.18}$$

$$C_{2B} = (1 - \alpha) Y_B / P_{2B} \tag{6.19}$$

The producers of good 1 sector in country B maximize the profit function (6.20) subject to the production function (6.21).

$$\pi_{1B} = P_{1B}Q_{1B} - r_B k_{1B} - w_B l_{1B} \tag{6.20}$$

$$Q_{1B} = k_{1B}^a l_{1B}^{1-a} \tag{6.21}$$

where π_{1B}, Q_{1B}, k_{1B}, and l_{1B} are, respectively, profit, amount of production, capital input, and labor input, in the good 1 sector of country B. r_B and w_B are rental rate of capital and wage rate of labor, respectively, in country B.

Solving the profit maximization problem, the following equilibrium conditions are obtained.

$$r_B = P_{1B} a k_{1B}^{a-1} l_{1B}^{1-a} \tag{6.22}$$

$$w_B = P_{1B}(1 - a)k_{1B}^a l_{1B}^{-a} \tag{6.23}$$

Similarly, the production of good 2 in country B is characterized by the following four equations, which correspond to equations (6.20), (6.21), (6.22) and (6.23) for good 1 production.

$$\pi_{2B} = P_{2B}Q_{2B} - r_Bk_{2B} - w_Bl_{2B} \tag{6.24}$$

$$Q_{2B} = k_{2B}^b l_{2B}^{1-b} \tag{6.25}$$

$$r_B = P_{2B}bk_{2B}^{b-1}l_{2B}^{1-b} \tag{6.26}$$

$$w_B = P_{2B}(1-b)k_{2B}^b l_{2B}^{-b} \tag{6.27}$$

Since domestic labor supply is assumed to be given, the sum of labor input in two sectors is equal to the sum of the domestic labor supply (L_B) minus the number of emigrated workers (L_F) from country B to country A.

$$l_{1B} + l_{2B} = L_B - L_F \tag{6.28}$$

Similarly, the amount of labor input in two sectors is equal to the domestic capital supply (K_B) plus the amount of receiving FDI from country A into country B.

$$k_{1B} + k_{2B} = K_B + K_F \tag{6.29}$$

Since the tariff revenue accrued to the government is assumed to be distributed to domestic consumers in a lump-sum fashion, and since there is no profit in equilibrium, the national income (GNP rather than GDP), which does not include the income accrued to the imported factor but does include the income accrued to the exported factor, is as follows.

$$r_BK_B + w_B(L_B - L_F) + w_AL_F + P_{1B}(t_B/(1+t_B))(C_{1B} - Q_{1B}) = Y_B \tag{6.30}$$

where t_B is the tariff rate imposed on the imported goods (good 1). Note that, since we are dealing with interior solutions here, capital-scarce (or labor-abundant) country B is importing capital-intensive good 1.

(Tariff wedge under no price discrimination by the firm)
In the model, firms are assumed to have no monopolistic power to exercise price discrimination among the different markets. Therefore, the domestic

price of good 2 in country A (P_{2A}) is higher by t_A than the domestic price of good 2 in country B (P_{2B}).

$$P_{2A} = (1 + t_A)P_{2B} \qquad (6.31)$$

Similarly, the following relationship holds for the price of good 1.

$$P_{1B} = (1 + t_B)P_{1A} \qquad (6.32)$$

(World market clearance)
Since the amount of total production of each good must be equal to the amount of total consumption of the good in equilibrium, we have the following two equations.

$$C_{1A} + C_{1B} = Q_{1A} + Q_{1B} \qquad (6.33)$$

$$C_{2A} + C_{2B} = Q_{2A} + Q_{2B} \qquad (6.34)$$

The above model is complete, and the system of 28 equations ((6.1), (6.3), (6.4), (6.6), (6.7), (6.8), (6.10), (6.11), (6.12), (6.13), (6.14), (6.15), (6.16), (6.18), (6.19), (6.21), (6.22), (6.23), (6.25), (6.26), (6.27), (6.28), (6.29), (6.30), (6.31), (6.32), (6.33), and (6.34)) determines the equilibrium values of 28 endogenous variables in the model (U_A, U_B, C_{1A}, C_{2A}, C_{1B}, C_{2B}, Q_{1A}, Q_{2A}, Q_{1B}, Q_{2B}, k_{1A}, k_{2A}, k_{1B}, k_{2B}, l_{1A}, l_{2A}, l_{1B}, l_{2B}, P_{1A}, P_{2A}, P_{1B}, P_{2B}, r_A, w_A, r_B, w_B, Y_A, Y_B). Note that one of the 28 equations is redundant by Walrus's law and that one of the prices (for example, w_B) can be set to unity as the numeraire. Hence, the above model consists of 27 independent equations that can be solved for 27 endogenous variables. Therefore, as soon as the values of parameters (α, a, b, K_A, L_A, K_B, L_B, K_F, L_F, t_A, t_B) are identified, the model can be solved to obtain the equilibrium values of endogenous variables for the parameter values.

In order to evaluate the impact of migration (FDI), all we have to do is to solve the model for the different values of L_F (K_F) and compare the values of endogenous variables in each situation. Similarly, for evaluation of the impact of trade liberalization, we can solve the model for reduced values of t_A and t_B.

(2) Impact of Asian Migration to Japan: Illustrative Simulation

(a) Method for simulation

(i) Basic strategy of simulation   In what follows, I will calibrate the model developed above in order to present an integrated analysis of migration, FDI

and trade liberalization. While in many cases the effect of migration has been analyzed separately from the effects of FDI and of trade liberalization, I will analyze the impact of migration under the situation where FDI and international trade also exist, and compare the effects of migration with those of FDI and trade liberalization. Therefore my model is a little more complicated and sophisticated than traditional frameworks for the analysis of migration, where 'no trade' or 'free trade' has often been assumed and FDI has been assumed away. The motivation for my taking a more complicated approach is twofold.

First, contrary to the assumption of the traditional framework, migration, FDI and trade barriers coexist in the real world. For example, while East Asian countries are exporting workers to Japan and other developed countries, they are also admitting many multinational corporations from Japan and other countries (for example, SONY, Panasonic, Toyota, to name a few). In addition to the movement of production factors (labor and capital), countries are integrated with each other through international trade that is subject to tariffs and non-tariff barriers. As discussed in section 3 above, the effect of migration in the partially-opened economy, that is, in the economy with international trade subject to trade barriers, is very much different from that in the economy without trade. Therefore, in order to evaluate the impact of migration more precisely, we have to incorporate the impact of trade barriers and capital movement simultaneously.

Second, as is often argued, there are various alternatives to migration. Instead of moving workers from East Asia to Japan, the Japanese firms may be able to move their plants to East Asia and employ workers there. Also, instead of importing labor, Japan can import labor-intensive goods such as textiles and clothing from neighboring developing countries. In other words, Japan can *indirectly* utilize labor in East Asia through international trade. In view of the fact that there are alternatives to migration, for policy discussions at least, benefits and costs of migration should be compared with those of alternatives such as trade liberalization or foreign direct investment, because, if all the benefits of migration can be achieved by an alternative measure with fewer costs, the alternative is superior to migration. As will become clearer below, trade liberalization is generally superior to migration as a means of enhancing welfare in sending countries as well as receiving countries.

In the simulation below, I will analyze the economic relationship between Japan and East Asia as an aggregate, as an example.[7] So, Country *A* in the model means Japan, and country *B* is the aggregated entity of seven countries in East Asia, that is, China, Indonesia, Korea, Malaysia, Philippines, Thailand, and Taiwan province of China. These seven countries are chosen because they are major exporters of migrant workers to Japan. Also, the group of seven countries corresponds to the group of ASEAN and Asian NIEs plus China, minus Hong Kong and Singapore. As is well known, per capita income in Hong Kong and Singapore is so high that they are importers of migrant workers rather than exporters. In fact, according to the statistics compiled by the Japanese Government, there is very little immigration to Japan from Hong Kong or Singapore.

The basic strategy of simulation is as follows: the model is solved for the base year using parameter values in 1997, and I obtain equilibrium values of endogenous variables. Next, the model is solved again using different (increased) numbers of migrant workers (L_F). While the actual number of migrant workers, both legal and illegal, from East Asia to Japan is estimated at 319 000 in 1997, the model is again solved for the three other values of L_F, that is, 419 000 (319 000 plus 100 000), 500 000, and one million, in order to evaluate the welfare impact of migration for both Japan and East Asia. Similarly, the model is solved using different values of t_A and $t_B(K_F)$ in order to evaluate the impact of trade liberalization (foreign direct investment). Note that the simulation result using different values of L_F is also compared with those using different values of t_A and t_B or K_F, in order to obtain some policy implications on the relative importance of migration and trade liberalization as a means of improving economic welfare.

(ii) Identification of parameter values of the model   As discussed above, since the model consists of 27 independent equations and 27 endogenous variables (plus the price of the numeraire good), it can be solved if values of parameters (α, a, b, K_A, L_A, K_B, L_B, K_F, L_F, t_A, t_B) are identified. I borrow some of the parameter values from Goto (1998) because he presented simulation analysis of the impact of admitting migrant workers on the Japanese economy. Although the focus and model of this chapter is different from that of Goto, we can borrow some of the parameters used there.

First, a and b in the production functions (6.21) and (6.25) must be identified.

$$Q_{1B} = k_{1B}^a l_{1B}^{1-a} \tag{6.21}$$

$$Q_{2B} = k_{2B}^b l_{2B}^{1-b} \tag{6.25}$$

Borrowing the values used in Goto, I obtained $a = 0.4242$ and $b = 0.3785$. As assumed in the above model, good 1 is more capital-intensive than good 2 because $a > b$.

Second, α in social utility function (6.1) (or (6.16)) must be identified.

$$U_A = C_{1A}^\alpha C_{2A}^{1-\alpha} \tag{6.1}$$

With the proportional adjustment of the values of superscripts in the utility function in Goto's three good model, I obtained $\alpha = 0.4509$. Namely, the share of consumption of capital-intensive goods in total expenditure is equal to 45 per cent.

Third, the magnitude of current trade barriers of both countries (t_A and t_B) must be identified. Note that t_A and t_B include both tariffs and non-tariff barriers. Although the data for tariffs exist, it is very hard to obtain the data for tariff equivalency of non-tariff barriers. Borrowing from Goto, I obtained $t_A = 0.1329$. In other words, the domestic price of imports in Japan is on average 13 per cent higher than the international price due to various trade barriers. In view of the fact that, generally speaking, trade restrictions imposed on capital-intensive imports in developing countries are much higher than trade barriers by industrialized countries,[8] I set, somewhat arbitrarily, t_B as double t_A (that is, $t_B = 0.2658$).

Fourth, amounts of endowments of capital and labor in both countries (K_A, L_A, K_B, L_B) must be identified. While Goto presented the data for Japan (that is, K_A and L_A), it is very hard to obtain the corresponding data for seven countries in East Asia, and, even if they existed, they do not seem very reliable. Moreover, when we deal with a multi-country model consisting of countries which are very different from each other in terms of education, training, technology, and so on, a simple headcount of the number of workers may be misleading. For example, the productivity of well-trained workers in Country A is likely to be higher than that of less-trained workers in Country B. Therefore, some measures of *effective workforce*, which incorporates difference in skills and education of workers and a difference in technology among countries, seems to be more desirable than a simple headcount of workers for the simulation here. In order to cope with such difficulties, I indirectly estimated K_A, L_A, K_B, and L_B, using the observed values of some endogenous variables. I used observed values of national incomes (Y_A and Y_B), the value of Japanese exports to East Asia ($P_{1A}(Q_{1A} - C_{1A})$), and the value of Japanese imports from East Asia ($P_{2B}(Q_{2B} - C_{2B})$). In other words, in this preliminary calibration, K_A, L_A, K_B, and L_B are treated as if they were endogenous variables. By this preliminary calibration, I obtained $K_A = 5055$, $K_B = 371$, $L_A = 10$, and $L_B = 15.1$. The values for K's do not show the dollar amounts of capital endowment due to the different choice of unit. Also, values for L's do not show the headcount of workers due to the choice of unit and, more importantly, due to the fact that they show the effective unit of labor endowment which embodies difference in education, training and so on.

Finally, by using the units for K's and L's, I proportionally adjusted the data of migration in Japan from East Asia (318 600) and the stock of FDI from Japan to East Asia ($60.45 billion), and obtained $K_F = 39.1$ and $L_F = 0.0052$.

(b)　Results of calibration

With values for all the parameters (obtained as above), the model can be solved for the 28 endogenous variables. The model was solved using the above parameter values for the base simulation first. Then, the model is repeatedly solved using different values of L_F, t_A and t_B, and K_F, in order to evaluate the impact of migration, trade liberalization and FDI. In what follows, the results of simulation are summarized for the selected endogenous variables. After presenting the welfare impact of the three different policy measures, that is, the increase in migration, trade liberalization and the increase in the Japanese FDI to East Asia separately, I will compare the magnitude of the welfare impact of migration with that of trade liberalization in order to get some insights into the relative effectiveness of alternative measures to enhance economic welfare.

(i)　Effect of increased migration from East Asia to Japan　First of all, let us examine how welfare in Japan (U_A) and East Asia (U_B) changes when the number of migrating workers from East Asia to Japan is increased either by Japan's open-door policy or increased efforts for emigration by sending countries. In addition to the base simulation for the actual situation in 1997, I repeated the simulation using different values of L_F. In Table 6.4, three simulation results are reported: Case A-1 where $L_F = 419\,000$ (that is, $100\,000$ increase from the current number of $319\,000$), Case A-2 where $L_F = 500\,000$, and Case A-3 where $L_F =$ one million. Other parameters are kept constant for these three cases.

As shown in the table, the economic welfare of East Asia (country B) increases as the amount of emigration to Japan increases because these emigrated workers earn higher wages than they could in their home country. They are more productive in the labor-scarce country than in the labor-abundant country. However, the economic welfare of Japan (country A) decreases as the amount of migration from East Asia increases. While it may seem a little counter-intuitive, the mechanism of this 'trade barrier' effect has already been discussed in section 2. The trade barrier effect is also known as the Brecher–Diaz-Alejandro effect (or Uzawa effect), as they analyzed capital inflow to developing countries when their imports of capital-intensive goods are restricted by tariffs. As discussed above, a similar argument can be made for the imports of labor when the imports of labor-intensive goods are restricted by tariffs. Due to the tariffs imposed by Japan on labor-intensive imports, the prices of the labor-intensive good and of the factor intensively used in that sector (that is, labor) are in some sense inflated in Japan. If migrant workers are paid by this inflated wage, the welfare of the labor-importing country declines. Hence, the welfare of Japan is decreased by the further admission of migrant workers from East Asia.

Table 6.4   Result of simulation A: impact of migration

	Base	Case A-1 (small)	Case A-2 (middle)	Case A-3 (large)
Migration (LF) (thousand)	319	419	500	1000
Japanese Trade Barrier (TA) (%)	13.29	13.29	13.29	13.29
East Asian Trade Barrier (TB) (%)	26.58	26.58	26.58	26.58
Stock of FDI (KF) ($billion)	60.45	60.45	60.45	60.45
Japanese Welfare (UA) change	100 000 0	99 997 −3	99 994 −6	99 980 −20
East Asian Welfare (UB) change	100 000 0	100 029 29	100 049 49	100 176 176

Source: Author's simulation (see main text for detail).

However, note that the magnitude of the increase in the welfare of East Asian countries is larger than the magnitude of the decrease in the welfare of Japan. For example, when one million migrant workers are admitted to Japan, the welfare index of East Asia increases by 176 while the Japanese welfare index decreases only by 20.[9]

(ii)   Effect of trade liberalization   Let us examine how welfare of Japan (U_A) and East Asia (U_B) changes when both countries decrease their trade barriers by reduction of tariffs and/or lifting some non-tariff barriers. As is well known, tariffs have been lowered by a series of world trade negotiations such as the Tokyo Round and the Uruguay Round. Recently, there have been various initiatives to realize trade liberalization in Asia and the Pacific. For example, as manifested in the Bogor Declaration of 1994, APEC members agreed to achieve free and open trade and investment in Asia and the Pacific by 2010 for industrialized countries and by 2020 for developing countries. In order to evaluate the impact of such efforts toward trade liberalization, I repeated the simulation using different values of t_A and t_B. In Table 6.5, three simulation results as well as the base simulation result are reported: Case B-1 where t_A=12.63 per cent and t_B=25.25 per cent (that is, 5 per cent decline in tariff rates in both countries from the base simulation); Case B-2 where t_A=11.96 per cent and t_B=23.92 per cent (that is, 10 per cent decline from the base simulation); Case B-3 where t_A=9.30 per cent and t_B=18.60 per cent (that is, 30 per cent decline from the base

Table 6.5   *Result of simulation B: impact of trade barrier*

	Base	Case B-1 (small)	Case B-2 (middle)	Case B-3 (large)
Migration (LF) (thousand)	319	319	319	319
Japanese Trade Barrier (TA) (%)	13.29	12.63	11.96	9.3
East Asian Trade Barrier (TB) (%)	26.58	25.25	23.92	18.61
Stock of FDI (KF) ($billion)	60.45	60.45	60.45	60.45
Japanese Welfare (UA)	100 000	100 087	100 185	100 543
change	0	87	185	543
East Asian Welfare (UB)	100 000	100 780	102 088	105 937
change	0	780	2088	5937

Source: Author's simulation (see main text for detail).

simulation), to evaluate the welfare impact of trade liberalization. Other parameters are kept constant for these three cases.

As shown in the table, the economic welfare of East Asia (country *B*) increases as trade liberalization continues, because after the liberalization, consumers benefit from cheaper foreign goods and because producers in the exporting good (good 2) sector benefit from increased demand abroad. In comparison with the effect of migration, the magnitude of welfare increase by trade liberalization is large. When 5 per cent, 10 per cent, and 30 per cent trade liberalization are achieved, the East Asian welfare increases by 780, 2088 and 5937, respectively.

Note that through trade liberalization, the economic welfare of Japan also increases, and the magnitude of such an increase is large. When 5 per cent, 10 per cent, and 30 per cent trade liberalization are achieved, the Japanese welfare increases by 87, 185 and 543, respectively. Thus, trade liberalization substantially benefits not only labor-exporting East Asia but also labor-importing Japan. The result conforms to the theoretical analysis of Goto (1998).

(iii)   *Effect of the increase in Japanese FDI to East Asia*   Next, let us examine how welfare of Japan (U_A) and East Asia (U_B) changes when the amount of Japanese FDI to East Asia increases. In order to evaluate the impact of such efforts to increase the FDI, I repeated the simulation using different values of K_F. In Table 6.6 three simulation results as well as the base

Table 6.6   Result of simulation C: impact of FDI

	Base	Case C-1 (small)	Case C-2 (middle)	Case C-3 (large)
Migration (LF) (thousand)	319	319	319	319
Japanese Trade Barrier (TA) (%)	13.29	13.29	13.29	13.29
East Asian Trade Barrier (TB) (%)	26.58	26.58	26.58	26.58
Stock of FDI (KF) ($billion)	60.45	61.45	65.45	70.45
Japanese Welfare (UA)	100 000	100 045	100 229	100 457
change	0	45	229	457
East Asian Welfare (UB)	100 000	99 895	99 470	98 943
change	0	−105	−530	−1057

Source: Author's simulation (see main text for detail).

simulation result are reported: Case C-1 where $K_F = \$61.45$ billion (that is, $1 billion increase from the base value of $60.45 billion); Case C-2 where $K_F = \$65.45$ billion (that is, $5 billion increase from the base value), and Case C-3 where $K_F = \$70.45$ billion (that is, $10 billion increase from the base value of $60.45 billion). Other parameters are kept constant for these three cases.

As shown in the table, the economic welfare of Japan (country *A*) increases as the amount of Japanese FDI increases because outgoing capital earns higher returns than it would in its home country. Capital is more productive in the capital-scarce (and labor-abundant) country. When the stock of Japanese FDI in East Asia increases by $1 billion, $5 billion and $10 billion, the economic welfare of Japan increases by 45, 229 and 457, respectively.

However, the economic welfare of East Asia (country *B*) decreases as the amount of Japanese FDI increases. The Brecher–Diaz-Alejandro effect (or Uzawa effect) is clearly working here. When the stock of Japanese FDI in East Asia increases by $1 billion, $5 billion and $10 billion, the economic welfare of East Asia decreases by 105, 530 and 1057, respectively. Namely, unless a negative Brecher–Diaz-Alejandro effect is compensated by some other external benefit, such as technology transfer, the increase in FDI tends to give negative effects on the receiving country under the tariff-distorted world economy.

(c)   Migration vs. trade liberalization: some policy implications
So far, I have examined the impact of migration, trade liberalization and FDI separately. At the end of the calibration section of the chapter, let us

discuss the relative benefits of migration and other alternatives, especially trade liberalization. First of all, if we are interested in the welfare improvement of a labor-importing developed country such as Japan, migration is the worst measure of three alternatives. Migration tends to reduce the welfare in Japan at least under such a range of the amount of migration,[10] while the other two alternatives make a positive impact on Japanese welfare. However, we may well argue that the welfare improvement of East Asia is more important than the (small) decline in Japanese welfare, because, in view of the huge income gap between Japan and East Asian countries, Japan has some international obligation to contribute to the economic development of her neighbors.

In what follows, I will examine the relative effectiveness of migration and trade liberalization as a means of improving the welfare of East Asia (U_B). For that purpose, I repeat the simulation exercise using many different values of L_F, to find out how many migrant workers (L_F) have to be admitted to achieve the same values of U_B as those achieved by trade liberalization in Case B-1, Case B-2 and Case B-3, respectively. In other words, through repeated simulations, I tried to find how many migrant workers must be admitted to Japan, if we want to achieve the same welfare improvement in East Asia as the improvement achieved by various degree of trade liberalization. Table 6.7, which is probably the most important table in this chapter, summarizes the result of simulations. As the table shows, when a 10 per cent reduction in trade barriers is achieved for both t_A (from 13.29 per cent to 11.96 per cent) and t_B (from 26.58 per cent to 23.92 per cent), the welfare of East Asian improves by 2088. If we achieve this 2088 improvement of the East Asian welfare through migration to Japan, the number of East Asian migrant workers into Japan has to be increased to 8.7 million from the current 0.3 million. While a 10 per cent reduction in trade barriers does not seem very difficult to achieve, the admission of East Asian migrant workers to Japan by 8.7 million is far from being realistic (at least in the near future). Similarly, if we want to achieve the improvement of East Asian welfare realized by a 30 per cent reduction in trade barriers (that is, t_A from 13.29 per cent to 9.30 per cent and t_B from 26.58 per cent to 18.61 per cent), the number of East Asian migrant workers has to be increased to 24.9 million from the current 0.3 million. In view of the fact that the current number of employees in Japan is 53.7 million, the admission of 24.9 million (or about half of the total number of Japanese workers) is far from realistic.

Thus, it seems to me that trade liberalization is a more effective (and realistic) way to improve the welfare in labor-exporting countries in East Asia than migration. Moreover, it should be noted that trade liberalization also improves the welfare of Japan, a labor-importing country.

Table 6.7   Migration vs. trade liberalization

	Base	Trade Liberalization	Migration
Comparison with 5% reduction			
Migration (LF) (thousand)	319	319	3398
Japanese Trade Barrier (TA) (%)	13.29	12.63	13.29
East Asian Trade Barrier (TB) (%)	26.58	25.25	26.58
Stock of FDI (KF) ($billion)	60.5	60.5	60.5
Japanese Welfare (UA)	100 000	100 087	99 913
change	0	87	−87
East Asian Welfare (UB)	100 000	100 780	100 780
change	0	780	780
Comparison with 10% reduction			
Migration (LF) (thousand)	319	319	8662
Japanese Trade Barrier (TA) (%)	13.29	11.96	13.29
East Asian Trade Barrier (TB) (%)	26.58	23.92	26.58
Stock of FDI (KF) ($billion)	60.5	60.5	60.5
Japanese Welfare (UA)	100 000	100 185	99 770
change	0	185	−230
East Asian Welfare (UB)	100 000	102 088	102 088
change	0	2088	2088
Comparison with 30% reduction			
Migration (LF) (thousand)	319	319	24 875
Japanese Trade Barrier (TA) (%)	13.29	9.30	13.29
East Asian Trade Barrier (TB) (%)	26.58	18.61	26.58
Stock of FDI (KF) ($billion)	60.5	60.5	60.5
Japanese Welfare (UA)	100 000	100 543	99 371
change	0	543	−629
East Asian Welfare (UB)	100 000	105 937	105 937
change	0	5937	5937

Source: Author's simulation (see main text for detail).

However, some caveats may be necessary. The above conclusion, based on the simulation results reported in Table 6.7, does not incorporate (positive or negative) externalities nor does it include adjustment costs associated with international migration. Migration is not a mere movement of labor as a production factor but the movement of human beings as a whole across the border. Migration involves various externalities. For example, when a Japanese university hires a chemistry professor from the Philippines, the professor might increase the productivity of fellow Japanese professors of economics by familiarizing them with the economic development of the Philippines and other East Asian countries. Similarly, when the Filipino professor goes back to his country, he may bring back some advanced technology from Japan. The degree of positive externality would depend on the type of work performed by the migrant worker. If he (she) works as a professional and skilled worker, such as professor, doctor or lawyer, positive externalities are easily expected. However, if the migrant worker is employed as an unskilled worker, which is the case for most migrant workers in East Asia, it is hard to expect him (her) to bring about a large degree of positive externalities to the Japanese economy, and to bring home advanced technology from Japan. On the other hand, the movement of workers may involve greater adjustment cost than the movement of goods. If this is the case, the case for trade liberalization over migration is further strengthened.

5. THE AGEING POPULATION AND LABOR MARKET POLICY

In the previous sections, I have analyzed the welfare impact of international movements of labor, money and goods. In what follows, let us discuss some empirical issues on the relative benefit of various measures to cope with a possible labor shortage caused by the ageing population in Japan. As I have argued elsewhere,[11] the population policy may be powerless to prevent the dependency ratio (and old population ratio) from rapidly rising in the next 20 years or so. However, the labor market policy seems promising in preventing the actual burden on the working population by keeping the balance between labor demand and labor supply. First of all, it should be noted that the decline in numbers of the working-age population does not necessarily cause a labor shortage or an increased burden on the working population. The labor market balance is also determined by the demand-side factor (how much labor is demanded by the national economy) and by the supply-side factor (what percentage of the working-age population actually works). Therefore, if the Japanese economy makes a structural change to the labor-saving economy, and if the labor participation rate is increased by a rise in numbers of female workers, the decline in the working-age population does not necessarily result in a labor shortage.

One of the most important measures to avoid a labor shortage or an increase in the burden on the working population is, needless to say, to increase labor productivity, because, even if the number of workers decreases in the future, the productivity increase can compensate for the decline. As discussed above, the working-age population in Japan is expected to decline by 9.8 million in 15 years, or an annual decline of 0.7 per cent. On the other hand, labor productivity in Japan (at least until the recent recession) has been increasing by about 3 per cent a year mainly due to the active investment by Japanese firms. So, if the Japanese economy is put on track again and if the age of the IT revolution comes, a 0.7 per cent annual decline in the working-age population is easily offset by the increase in labor productivity.

In addition to the increase in labor productivity, various measures can be taken to prevent a labor shortage in the future. In what follows, I will discuss two types of measures; (1) measures to utilize Japanese labor effectively (for example, female participation and rationalization of agriculture); and (2) measures to utilize foreign labor *indirectly* (for example, trade liberalization and outflow of foreign direct investment).

First, female participation seems most promising. Although more and more women have entered the labor market in recent years, there are still large numbers of women who want to work but cannot do so due to family responsibilities such as housework, small children, or sick parents. So, if a better working environment is provided for women, such as an adequate number of good quality daycare centers, the supply of female labor will be increased, thereby mitigating the expected labor shortage in Japan.

Second, the rationalization of inefficient industries, such as agriculture and distribution sectors, is important. While the number of agricultural workers has been steadily declining, labor productivity in the agriculture sector is still much lower than in many countries, if Japanese agricultural products are evaluated at international prices. So, if the further rationalization of Japanese agriculture makes it possible to reallocate agricultural workers to other sectors, the labor shortage in the Japanese economy as a whole will be relieved by that much.

Third, trade liberalization is also promising. If (instead of producing goods in Japan using Japanese workers) Japan imports more foreign-made products, which are produced by foreign labor in foreign countries, she can save domestic labor by that much. The import of labor-intensive products, such as textile and clothing, seems particularly promising.

Fourth, closely related with the third point, the curb on export drive should yield results. Ever since the *Meiji* Restoration, Japan has been encouraging export of goods made in Japan, and in recent years the accumulation of trade surplus has brought about trade conflicts with many countries. If Japan curbs this strong export drive and reduces the export of at least labor-intensive products, the labor demand by the Japanese economy will be substantially decreased.

Fifth, foreign direct investment (FDI) is also important. Instead of building factories in Japan and hiring Japanese workers, Japanese firms can move production sites to foreign countries, where they can produce goods

Table 6.8   Labor saving and labor creation: a simulation (thousands)

	Normal	High speed
Female participation	379	783
Efficient agriculture	223	325
Trade liberalization	153	304
Curb on the export drive	96	96
FDI	158	158
Total of the above	1009	1666

Note: The expected decline in working-age population in 2000–2015 is 9.8 million.

Source: Goto (1993).

by hiring foreign workers there. The outflow of Japanese FDI will create jobs in foreign countries, and, at the same time, save labor in Japan.

How great is the effect of the above five measures? I have made a simple simulation of the magnitude of the labor-creation and labor-saving effects of the above measures (see Goto, 1993). Table 6.8 is the result of the simulation. It shows the total size of the labor-saving (and labor-creating) effect ranging from 10 million to 17 million, depending on the underlying assumptions. These figures are larger than the expected decline in the working-age population in the early twenty-first century (9.8 million). Thus, at least in aggregate, the decline in working-age population and the resulting increase in the burden on the working population seem to be compensated if various measures are taken effectively.

6.   CONCLUDING REMARKS

In the above, I have theoretically and empirically examined the impact of migration on both the host country and the home country in East Asia, because it is often pointed out that, in order to cope with a serious labor shortage, Japan should open the door to international migration, and because many people argue that the increased migration to Japan would benefit sending countries as well through remittance and employment creation.

In section 2, I have briefly reviewed the ageing situation in Japan. The Japanese population is rapidly ageing and the fertility rate is steadily declining. In view of this, it is widely argued that, in order to cope with a possible labor shortage in the near future, Japan should make every effort to raise the fertility rate now. However, as discussed in detail in section 2, since the rapid ageing trend will continue only for 20 years or so in the early twenty-first century, and since it takes about 20 years before those born today can start working, the increase in fertility rate now will increase, rather than decrease, the burden on the working population.

As demonstrated in section 3, the economic effect of immigration is not necessarily beneficial to the host country, because the negative trade barrier effect (Brecher–Diaz-Alejandro effect) dominates other positive effects in many cases. This implies that, at least in the long run, the admission of guest workers may not be a desirable policy, unless the above negative effect is compensated by some positive externalities. As argued above, the migration by professional and skilled workers is more likely to have positive externalities than that by unskilled workers. Unfortunately, however, the majority of the current intra-Asian migration consists of the movement of unskilled workers, such as maids and construction workers. In addition to the economic impact on the host country, the impact on the home country and the social effects have also been examined in section 3.

In section 4, after developing a simple $2\times2\times2$ CGE model, which incorporates international migration, FDI and trade liberalization, the economic effects of migration, FDI and trade liberalization are compared with each other, taking the economic relationship between Japan and seven East Asian countries as an example. Through a series of simulation exercises, I found that migration tends to give negative welfare effects to the receiving country (Japan), although it has a positive welfare impact on the host country as well as on home countries. It was demonstrated that, in order to achieve a positive economic impact on the home country, such as income creation and alleviation of unemployment, there are alternative measures such as the increased flow of goods through trade liberalization by both parties. The simulation results suggest that trade liberalization is a far more desirable policy than international migration to enhance the economic welfare of the sending country. Moreover, it should be noted that trade liberalization is beneficial to both the host country and home countries in East Asia, while migration tends to benefit only sending home countries. Thus, even from a pure economic viewpoint, trade liberalization seems to be a superior policy to migration.

In section 5, I discussed some empirical issues on the relative benefit of various measures to cope with a possible labor shortage caused by the ageing population in Japan. I have found that, at least in aggregate, the decline in working-age population and the resulting increase in the burden on the working population seem to be compensated if various measures, such as utilization of female labor, are taken effectively.

NOTES

1. Note the difference between the gross domestic product (GDP) and the gross national product (GNP). GDP of Country 1 is defined as the total value of the product produced in Country 1, which does not include the value of the product produced by the migrant workers from Country 1 to Country 2 even if they are still the citizens of Country 1. On the other hand, GNP includes the income of these migrant workers as long as they remain the citizens of Country 1.
2. Note that this argument is based on the full-employment assumption. If the emigrant workers were totally unemployed before migration, total income of these migrant workers is a net gain to Country 1.
3. For those who are interested in a more rigorous mathematical model and proofs, see Goto (1998), pp. 63–83.
4. Note that the argument here assumes that both native workers and migrant workers are paid according to their labor productivity, and therefore, there is no genuine wage discrimination. In reality, however, it is often reported that migrant workers are paid substantially less than native workers. In the event that such wage discrimination exists, the magnitude of the negative trade barrier becomes smaller. (If the wage discrimination is severe, the effect can be positive to the host country.)
5. For a more rigorous argument, see Goto (1998).
6. Note that here we are assuming that capital abundant (and labor scarce) country A imports labor and exports capital. However, the export of labor (capital) can be incorporated by putting a negative number into $L_F (K_F)$.
7. Needless to say, the model is so general that we can also analyze other situations when parameter values of those situations are identified.
8. It is often the case that the tariff rate imposed by developing countries on capital-intensive 'luxury' goods, such as cars, is as high as 100 per cent.
9. Although, at the first glance, the changes in welfare by 20 or by 176 (from 100 000) may look very small and close to zero, we should note that the number of migrant workers here (one million) is also very small in comparison with the total population of the seven countries in East Asia (1.7 billion). Therefore, the important thing is the relative number rather than absolute number. Also, note that the utility is expressed as an ordinary number, rather than a cardinal number.
10. As discussed earlier, very large scale of admission of migrant workers may increase the welfare of recipient country. See Goto (1998) for detailed discussions on this point.
11. See Goto (2001) for a detailed discussion of this issue.

BIBLIOGRAPHY

Brecher, R. and C.F. Diaz-Alejandoro (1977), 'Tariffs, foreign capital, and immiserizing growth', *Journal of International Economics*, 7, 317–22.

Goto, Junichi (1990), *Labor in International Trade Theory: A New Perspective on Japanese–American Issues*, Baltimore MD: The Johns Hopkins University Press.

Goto, Junichi (1993), *Gaikokujin Rodosha to Nihon Keizai* (Migrant Workers and the Japanese Economy), Tokyo: Yuhikaku Ltd.

Goto, Junichi (1998), 'The impact of migrant workers on the Japanese economy: trickle vs. flood', *Japan and the World Economy*, **10**, 63–83.

Goto, Junichi (2001), 'Aging society and the labor market in Japan: should the fertility rate be raised now? – No', *Japan Labor Bulletin*, **40**(9), 6–11.

International Labor Organization (1999), *Towards Full Employment: Prospects and Problems in Asia and the Pacific*, Geneva: International Labor Organization.

Schiff, Maurice (1999), 'Trade, migration, and welfare', Policy Research Working Paper (#2044), The World Bank.

Todaro, M.P. (1986), 'International migration, domestic unemployment, and urbanization: a three-sector model', Center for Policy Studies Working Paper (#124), London.

7. Retirement in non-cooperative and cooperative families*

Erik Hernæs, Zhiyang Jia and Steinar Strøm

1. INTRODUCTION

An increasing proportion of elderly persons in the population, falling labor force participation of older males and maturing of the public pension system all combine to threaten the financial stability of pay-as-you-go public pension systems in many industrialized countries. In Norway, problems have been exacerbated by the introduction of an early retirement program, hereafter called AFP (a Norwegian abbreviation). From a policy point of view, knowledge about how economic incentives affect workers' retirement, and to what extent they will respond to policy changes are therefore important.

Most of the literature on retirement behavior has focused on single individuals; see Lumsdaine and Mitchell (1999) for references. However, since a majority of older men and women are married or cohabiting, it is important to account for the fact that labor market behavior may be due to joint decisions by married couples. Among the relatively few empirical studies of retirement behavior in a household context, most have focused on patterns of family retirement, like 'wife first', 'joint retirement' and 'husband first'; see Henretta and O'Rand (1983) for an early contribution. In recent studies Gustman and Steinmeier (2000) find a tendency for spouses to retire together, which they attribute to correlation in preferences for (joint) retirement. Baker (2002) finds that the propensity to retire among males is around 5–10 percentage points higher when the wife is eligible for a supplementary pension. Blau (1997) finds 'strong associations between the labor force transition probabilities of one spouse and the labor force status of the other spouse'.

Lately, there have been retirement studies that explicitly model family behavior as the outcome of non-cooperative behavior. Hiedemann (1998) uses a Stackelberg model with male leadership to model the joint social security acceptance decisions and finds that it depends on several individual and household characteristics as well as financial incentives. But we have not seen much empirical evidence in the literature on how the decision process within the family really works. Do they cooperate in the sense that they share common interests and make the decision to maximize a 'family utility' function as if there were a benevolent dictator? Or do they maximize their own utility functions so that the family labor supply is just an outcome of a non-cooperative game?

In our analysis, we use the introduction of the AFP program as an opportunity to study the retirement decision of elderly, married couples and the responsiveness of that decision to the level of current earnings and potential pension benefits. The main purpose is to contrast different models for retirement behavior. We specify models for non-cooperative behavior as well as models for cooperative behavior within families. We follow Bresnahan and Reiss (1991) and Kooreman (1994) in calculating Nash and Stackelberg equilibrium. In Kooreman (1994) reaction functions are derived from linear utility functions of the spouses, while we allow more general (flexible) functional forms of the deterministic part of the utility functions (non-linear function of disposable income and leisure), with linear and Cobb–Douglas function as special cases. The models are estimated on Norwegian data from 1994–1998. Since the husband is usually older than the wife, on the average by three years, we restrict the sample to couples in which the husband becomes eligible, over a period when the eligibility age was 64, whereas the wife does not qualify. In contrast to the studies referred to above, we observe the exact date of retirement and we also observe all details of the budget sets, including pension benefits and taxes paid. The estimates of the different models are compared using econometric tests of how well the different models predict observed labor market attachments. We conclude that the Stackelberg model, with male leadership, performs best among the models we have studied, although they give quite similar parameter-estimates. The models are then employed to simulate the impacts on the labor supply of the families of replacing the rather generous taxation of pension benefits with the taxation of earnings for all kinds of income. It is shown that this policy change has a strong and negative impact on the propensity to retire early.

In section 2 we describe briefly the institutional setting in Norway. Section 3 presents the model, and section 4 give a basic description of data sources and the sample used in the analysis. Estimates and policy simulation are given in section 5. Section 6 concludes.

2.   INSTITUTIONAL SETTINGS

The institutional settings are described in detail in Hernæs et al. (2000). Briefly summed up, an early retirement program (AFP) came into effect in

Norway in 1989, as part of the national wage settlements of 1988. This program allows retirement before the standard retirement age of 67, when the ordinary old age pension can be received. The AFP age was 66 from 1 January 1989, 65 from 1 January 1990, 64 from 1 October 1993, 63 from 1 October 1997 and 62 from 1 March 1998.

The AFP program covers all government employees (of local and central government), and private sector employees of companies that have joined the program; in total about 60 per cent of the labor force. Participation is voluntary on the part of the private companies, and will usually be a part of the tariff agreement with the union. Self-employed and private employees of companies not participating are not covered. There are also individual requirements for being eligible for AFP, as only those are eligible who:

- had been employed in the company the last 3 years or had been employed in another company also operating the AFP scheme for the last 5 years,
- had earnings at a level at least corresponding to the basic pension (G) when AFP was taken up,
- had earnings at least equal to the basic pension the year before,
- had an average proportion between earnings and the basic pension of at least 1 in the 10 best years after the age of 50 and
- had at least 10 years in which earnings were at least twice the basic pension.

Persons meeting individual criteria while working in companies covered by the program become eligible from the month after they turn the required age. With information on the birth date, we are therefore able to identify exactly the date of eligibility.

Although the AFP program is a negotiated agreement, the benefits received are the same as in the ordinary public old age pension system. Private employees receive an AFP pension equal to the ordinary public old age pension, based on their actual earnings history and a projection of earnings from AFP take-up and up to age 67. This pension is also the pension they will receive from age 67, so that there is no penalty on early retirement. A detailed explanation of how this pension is calculated is given in Hernæs and Strøm (2000). With the pension level and exchange rate prevailing in the Autumn of 2001, it varies between 9000 USD and 22 000 USD per year; income above 68 000 USD does not count towards the pension. The system is therefore strongly re-distributive.

The AFP pension for (local and central) government employees is the same as for private employees up to age 65, when it becomes equal to the old age pension for public sector employees. Over the observation period, this latter pension equaled about 2/3 of income up to 45 000 USD and 2/9 of any part of the income between that level and the maximum level for accrual at 68 000 USD. Details can be found in Hernæs and Strøm (2000).

There are also special tax rules, which apply to retirement benefits. These are briefly described below, but all details are given in Haugen (2000). In the early retirement program a tax-free lump-sum amount is given to those who retire from a job in the private sector. In the government sector a higher, but taxed lump-sum amount is awarded.

Pensions for private employees are financed by a state subsidy of 40 per cent from age 64, and with the balance financed by the employers. In some industries the company of the incumbent pays 10 per cent of the pension whereas the rest is paid from pooled contributions levied according to the wage sum of the company. In other industries the contribution of the company equals the pensions of its (former) employees. Pensions for government employees are paid directly by the government.

3.   METHODOLOGY

3.1   The Models

We want to analyze the labor market decisions of elderly couples, when a new option (early retirement) becomes available to the husband. We assume that the decisions are results of either a two-player non-cooperative game or more traditionally the maximization of a joint utility.

The available choices for the husband are:

$$y_m = \begin{cases} 1 & \text{if he decides to take early retirement} \\ 0 & \text{if he decides to continue to work} \end{cases}$$

Similarly, the wife's choices set is:

$$y_f = \begin{cases} 1 & \text{if she decides not to work} \\ 0 & \text{if she decides to work} \end{cases}$$

3.1.1   Non cooperative model: separate utility functions for husband and wife

We first assume that the husband and the wife have his/her own utility function, and both of them try to maximize his/her own utility. As econometricians we do not know the preferences of the individuals and thus we have to deal with random utilities, although they may be assumed to be common knowledge within the household. Thus we assume the following random utility functions:

$$\begin{cases} U_m(y_m,y_f) = v_m(y_m,y_f) + \varepsilon_m(y_m) \\ U_f(y_m,y_f) = v_f(y_m,y_f) + \varepsilon_f(y_f) \end{cases}$$

where $v_k(.)$; $k=f, m$ are the deterministic parts of the utility functions and $\varepsilon_k(.)$; $k=f, m$ are the random parts. We recognize that it is actually a two-person discrete choice problem. One way to solve the problem is to use the multivariate qualitative model (see for example Maddala, 1983), which is an extension of univariate LOGIT or PROBIT. The choice then is determined by the following simultaneous equation system with discrete endogenous variables (endogenous dummy variables):

$$\begin{cases} y_m^* = v_m(1,y_f) - v_m(0,y_f) + e_m & \text{where } e_m = \varepsilon_m(1) - \varepsilon_m(0) \\ y_f^* = v_f(y_m, 1) - v_f(y_m, 0) + e_f & \text{where } e_f = \varepsilon_f(1) - \varepsilon_f(0) \\ y_l = 1 & \text{if } y_l^* > 0 \quad l=m, f \\ y_l = 0 & \text{otherwise} \end{cases} \tag{7.1}$$

where we assume that e_m and e_f are logistic distributed with correlation ρ across the husband and wife. But as argued by Heckman (1978) and Maddala (1983), some coherency conditions are required for the equation system to be well defined. As a result of imposing these coherency conditions, the simultaneity, which is essential in our analysis, is unfortunately eliminated.

Bresnahan and Reiss (1991) model the multi-person discrete choice behavior as the result of a multi-player game, and use solution concepts such as Nash equilibrium or Stackelberg equilibrium, rather than the equation system (7.1). Kooreman (1994) discusses the estimation problem of the econometric models of discrete games.

In our analysis, we follow the approach developed in Kooreman (1994) to model the observed behavior. In the game discussed here, husband and wife can take one of two actions, working or not working. The pay-off is his/her utility function: $U_k(y_m, y_f)$; $k=m, f$; The pay-off matrix of the game is given in Table 7.1.

Two solution concepts of this one-shot game will be employed below.

Nash equilibrium Each player is assumed to maximize his/her utility function, given the action of the other player. Both players then adjust their

Table 7.1   The pay-off matrix of the game

Husband	Wife	
	Works, $y_f=0$	Home, $y_f=1$
Works, $y_m=0$	$U_m(0,0),\ U_f(0,0)$	$U_m(0,1),\ U_f(0,1)$
Retired, $y_m=1$	$U_m(1,0),\ U_f(1,0)$	$U_m(1,1),\ U_f(1,1)$

actions until their decisions are mutually consistent. Or mathematically, choice (y_m, y_f) is a Nash equilibrium (NE) if:

$$U_m(y_m, y_f) > U_m(1 - y_m, y_f) \quad \text{and}$$

$$U_f(y_m, y_f) > U_f(y_m, 1 - y_f); \quad y_m, y_f = 0, 1 \tag{7.2}$$

A two-player game may have more than one NE or have no NE at all. Jia (2001) shows that the necessary and sufficient condition for (y_m, y_f) to be a NE for the above game is that it is a solution to the equation system (7.1). So the problem of equilibria non-uniqueness for the game is essentially the coherency problem for the simultaneous endogenous dummy model referred to above and vice versa.

There are several ways to solve the problems, as discussed both in Bresnahan and Reiss (1991) and Kooreman (1994). We make the simplest assumptions following Kooreman (1994):

- If there is only one NE, the household will choose it.
- If there is more than one NE, we assume the household picks any one of them by random.
- If there is no NE, we assume each available choice is chosen with equal probability.

As shown in Table 7A.1 in Appendix 7.1, we can specify the NE corresponding to each of the 16 possible combinations. Under the assumptions, we can calculate the probability of the household choosing (y_m, y_f) for y_m, $y_f = 0, 1$.

For example:

$$\Pr(\text{husband retire, wife not work}) = \Pr(1, 1)$$

$$= \Pr(e_m > (v_m(0, 1) - v_m(1, 1)) \ \wedge \ e_f > (v_f(1, 0) - v_f(1,1)))$$

$$- \tfrac{1}{2}\Pr((v_m(0, 0) - v_m(1, 0)) > e_m > (v_m(0, 1) - v_m(1, 1))$$

$$\wedge \; (v_f(0, 0) - v_f(0, 1)) > e_f > (v_f(1, 0) - v_f(1,1)))$$

$$+ \tfrac{1}{4}\mathrm{Pr}((v_m(0, 0) - v_m(1, 0)) > e_m > (v_m(0, 1) - v_m(1, 1))$$

$$\wedge \; (v_f(1, 0) - v_f(1, 1)) > e_f > (v_f(0, 0) - v_f(0, 1)))$$

$$+ \tfrac{1}{4}\mathrm{Pr}((v_m(0, 1) - v_m(1, 1)) > e_m > (v_m(0, 0) - v_m(1, 0))$$

$$\wedge \; (v_f(0, 0) - v_f(0, 1)) > e_f > (v_f(1, 0) - v_f(1, 1)))$$

The likelihood function simply follows.

Stackelberg equilibrium Instead of the symmetric Nash game we can assume that the roles of husband and wife are asymmetric, that is one of them is assumed to be the leader, the other acts as a follower. Then we have a Stackelberg game. Note that the solution we get using this equilibrium concept is not the solution for the equation system (7.1).

It is easy to see that Stackelberg equilibrium always exists and that it is unique. Table 7A.2 in Appendix 7.1 shows the probability of the couple choosing state (y_m, y_f) for the case of male as the leader. Detailed deductions can be found in Hiedemann (1998). Similar to the case of Nash equilibrium, we can construct the likelihood function.

Notice that neither Nash equilibrium nor Stackelberg equilibrium is generally Pareto optimal. So the use of the non-cooperative game is controversial. Kooreman (1994) tried to estimate a model implying Pareto-optimality of observed outcomes. With a very simple structure, that is linear reaction functions, he was not able to get convergence. Although he managed to succeed in estimating a mixed model of Pareto-optimality and Nash equilibrium, we have not tried to estimate a model along his line.

3.1.2 Joint utility for the couple: cooperative households

One possible way to account for cooperative behavior is to assume that the couple has one joint utility function. Or, that the decisions within the family are made in a cooperative setting. In the literature, there is an increasing interest in models of household behavior as the result of a cooperative game, particularly a Nash bargaining game. See for example Bourguignon and Chiappori (1992) for a review. But it turns out that the empirical estimation of such a model is very difficult, since we would like to estimate simultaneously the individual preferences of the spouses and the threat point. At the present stage, we are not able to do so. On the other hand no definite conclusion about which approach is better (joint utility versus Nash bargaining) has been made yet. Kapteyn and Kooreman (1992) argued that more about the players' preferences should be known before one can discriminate between these two kinds of models empirically. We will therefore use the neoclassical joint utility for couples and assume the following random utility function:

$$U(y_m, y_f) = v(y_m, y_f) + \varepsilon(y_m, y_f) \tag{7.3}$$

Under the assumption of $\varepsilon(y_m, y_f)$ being extreme value distributed with a location parameter η and a scale parameter σ, and the assumption of utility maximization, the probability that alternative (y_m, y_f) is chosen by the decision maker (household) is:

$$P(y_m, y_f) = \Pr(U(y_m, y_f) \geq U(k, s), \ \forall \ (k, s) \in (1, 0) \times (1, 0)). \tag{7.4}$$

Then we have

$$P(y_m, y_f) = \frac{e^{\sigma v(y_m, y_f)}}{\sum_k \sum_s e^{\sigma v(k, s)}}; \quad y_m, y_f = 1, 0. \tag{7.5}$$

3.2 The Utility Function and the Economic Attributes in the Alternatives

In the game theoretical models, we specify the deterministic part of the utility function as a Box–Cox transformation of household disposable income, his/her leisure and the leisure of the spouse. There are two points we need to clarify. First, we assume that there is some kind of income sharing within the household, and the sharing factor θ is absorbed into the parameter of income for male and female. So the household disposable income enters the utility instead of individual disposable income. Second, we assume that the preference is so-called 'altruistic' – one spouse's leisure enters the other member's utility function.

The utility functions for the husband and the wife are:

$$\begin{cases} U_m(i, j) = \alpha_m \dfrac{C_{ij}^{\lambda} - 1}{\lambda} + \beta_m \dfrac{L_{mi}^{\lambda} - 1}{\lambda} + \beta_{mf} \dfrac{L_{fj}^{\lambda} - 1}{\lambda} + \varepsilon_m(i) \\[2mm] U_f(i, j) = \alpha_f \dfrac{C_{ij}^{\lambda} - 1}{\lambda} + \beta_f \dfrac{L_{fj}^{\lambda} - 1}{\lambda} + \beta_{fm} \dfrac{L_{mi}^{\lambda} - 1}{\lambda} + \varepsilon_f(j) \end{cases} \tag{7.6}$$

where

$U_k(i, j) =$ utility of spouse k, the husband is in state i and the wife in state j; $i, j = 0, 1$ and $k = m, f$,

Disposable income C_{ij} and leisure L_{mi} and L_{fj} are defined below.

$\alpha_k = \alpha_{k0} + \alpha_{k1}$ (Household wealth); $k=m, f$

$\beta_m = \beta_{m0} + \beta_{m1}$ (Age difference) $+ \beta_{m2}$ (Sickness history) $+ \beta_{m3} D_m$,

$\beta_f = \beta_{f0} + \beta_{f1}$ (Age$_f$)

$D_m = 1$ if the husband worked in the private sector before retirement,

$\quad = 0$ otherwise,

$\varepsilon_k(i)$ is an extreme value distributed random variable which may be correlated across spouses; $k = m, f$. Since only the difference e_k enters into the likelihood function, we simply assume corr$(e_m, e_f) = \rho_{mf}$ instead of directly assuming a correlation structure across $\varepsilon_k(i)$.

As can be seen from the specification of the utility function, we assume that the shape coefficient, λ, is the same for both spouses and all alternatives, while all scale coefficients are allowed to vary.

Disposable income, C_{ij}, is equal to annual after-tax income when the husband is in state i and the wife is in state j. Thus $C_{ij} = r_{Mi} + r_{Fj} - T(r_{Mi}, r_{Fj})$; $i, j = 0, 1$; where r_{Mi} is the gross income of the husband when he is in state i, and r_{Fj} is the gross income of the wife when she is in state j, and $T(.)$ is the tax function. On average, pension income is taxed at lower rates than labor income. The unit of tax calculation is the couple, not the individual, which means that the taxes paid by the couple depend on the labor market states of both members of the household. The marginal tax rates are not uniformly increasing with income and therefore the tax rules imply non-convex budget sets. In the estimation of the model, all details of the tax structure, including the non-convexity of the budget sets, are accounted for.

Leisure, L_k, $k = F, M$, is defined as one minus the ratio of hours of work to total annual hours. Thus, when the husband is retired or the wife is not working, $L_k = 1$; when the husband works full time, $L_m = 1 - (37.5*46)/8760$.

Because the individual can be observed in one state only, we can observe the gross income of the individual only in that state. In order to model different possible outcomes, we need to impute or simulate the gross income also in those states in which the individual is not observed. These include the following:

- If the husband or the wife is observed working in the current period or in the year prior to the date of the husband's eligibility, then working is characterized by their observed earnings and leisure. A justification for this assumption is that at the age of the individuals considered here there is some rigidity in the labor market attachments.
- If the wife is observed to be out of the labor force during the current and the previous period, then working is characterized by predicted earnings based on a log earnings function estimated on earnings data among those women working full time. Leisure is predicted as leisure

consistent with the working load related to the earnings that are assigned to the women. The estimated log earnings function is given in Appendix 7.2.

- For the husband, the potential pension following eligibility is calculated according to rules applied to his earnings history, which is observed. Details about pension rules are set out in Haugen (2000).

Household wealth is defined as financial wealth and we expect that the marginal utility of income of both spouses (evaluated by the deterministic part of the utility function) will decrease with wealth. As alluded to in the next section, all males are 64 years old and thus it makes no sense to let the marginal utility of male leisure depend on the age of the male. However, the age difference, defined as husband's age minus wife's age, may have an impact on the marginal utility of male leisure. We expect that the larger this difference is, the less is the marginal utility of male leisure. Sickness history is measured as the ratio of sick leave to working hours in the 15 months prior to AFP-eligibility. We expect that the marginal utility of male leisure is increasing in the sickness history of the male. For the males belonging to the cohorts studied here, working in the private sector may have been more strenuous than working in the public sector. Thus we expect that the marginal utility of leisure is higher among private sector employees than among those working in the public sector. The age of the wife may vary across the sample and we therefore let the marginal utility of female leisure depend on her age. The higher the age is, the higher we expect the marginal utility of leisure to be. Similarly, we define the joint utility function as follows:

$$U(i,j) = \alpha \frac{C_{ij}^{\lambda} - 1}{\lambda} + \beta_m \frac{L_{mi}^{\lambda} - 1}{\lambda} + \beta_f \frac{L_{fj}^{\lambda} - 1}{\lambda} + \varepsilon_{ij}$$

where

$\alpha = \alpha_0 + \alpha_1$(Household wealth),

$\beta_m = \beta_{m0} + \beta_{m1}$(Age difference) + β_{m2} (Sickness history) + $\beta_{m3}D_m$,

$\beta_f = \beta_{f0} + \beta_{f1}(\text{Age}_f)$

To some extent, we can regard the joint utility function as a weighted sum of the two members' utility function. The discussion about the expected property of the coefficient estimates should hold also in the joint utility case.

3.3   Identification of the Parameters

One key factor when examining the identification problem in a discrete choice setting is that only the difference in utility counts. When taking the difference, the common factor in utilities of different alternatives is eliminated and we will not be able to identify the parameters that only appear in these factors. For instance, given our structure of the utility function, neither of the 'altruistic' parameters β_{mf} and β_{fm} can be recovered in the Nash setting. The reason is as follows. In the Nash settings, both husband and wife take the other's action as given when they make their own decision, that is they compare either the state pair $(1, y_f)$ and $(0, y_f)$ or $(y_m, 1)$ and $(y_m, 0)$. Since the 'altruistic' parts depend only on the leisure of the other member, those parts become common factors in the utility function comparison, and cancel out in the likelihood function. So both β_{mf} and β_{fm} are not identified. It is the same reason that β_{fm} in the Stackelberg setting is not identified. However, the husband's 'altruistic' parameter β_{mf} can be identified, since he has to make a comparison between the state pair where the wife is in different state, such as $(1,1)$ and $(0,0)$.

Another important issue is the scale of the estimated parameters. It is well known that we are not able to identify the parameters that enter the utility function linearly, because the variance of the disturbance σ is absorbed in these scale coefficients. However, the shape parameter of the utility function, λ, is identified.

4. DATA

The empirical basis for the analysis is register files held by Statistics Norway. The files are all based on an encrypted personal identification number that allows linking of files with different kinds of information and covering different periods in time. Details about the data sources can be found in Hernæs and Strøm (2000).

For the present study, we used register files covering the entire population and spanning the period 1993–98. The data sets give detailed information on employment spells (including identification of the employer), earnings (based on tax reports, implying that all earnings are included, possibly from more than one employer) and benefits of various types (including pension income), wealth (from tax reports), gender, age (including birth date), marital status, educational attainment, sickness history and place of residence.

Eligibility for the AFP is determined in two steps. In the first step we identify all persons employed in companies in which some employees have previously taken out AFP. In the second step we use information on current and previous employment to identify those persons who meet the individual requirements. Then, we include information about the month in which the retirement option becomes available and the month in which it is taken out.

During the observation period, 50 per cent of earnings in excess of the basic amount in the public pension system (USD 5600) when retired were deducted from the pension. With a marginal tax rate on earnings and pension at, say, 40 per cent, the effective tax rate on earnings was 70 per cent. We have therefore disregarded the option of combining earnings and early retirement (partly retired).

The earnings history is available from 1967 in the form of accrued rights in the public sector pension system, via year-by-year total pension-accruing income and pension points in the public pension system. This is the basis for predicting the potential public pension and thus also the potential pension in the AFP program.

Starting with eligible persons, we restrict the sample in this study to comprise all married couples in which the husband qualified during the period from 1 October 1994 until 31 December 1996. Since the eligibility age was 64 from 1 October 1993 until 1 October 1997, the couples in the sample then knew at least one year in advance that retirement would become possible, and could plan retirement. Previous studies (Røgeberg, 1999) have shown that a sudden change in the eligibility age entails a lagged response. We then restrict the data to couples in which the wife did not qualify and in which the wife is younger than the husband. These restrictions are imposed in order to make sure that the options postulated for the two spouses are reasonable. The restrictions reduce the sample from 12 475 couples in which the husband qualifies, to 8210 that fulfill all the criteria. Some descriptive statistics are given in Table 7.2.

Table 7.2 Descriptive statistics

Variable	Average value	Minimum value	Maximum value
Household disposable income, when both are working (100 000 NOK)	3.0642	1.1425	29.5826
Household disposable income, when husband is working but wife is not	1.8474	0.5052	27.7983
Household disposable income, when wife is working but husband is not	2.5060	1.1072	7.9971
Household disposable income, when husband takes early retirement and wife is not working	1.2892	0.7056	1.6440
Wealth (100 000 NOK)	5.6966	0	1930.93
Age of wife	58.8996	33	63
Sick history (proportion of previous 15 months on sick leave)	0.0231	0	0.8667
Private sector dummy (=1, if works in private sector)	0.4534	0	1

5. THE ESTIMATIONS AND POLICY SIMULATION

5.1 The Game Theoretical Model

We would like to estimate the shape parameter λ together with other parameters using maximum likelihood method. However, the log-likelihood functions for both the Nash and Stackelberg case are not differentiable w.r.t. λ.[1] This means that although consistency can still be guaranteed, asymptotic normality is questionable, thus we will not be able to do the conventional inferences.[2] This problem calls for a new strategy of estimation.

Note that for any given λ, the likelihood function is well behaved, so we will be able to avoid the non-smooth problem if we assume λ to be a constant as Kooreman (1994) and Hiedemann (1998) did. However, there is no obvious theoretical argument favoring any particular value. In the literature, linearity or log-linearity is often assumed, but it is mainly because of the computational convenience. In our case, we think that we should let the data decide. So we do the estimation in two steps. First, we obtain a consistent estimate λ^* for λ. Note that the fact that the MLE is consistent despite non-differentiability, we simply maximize the log-likelihood function w.r.t. all unknown parameters of the model to obtain λ^*. Then we estimate the model using MLE based on the assumption that $\lambda = \lambda^*$. The estimation results for the game theoretic models are given in Table 7.3.

We observe that the estimates of these two game models are quite similar. Because these two models are estimated on the same data set, one simple way to tell if one is better than the other is using the goodness-of-fit criteria. In our case, according to the log-likelihood values, the Stackelberg model, with male as the leader, performs slightly better. There are some tests available to test the non-nested hypothesis as well as to be used in model selections. Ben-Akiva and Swait (1984) shows that under the null hypothesis where model A is the true specification, the following holds asymptotically,

$$\Pr(\bar{\rho}_B^2 - \bar{\rho}_A^2 > z) \leq \Phi\{-[-2z\ell(0) + (K_B - K_A)]^{1/2}\}, \quad z > 0 \quad (7.7)$$

where

$\bar{\rho}_l^2$ = the adjusted likelihood ratio index for model l, $l = A, B$
K_l = the number of parameters in model l.
Φ = the standard normal cumulative distribution function.
$l(0)$ = is the log-likelihood when the number of parameters are set equal to zero.

Table 7.3   Estimates of Nash and Stackelberg model

The shape parameter		Nash		Stackelberg (husband leader)	
		$\lambda = 0.5690$		$\lambda = 0.5522$	
Coefficient	Variable	Estimate	Asy t-value	Estimate	Asy t-value
	Wife's utility function				
α_{f0}	Household disposable income: constant	5.3268	31.5004	5.3372	31.4340
α_{f1}	Household disposable income: linear in wealth	−0.0015	−1.2315	−0.0014	−1.2839
β_{f0}	Female leisure: constant	−0.7550	−0.3569	−1.0900	−0.5135
β_{f1}	Female leisure: linear in age	0.4228	12.8205	0.4192	12.6995
	Husband's utility function				
α_{m0}	Household disposable income: constant	1.3340	12.0470	1.3349	10.1122
α_{m1}	Household disposable income: linear in wealth	−0.0028	−1.4396	−0.0027	−1.1829
β_{m0}	Male leisure: constant	−2.1609	−7.3752	−1.9968	−6.7869
β_{m1}	Male leisure: linear in age difference	−0.1240	−3.8367	−0.1285	−3.9568
β_{m2}	Male leisure: linear in sick history	13.6448	8.9227	13.6734	8.8327
β_{m3}	Male leisure: private sector	4.2346	18.0343	4.3160	18.1141
β_{mf}	Female leisure	NA	NA	9.0977	4.8238
	In both utility functions				
ρ_{mf}	Correlation	0.1668	9.2157	0.1655	9.1949
	Observations	8210		8210	
	Log-likelihood	−9837.61		−9826.17	
	$\rho^{2,3}$	0.1356		0.1367	
	$\bar{\rho}^2$	0.1346		0.1355	

If we think the model with the greater $\bar{\rho}^2$ is the right one, the probability of erroneously choosing the incorrect model is less than the expressions to the right in (7.7). Alternatively we can perform the likelihood ratio test developed by Vuong (1989) to test the hypothesis that these two models are equivalent against the hypothesis that one is better than the other. Details of the test are given in Vuong (1989).

When we performed these two tests, both tests rejected the Nash model in favor of the Stackelberg model at a very low level of significance (<0.001), even though the log-likelihood is quite close. Even so we cannot then be sure that Stackelberg is the right model while the Nash is not in the household decision-making process. It only means that the Stackelberg model may be a better description of the data used in the present study. It may just be a special phenomenon for the age cohorts studied here. (The males in this study were born between 1930–1935.)

The shape coefficients, the λ's, are very close to 0.5. This is a value that has been found in psychophysical experiments; see Stevens (1975).

From the estimate of the deterministic part of the utility function we observe that:

- the marginal utilities of disposable income are positive and significantly different from zero; the effect of wealth on the marginal utility of disposable income is not significant;
- the marginal utility of female leisure is positive for all relevant age levels and it is increasing with age, which is in line with our expectations;
- the marginal utility of male leisure is positive for all relevant sickness history, it is higher if working in the private sector, and it increases with sickness history. It decreases with the age difference, which suggests that the older the husband is relative to the wife, the more likely it is that the husband delays his retirement – it can be interpreted as an appreciation of so-called 'joint leisure'. Hurd (1997) and Hiedemann (1998) have found a similar effect;
- the marginal utility of the wife's leisure for males is significant and positive. It may suggest that the husband does care about his wife's well-being. This result fits well the finding of Gustman and Steinmeier (2000), who found that the wife's retirement appears to have a larger effect on the husband's propensity to retire than vice versa, although they found only the joint effect to be significant;
- the unobserved variables affecting the utility levels of the spouses are positively correlated. This can be explained by common preferences, either because of why they got married in the first place or because of joint opinions forming during the long years of adjustments and compromises from both parties. Hiedemann (1998) reported similar results, but to a much greater extent. But since she used a grid search on the correlation instead of estimating it together with other parameters using a maximum likelihood method, we do have reason to question her estimates.

5.2 Joint Utility Model

The estimation results of the joint utility model are given in Table 7.4. From Table 7.4, we notice that the log-likelihood and the goodness of fit criteria $\bar{\rho}^2$ are well below both game theoretical models. If we perform the two-model selection tests on the joint model against the Stackelberg model, the same results are obtained: the joint model is rejected. But the joint model did recover the shape parameter very well. The sign of the coefficients entering the marginal utility of disposable income and leisure are as expected. We note that the shape parameter λ is very sharply determined. The estimate is almost identical to the estimates we obtained in the game case above. We can reject both log-linear utility function ($\lambda = 0$) and linear utility function ($\lambda = 1$).

5.3 Observed versus Predicted Proportion

Based on the estimates of the three models, we can calculate the average probability of choosing each state across the couples. Table 7.5 shows the observed proportions as well as the predicted average probabilities and average marginal probabilities.

Of most interest here is the marginal probability of male retirement. We notice that 35.69 per cent of the males decided to retire at the eligibility date. All three models give almost similar predictions that are very close to the observed fractions.

Table 7.4 Estimates of the joint utility model

Coefficient	Variable	Estimate	Asy t-value
α_0	Income female constant	2.9780	23.9090
α_1	Income female, linear in wealth	−0.0020	−1.3239
β_{f0}	Female leisure: constant	−14.4226	−7.2166
β_{f1}	Female leisure: linear in age	0.4590	13.8711
β_{m0}	Male leisure: constant	0.4089	1.5335
β_{m1}	Male leisure: linear in age difference	−0.1954	−6.1077
β_{m2}	Male leisure: linear in sick history	12.8957	8.4550
β_{m3}	Male leisure: private sector	4.8458	20.5799
λ	Shape parameter	0.5315	13.9872
	Observations	8210	
	Log-likelihood	−10041.3	
	ρ^2	0.1178	
	$\bar{\rho}^2$	0.1170	

Table 7.5   The observed proportions versus predicted probabilities

	Observed	Nash	Stackelberg (husband leader)	Joint
State (1,1)	0.1454	0.1556	0.1557	0.1396
State (1,0)	0.2115	0.2046	0.2085	0.2038
State (0,1)	0.2451	0.2794	0.2769	0.3053
State (0,0)	0.3981	0.3604	0.3590	0.3513
Male retires	0.3569	0.3602	0.3642	0.3434
Male works	0.6431	0.6398	0.6358	0.6566
Female do not work	0.3905	0.4349	0.4326	0.4449
Female works	0.6095	0.5651	0.5674	0.5551

Note: State (i,j) means male in state i and female in state j; $i,j = 1 =$ not work; $i,j = 0 =$ work.

We notice that we predict the labor market situation of the wife less well than the labor market situation of the husband. This may be because for males we are modeling the adjustment right after a new option has become available. For the wife, we are modeling the labor market affiliation that may follow from choices related to the life cycle. The economic incentives incorporated are primarily related to the current situation, and may therefore be insufficient to explain the wife's labor market situation.

5.4   Policy Simulation

In order to illustrate the magnitude of the estimated relationship and the corresponding impact of potential policy changes, we have performed a policy simulation based on the estimated models. In the simulation, pension benefits are taxed the same way as labor earnings.

Table 7.6 shows how the average choice probabilities across the sample are affected by the policy changes and how the marginal probabilities of work and leisure across gender are affected.

As seen from Table 7.6, the tax system favors retirement. Therefore, making the taxation of pension benefits less generous, (equal to the taxation of labor income) reduces early retirement. We also observe that although the three models had almost the same prediction of within-sample frequencies, the joint utility model differs considerably from the two game models with regard to the prediction of a change in policy rules. Based on the joint utility model the predicted reduction in the marginal probability of male retirement averages around 13 percentage points, while

Table 7.6   Choice probabilities in policy simulations

	Nash		Stackelberg (husband leader)		Joint	
	Model	Policy	Model	Policy	Model	Policy
State (1,1)	0.1556	0.1001	0.1557	0.0997	0.1396	0.0748
State (1,0)	0.2046	0.1943	0.2085	0.2191	0.2038	0.1399
State (0,1)	0.2794	0.3157	0.2769	0.2941	0.3053	0.3651
State (0,0)	0.3604	0.3900	0.3590	0.3872	0.3513	0.4202
Male retires	0.3602	0.2943	0.3642	0.3187	0.3434	0.2147
Male works	0.6398	0.7057	0.6358	0.6813	0.6566	0.7853
Female do not work	0.4349	0.4158	0.4326	0.3938	0.4449	0.4399
Female works	0.5651	0.5842	0.5674	0.6062	0.5551	0.5601

in the case of game models the average reduction amounts to 5–7 percentage points. We probably should pay more attention to the predictions of the Stackelberg model, for the two tests we performed are in favor of it. According to the test, the joint model is the worst among the three, so to some extent it may be misleading to rely on the policy simulations in this case.

But anyway, these results indicate that the current tax system favors retirement and that the change in the tax rules described above may have a large and positive impact on the male labor supply among those males who are eligible for early retirement.

In our simulations, the female labor supply does not change much due to the shift in policy. If anything, a slight increase in labor supply is predicted. This is the same across models. Thus, the considered change in the taxation of pension incomes clearly increases labor supply among the elderly men eligible for early retirement, with a modest but positive impact on their wives' labor supply. Thus, the considered change in tax rules is a good policy candidate, if one wants to counteract the negative effects on labor supply implied by the early retirement programs.

6.   CONCLUSIONS

The chapter makes a first attempt to compare non-cooperative game-theoretic and joint utility models of early retirement and labor force participation for married couples, using detailed Norwegian micro data. Although the estimates indicate that the marginal utility of leisure and the shape coefficient is rather similar across models, based on some model selection tests, both the joint utility model and the Nash model are rejected against the Stackelberg model with the male as leader.

We are not yet able to estimate a cooperative game model such as a Nash bargaining model, which at the focus of the literature on household behavior analysis (see for example McElroy and Horney, 1981; 1990 and Chiappori, 1988; 1991). Thus we have not been able to compare the Stackelberg model with a Nash bargaining model. This we leave for future research.

The three models do not differ to any great extent with regards to how within-sample fractions are predicted. However, they vary more with respect to the prediction of choice probabilities generated by a change in taxation. All simulations indicate that the lenient taxation of pension income favors early retirement. Taxing pension income by the rules of earning reduces on average the marginal probability of male retirement by 5–7 percentage points in the game models and by as much as 13 percentage points in the joint utility model. In all three models the female labor supply is predicted to increase slightly.

It should be noted that the results in this chapter are based only on observations of couples in which only the husband qualifies for early retirement. Another topic for further research will be to estimate the models on observations of couples over a period in which both spouses qualify. The indication of a positive correlation in retirement behavior is found in previous research, for instance Blau (1997), Zweimüller et al. (1996) and Hiedemann (1998).

NOTES

* This chapter is part of the project *The Ageing Population* financed by the *Economic and Social Research Institute, Cabinet Office, the Government of Japan*, and of the project *Pension Schemes, Work and Retirement Behavior* financed by the *Research Council of Norway*. We thank both sponsors for generous support. We also thank Statistics Norway for excellent service in providing the necessary data. Part of the paper was written during Steinar Strøm's visit to CES, Munich. The hospitality of CES is gratefully acknowledged.
1. See Appendix 1 for the explanation.
2. Discussions of some general results on asymptotic distribution theory for estimators derived from non-smooth objective function can be found in Newey and McFadden (1994). Unfortunately, we were not able to derive asymptotic normality for our case based on their results.
3. ρ^2 and $\bar{\rho}^2$ are both informal goodness-of-fit measures, defined as $\rho^2 = 1 - [\ell(\hat{\beta})/\ell(0)]$ and $\bar{\rho}^2 = 1 - [(\ell(\hat{\beta}) - K)/\ell(0)]$ respectively, which are used in a fashion similar to R^2 in regression analysis. K is the number of parameters.

REFERENCES

Baker, M. (2002), 'The retirement behavior of married couples: evidence from spouse's allowance', *Journal of Human Resources*, **37**(1), 1–34.

Ben-Akiva, M. and J. Swait (1984), 'The Akaike likelihood ratio index', Working paper, Department of Civil Engineering, MIT, Cambridge, Mass, USA.

Blau, D.H. (1997), 'Social security and the labor supply of older married couples', *Labour Economics*, **4**, 373–418.

Bourguignon, F. and P.A. Chiappori (1992), 'Collective models of household behavior, an introduction', *European Economic Review*, **36**, 355–64.

Bresnahan, T.F and P.C. Reiss (1991), 'Empirical models of discrete games', *Journal of Econometrics*, **48**, 57–81.

Chiappori, P.A. (1988), 'Nash-bargained household decisions: a comment', *International Economic Review*, **29**, 791–6.

Chiappori, P.A. (1991), 'Nash-bargained household decisions: a rejoinder', *International Economic Review*, **32**, 761–2.

Gustman, A.L. and T. Steinmeier (2000), 'Retirement in dual-career families: a structural model', *Journal of Labor Economics*, **18**(3), 503–45.

Haugen, F. (2000), 'Insentivvirkninger av skatte- og pensjonsregler', Master Thesis, Department of Economics, University of Oslo (in Norwegian only).

Heckman, J.J. (1978), 'Dummy endogenous variables in a simultaneous equation system', *Econometrica*, **46**(7), 931–59.

Henretta, J.C. and A.M. O'Rand (1983), 'Joint retirement in the dual worker family', *Social Forces*, **62**, 504–20.

Hernæs, E. and S. Strøm (2000), 'Family labor supply when the husband is eligible for early retirement', *Memorandum from Department of Economics*, University of Oslo, No. 13.

Hernæs, E., M. Sollie, and S. Strøm (2000), 'Early retirement and economic incentives', *Scandinavian Journal of Economics*, **102**(3).

Hiedemann, B. (1998), 'A Stackelberg model of social security acceptance decisions in dual-career households', *Journal of Economic Behavior & Organization*, **34**, 263–78.

Hurd, M.D. (1997), 'The joint retirement decisions of husbands and wives', in David A. Wise (ed.), *Issues in the Economics of Aging*, Chicago: University of Chicago Press, pp. 231–54.

Jia, Z. (2001), *A Note on Discrete Choice Model of Two Agents*, Manuscript, University of Oslo.

Kapteyn, A. and P. Kooreman (1992), 'Household labor supply: what kind of data can tell us how many decision makers there are?', *European Economic Review*, **36**, 365–71.

Kooreman, P. (1994), 'Estimation of econometric models of some discrete games', *Journal of Applied Econometrics*, **9**, 255–68.

Lumsdaine, R.L. and O.S. Mitchell (1999), 'New developments in the economic analysis of retirement', in O. Ashenfelter, and D. Card (eds), *Handbook of Labor Economics*, Volume 3, Elsevier Science BV.

Maddala, G.S. (1983), *Limited-Dependent and Qualitative Variables in Econometrics*, Econometric Society Monographs No.3, Cambridge University Press.

McElroy, M.B. and J.M. Horney (1981), 'Nash bargained decisions: towards a generalisation of the theory of the demand', *International Economic Review*, **22**, 333–49.

McElroy, M.B. and J.M. Horney (1990), 'Nash bargained decisions, a reply', *International Economic Review*, **31**, 237–42.

Newey, W.K. and D.L. McFadden (1994), 'Large sample estimation and hypothesis testing', in R.F. Engle and D.L. McFadden (eds), *Handbook of Econometrics*, volume 4, Elsevier, pp. 2113–48.

Røgeberg, Ole, J. (1999), *Married Men and Early Retirement Under the AFP Scheme*, Master Thesis, Department of Economics, University of Oslo.

Stevens, S.S. (1975), *Psychophysics: Introduction to its Perceptual Neural and Social Prospects*, New York: Wiley.

Vuong, Q.H. (1989), 'Likelihood ratio tests for model selection and non-nested hypotheses', *Econometrica*, **57**(2), 307–33.

Zweimüller, Josef, Rudol Winter-Ebmer and Josef Falkinger (1996), 'Retirement of spouses and social security reform', *European Economic Review*, **40**, 449–72.

APPENDIX 7.1   NASH AND STACKELBERG EQUILIBRIUM

Table 7A.1   Nash equilibrium (NE)

	$U_m(1,1)-$ $U_m(0,1)>0$ $U_m(1,0)-$ $U_m(0,0)>0$	$U_m(1,1)-$ $U_m(0,1)>0$ $U_m(1,0)-$ $U_m(0,0)<0$	$U_m(1,1)-$ $U_m(0,1)<0$ $U_m(1,0)-$ $U_m(0,0)>0$	$U_m(1,1)-$ $U_m(0,1)<0$ $U_m(1,0)-$ $U_m(0,0)<0$
$U_f(1,1)-$ $U_f(1,0)>0$ $U_f(0,1)-$ $U_f(0,0)>0$	(1,1)	(1,1)	(0,1)	(0,1)
$U_f(1,1)-$ $U_f(1,0)>0$ $U_f(0,1)-$ $U_f(0,0)<0$	(1,1)	(1,1) or (0,0)	No pure NE	(0,0)
$U_f(1,1)-$ $U_f(1,0)<0$ $U_f(0,1)-$ $U_f(0,0)>0$	(1,0)	No pure NE	(1,0) or (0,1)	(0,1)
$U_f(1,1)-$ $U_f(1,0)<0$ $U_f(0,1)-$ $U_f(0,0)<0$	(1,0)	(0,0)	(1,0)	(0,0)

Table 7A.2   Stackelberg equilibrium (SE) (male as leader)

$y_f(1)=1$ $y_f(0)=1$	$e_f> \max[v_f(1,0)-v_f(1,1), v_f(0,0)-v_f(0,1)]$	$e_m>v_m(0,1)-v_m(1,1)$	(1,1) is SE
		$e_m<v_m(0,1)-v_m(1,1)$	(0,1) is SE
$y_f(1)=1$ $y_f(0)=0$	$v_f(0,0)-v_f(0,1)>e_f> v_f(1,0)-v_f(1,1)$	$e_m>v_m(0,0)-v_m(1,1)$	(1,1) is SE
		$e_m<v_m(0,0)-v_m(1,1)$	(0,0) is SE
$y_f(1)=0$ $y_f(0)=1$	$v_f(1,0)-v_f(1,1)>e_f> v_f(0,0)-v_f(0,1)$	$e_m>v_m(0,1)-v_m(1,0)$	(1,0) is SE
		$e_m<v_m(0,1)-v_m(1,0)$	(0,1) is SE
$y_f(1)=0$ $y_f(0)=0$	$e_f< \min[v_f(0,0)-v_f(0,1), v_f(1,0)-v_f(1,1)]$	$e_m>v_m(0,0)-v_m(1,0)$	(1,0) is SE
		$e_m<v_m(0,0)-v_m(1,0)$	(0,0) is SE

The Non-differentiability of the Likelihood Functions

Note that in our probability formula for both the Nash and Stackelberg case, the likelihood functions involve the terms similar to:

$$\Pr(v_f(1, 0) - v_f(1, 1) < e_f < v_f(0, 0) - v_f(0, 1) \; \wedge e_m < v_m(0, 0) - v_m(1, 1))$$

$$= \Pr\left((\alpha_f \frac{C_{10}^\lambda - C_{11}^\lambda}{\lambda} + \beta_f \frac{L_{f0}^\lambda - L_{f1}^\lambda}{\lambda} < e_f < \alpha_f \frac{C_{00}^\lambda - C_{01}^\lambda}{\lambda} + \right.$$

$$\left. \beta_f \frac{L_{f0}^\lambda - L_{f1}^\lambda}{\lambda} \; \wedge e_m < v_m(0, 0) - v_m(1, 1) \right)$$

Let

$$b = v_m(0,0) - v_m(1,1)$$

$$a = \beta_f \frac{L_{f0}^\lambda - L_{f1}^\lambda}{\lambda}$$

and let $F(x, y, \rho)$ be the CDF for (e_m, e_f)
then the above term equals to

$$\begin{cases} F(b, \alpha_f \dfrac{C_{00}^\lambda - C_{01}^\lambda}{\lambda} + a, \rho) - F\left(b, \alpha_f \dfrac{C_{10}^\lambda - C_{11}^\lambda}{\lambda} + a, \rho\right) & \text{if} \quad \dfrac{C_{10}^\lambda - C_{11}^\lambda}{\lambda} < \dfrac{C_{00}^\lambda - C_{01}^\lambda}{\lambda} \\ 0 \quad \text{otherwise} \end{cases}$$

So we see immediately that this term is not differentiable w.r.t. λ. Neither is the log-likelihood function.

APPENDIX 7.2   FEMALE EARNINGS FUNCTION

If the wife is observed to be out of the labor force during the current and the previous period, then gross annual labour income, w, is predicted from the estimated annual income function given below:

$$\ln w = X\lambda + \tau$$

where τ is a normal distributed error term. The covariates entering the X-vector are:

1. Constant term,
2. Age,
3. Education, number of years in schooling,
4. Dummy for work between 20 to 29 hours,
5. Dummy for work more than 30 hours.

The estimates are given in Table 7A.3.

Table 7A.3   Estimates of wage regression

	Estimate	Std.dev	t-value
1) C	11.2727	0.0456	247.1100
2) Age	−0.0069	0.0007	−9.3600
3) Education in years	0.0455	0.0011	40.2000
4) Dummy for work between 20 and 29 hours per week	0.1417	0.0086	16.4100
5) Dummy for work more than 30 hours	0.4783	0.0079	60.9300
R square	30.5%		
Adjusted R square	30.3%		

Index